DATE DUE

D0966125

FREEDOM OF THE PRESS VS. PUBLIC ACCESS

BENNO C. SCHMIDT, JR.

Sponsored by the
Aspen Institute Program on
Communications and Society
and the National News Council

The Praeger Special Studies program—utiliz-
ing the most modern and efficient book production techniques and a selective worldwide
distribution network—makes available to the
academic, government, and business communities significant, timely research in U.S. and
international economic, social, and political
development.

FREEDOM OF THE PRESS VS. PUBLIC ACCESS

Praeger Publishers   New York   Washington   London

PRAEGER SPECIAL STUDIES IN U.S. ECONOMIC, SOCIAL, AND POLITICAL ISSUES

Library of Congress Cataloging in Publication Data

Schmidt, Benno C., Jr.   1942-
   Freedom of the press vs. public access.

(Praeger special studies in U.S. economic, social, and political issues)
Includes bibliographical references and index.
   1. Liberty of the press—United States.   2. Press law—United States.
3. Broadcasting—Law and legislation—United States.
I. Aspen Institute Program on Communications and Society.
II. Title.
KF4774.S28   343'.73'0998   75-19818
ISBN 0-275-01620-X
ISBN 0-275-89430-4 pbk.

PRAEGER PUBLISHERS
111 Fourth Avenue, New York, N.Y. 10003, U.S.A.
5, Cromwell Place, London SW7 2JL, England

ASPEN INSTITUTE PROGRAM ON COMMUNICATIONS & SOCIETY
360 Bryant Street
Palo Alto, CA 94301

© 1976 by the Aspen Institue Program on Communications & Society
Printed in the United States of America
Book composition by Curt Chelin, San Francisco

To my teacher,

ALEXANDER M. BICKEL

1924-1974

Preface

Early in 1974, the National News Council invited me to write a background paper on the issue of guaranteed access to newspapers, a matter then pending before the Supreme Court in the case of *Miami Herald Publishing Co.* v. *Tornillo.* The project soon assumed larger dimensions, as the Council and I agreed that a more useful contribution might be made both by awaiting the Court's decision and by broadening the subject to include access to radio and television and such related issues of constitutional law as libel and the right of expression in "public forums." National News Council members read early drafts of this book and contributed excellent suggestions and generous encouragement. I should make clear, however, that the Council has made no effort to inject its views into this book, which represents my own positions only and should not be taken as the views of the Council or any of its members.

I am most grateful to the National News Council; to its first Chairman, the Honorable Roger J. Traynor, who helped me define this project; and to its current Chairman, the Honorable Stanley H. Fuld, who has seen the book through and generously contributed a foreword. Thoughtful criticism and support were also offered by the Council's advisors, especially the late Harry Kalven, Jr., William Arthur, the Executive Director, and Ned Schnurman, the Associate Director.

I also want to record my gratitude to the John and Mary R. Markle Foundation and to the New York State Bar Association for their generous grants to Columbia University to support teaching and research in the area of mass communications media and the First Amendment. These grants supported the development of courses and seminars in which Fred W. Friendly and I have tried to bring to bear the perspectives of journalism and law on problems of freedom of the press. I owe more to my collaboration with Fred Friendly than I can possibly reckon. Certainly this book is largely a product of that association.

I wish to thank the Aspen Institute Program on Communications and Society and its Director, Douglass Cater, for overseeing the publication of this book. Richard Kuhn has been extraordinarily helpful and constructive in supervising all aspects of the book's production, and I am greatly indebted to him. I am also grateful to my editors, Susan Rumsey and Mary Arbogast, for their skillful efforts and to the following persons, who submitted helpful reviews of the manuscript at the Aspen Institute's invitation: Ray E. Hiebert, Erwin G. Krasnow, Don R. LeDuc, and Charles Clift.

Finally, I want to record my appreciation to my friends and associates at Columbia Law School. Virginia Woods and her assistants in the secretariat have handled my typing needs with great skill and helpfulness. Fred Santillan and his crew in the machine room have been marvels of care and efficiency. Two gifted student assistants, Gerard E. Lynch and Stephen A. Smith, provided research help and useful criticism. I have had enlightening discussions about the book with W. Kenneth Jones, Alfred Hill, and Harlan Blake, and my warm thanks also go to Telford Taylor and Harold Edgar, who read drafts of this work and offered countless suggestions for improvement. Above all, I thank Herbert Wechsler, who has been a constant source of wisdom and encouragement.

TABLE OF CONTENTS

Foreword

by Stanley H. Fuld

In the Fall of 1972, a Twentieth Century Fund Task Force report entitled *A Free and Responsive Press* was completed following an eighteen-month study. The report urged the formation of a private and independent national news council to receive, examine, and report on complaints concerning the accuracy and fairness of news reporting in the United States, and to initiate studies on issues involving the freedom of the press. In the course of their report, its authors declared:

> *A free society cannot endure without a free press, and the freedom of the press ultimately rests on public understanding of, and trust in, its work.*
>
> *The public as well as the press has a vital interest in enhancing the credibility of the media and in protecting their freedom of expression. One barrier to credibility is the absence in this country of any established national and independent mechanism for hearing complaints about the media and for examining issues concerning freedom of the press.*

On August 1, 1973, the National News Council opened its doors for business. Since then it has received several hundred complaints from the public at large about unfair and inaccurate reporting in the media, as well as complaints from individuals associated with the media about infringements on their freedom of expression.

The media's reaction to the Council has been mixed. Many see the Council as it sees itself: an independent body dedicated to the preservation of the media's rights under the First Amendment, concerned with the public's confidence in the fairness and integrity of the media, providing a forum for ventilation for the public and the media, and opposing government regulation of the media.

Others are less than enthusiastic about the Council. They fear this attempt at reasonable examination of media by a non-governmental body may lead to abusive governmental regulation, and thus to a deterioration in the media's freedom of expression.

With regard to these varying views, it is worth noting the United States Supreme Court's references to the Council in the *Miami Herald Publishing Co.* v. *Tornillo*[1] decision. The Court referred four times to the Council and to the task force of distinguished citizens which urged formation of the Council. In one of those references, Chief Justice Burger characterized the Council as "an independent and voluntary body concerned with press fairness . . . to provide a means for neutral examination of claims of press inaccuracy."[2] Citing the Court's references to the Council, William B. Arthur, the Council's Executive Director, has written: "[A]t least in the eyes of the Supreme Court, the National News Council is one of the stones in the wall protecting the media's First Amendment rights against governmental encroachment, and not, as our critics never tire of suggesting, a Trojan horse that has slipped inside that wall."

Shortly after its inception, the Council decided to sponsor a study of the potential threat to a free press posed by increased demands for access to the media. Benno C. Schmidt, Jr., Professor of Law at Columbia Law School, was asked to undertake the assignment.

In announcing the study, Roger J. Traynor, former Chief Justice of the California Supreme Court and my predecessor as the Council's first chairman, termed the access question "one of thumping importance." In his remarks at that time, Justice Traynor framed the dilemma of forced access. This is what he wrote: "Once the government moves in to tell a medium what it must publish, there is a basic question whether such a command is an abridgment of freedom of the press." However, he also put this question: "If you don't allow government intrusion, what kind of relief is an injured person going to get?"

When the study was originally conceived, it was to be completed by the Spring of 1974. But, when the United States Supreme Court decided to consider the *Tornillo* case, the study's completion was delayed to include this court ruling. That was a wise decision for, as this study ably demonstrates, *Tornillo* has opened as many doors as it has closed.

In *Freedom of the Press vs. Public Access,* Professor Schmidt examines whether there is a constitutionally rooted right of access to the electronic and print media, and surveys the perimeters of constitutional restraints upon statutory rights of access. In doing so, he unpacks the concept of access, traces its development, defines the policies and considerations which give it sustenance, reviews the evolving views of the First Amendment, and relates questions of access to the law of defamation and the "rich variety of judicial decisions" testing rights to expression in public forums.[3]

Professor Schmidt examines, in considerable detail and insight, the law and intricate problems of access to electronic media. He outlines with clarity the public policy concerns for and against expanding access to radio and television, focuses at length on the "Equal Opportunites" provision of section 315(a) and the Fairness

Doctrine, and assays the relationship of access to cable television. Most interestingly, Professor Schmidt gives a thorough analysis of the Supreme Court's opinion in *Miami Herald Publishing Company* v. *Tornillo.* The "unprecedented" question raised by the *Miami Herald* case was the "constitutionality of a statute providing a right of access to newspapers," and it was raised at a time of "recent controversial developments in First Amendment Law."[4] The Court ruled that the Florida statute granting a right of reply to personal attacks carried in newspapers violated the First Amendment because it intruded into and infringed upon the editorial function.

Besides finding in the *Miami Herald* decision a "basic question . . . whether the constitutional status of radio and television is ripe for reconsideration,"[5] Professor Schmidt finds Chief Justice Burger, in his opinion for the Court, "surprisingly apologetic,"[6] making "a greater effort to describe the arguments favoring access guarantees than he did to refute them."[7] As a result, Professor Schmidt believes that the ruling in *Miami Herald* "probably is destined for uncharted qualifications and exceptions."[8]

With regard to future legislation requiring access to the print media, Professor Schmidt ventures the view that the Supreme Court "will probably adopt a skeptical, but not wholly resistant, attitude."[9] "Sweeping access rights will not be approved,"[10] he maintains, but "[n]arrow specific access guarantees, designed to implement particular and weighty social objectives with the least possible jeopardy to editorial autonomy, may be upheld."[11] He goes on to suggest that the *Miami Herald* decision should not be a bar to the "mandatory publication of retractions where defamation has been established,"[12] or to the application of access obligations to "commercial advertising where a medium has accepted other ads dealing with the same activity, and cannot claim that its refusal to take an ad reflects disapproval of the ad or the underlying activity."[13]

Professor Schmidt concludes that the Supreme Court has cloaked the print media with a broad grant of immunity from government regulation, which he generally supports. He urges, however, that the print media take to heart the Bob Dylan saying: "To live outside the law you must be honest,"[14] which I too support.

Freedom of the Press vs. Public Access is a distinguished piece of work. Professor Schmidt has written a stimulating and insightful analysis of a very complex issue which is laced with historical and economic concerns and which involves many competing social and individual interests. The study is a valuable contribution to a dynamic field, and the National News Council is proud to have been its sponsor.

Stanley H. Fuld
Chairman,
National News Council

PART I

ACCESS TO THE MEDIA:
GENERAL PERSPECTIVES

Congress shall make no law respecting an establishment of religion, or prohibiting the free exercise thereof; or abridging the freedom of speech, or the press; or the right of the people peaceably to assemble, and to petition the Government for a redress of grievances.

The First Amendment to the Constitution of the United States

[O]f freedom of thought, and speech . . . one may say that it is the matrix, the indispensable condition, for nearly every other form of freedom.

Justice Benjamin Cardozo[1]

Not since the rancorous period at the close of the eighteenth century, which generated the Sedition Act of 1798, has controversy about the freedom and the responsibilities of the press so preoccupied public discussion as in recent years. New, unusual strains on politics and social traditions have aggravated the normal tensions between government and the press. The Vietnam War brought an end to the general consensus that had existed between government and the press since World War I about the desirable aims of foreign policy and the propriety of using force to achieve these aims. The *Pentagon Papers* confrontation marked the passing of an era when those with knowledge of defense and foreign policy secrets could be counted on to operate within accepted boundaries of discretion in disseminating information deemed sensitive by public officials. Moreover, during the 1960s, the war and other sources of disenchant-

1

ment in American society led numerous political, cultural, and racial groups to commit themselves to goals which they regarded as transcending obligations of obedience to law.

As a result, the First Amendment was strained in two areas. Journalism and law began following a collision course. Reporters who gathered information about dissident groups became unwilling objects of interest to law enforcement authorities, and a destructive cycle followed of subpoenas, principled resistance, threats of contempt citations, and, in a few cases, jail sentences. The second area of strain developed as doctrines designed to protect parades, demonstrations, street corner orators, and other expressive activities in public places were subject to troubled review, both in and out of the courts, in light of the aggressive, sometimes violent, protest gatherings that increasingly occupied the "public forum" of the streets, campuses, and parks. In this atmosphere, the problems of freedom of expression were buffeted about between strident challenge and anxious commitment, rather than approached from generally shared premises.

Governmental efforts at outright suppression, the forcible extraction of information from journalists, and the right to use public places for expressive purposes have generated the loudest public clamor about the limits of freedom of expression. However, these issues are probably overshadowed in legal significance by other developments since 1960. In a series of important decisions, the Supreme Court substantially lessened the scope of libel law in defamation actions by government officials and public figures. Another critical event for the law of freedom of the press during this period was the Supreme Court's first serious attention to the First Amendment status of broadcasting, the most popular source of information and attitudes about public affairs.

Not only have political and social developments and important changes in legal doctrines generated contention about the performance of the press and the scope of its constitutional protection, but developments within the press itself have also significantly contributed to the nation's volatile mood about the First Amendment. Many citizens began to perceive that media had reached the point of monopoly, and they challenged traditions of press freedom premised on the existence of a diversity of viewpoints in the marketplace of ideas. Furthermore, the period since 1960 has seen growing concern about the objectivity and fairness of the press. As a tone of subjectivity, and even advocacy, displaced traditional objectivity in many journalistic quarters, many persons wondered if the First Amendment tradition of press autonomy from official oversight really did safeguard the public's need for a broad and balanced spectrum of information.

This recent period of exaggerated tension between government and press, combined with changes in the nature of the communications industry and agitation about First Amendment guarantees, has given rise to a major controversy over access to the media. That issue is whether private publications, such as newspapers, magazines, radio and television stations, and conceivably even books, should be obligated by law to present the viewpoint of some person or entity that the publisher would not present as a matter of editorial discretion. And it is not surprising that the access issue surfaced when it did. The issue is, to some extent, the product of recent constitutional developments concerning libel and expressive activities in public places. It is also a response to changes in the nature of communications media that have invited reconsideration of their constitutional status. But although the access issue has its roots in other First Amendment developments of recent years, it is more significant and complex than any of these other developments.

Should access to the press be guaranteed by law? At issue are fundamental questions about the functions of the communications media in modern society.* Demands for access challenge the *laissez-faire* premises of the First Amendment, asking whether a largely unregulated dissemination of ideas should give way to legal guarantees of effective expression.

The judicial decisions that make up the body of First Amendment law are most notable for an absence of unifying theory and a disinterest in confronting basic assumptions. In the provisional mode of the common law, these decisions tend to be historical in deriving values, analogical in extrapolating principle from one setting to another, and intuitive in analyzing the consequences and efficacy of specific judgments. Some critics complain that this tradition is not geared to relating the First Amendment to the mass communications enterprises of the present. "Our constitutional theory is in the grip of a romantic conception of free expression," asserts a leading proponent of access, "a belief that the 'marketplace of ideas' is freely

---

*"In broadest terms, the access question is nothing less than an inquiry into the proper structure and purpose of the American press." *Lange, The Role of the Access Doctrine in the Regulation of the Mass Media*, 52 N. CAR. L. REV. 1 (1973).

accessible."[2] The demand for access confronts assumptions developed in a past of multiple independent publications with economic data, the facts of information flow, and other matters unfamiliar both to constitutional adjudication and to the intuitive mode of most writing about the First Amendment. Moreover, no problem of free expression presents so clearly the tension between individual autonomy and equality. The access controversy is reminiscent of constitutional wrangles during the first third of this century about the function of private property rights in the enjoyment of constitutional freedoms. Should a publisher give expression only to those views it approves of? If so, the power of effective mass communication will depend on individual variables such as wealth, skill at communication and organization, inherited enterprises, and other personal and legal attributes. Or should equality in public expression be sought through rights of access, even at the expense of the autonomy of private publishers?

Despite the importance of these basic theoretical and practical issues, the traditional print media have no historical experience with access requirements. By contrast, the electronic media have operated under explicit access rules from the beginning. But radio and television developed under a scheme of government licensing that is at odds with the historical conception of freedom of the press. The patterns of regulation derived from this scheme have not been applied to the print media. Nevertheless, there has been persistent pressure for a unitary First Amendment theory that would embrace both the print and the electronic media. This pressure emanates not only from the broadcast industry, but also, more generally, from what Professor Harry Kalven, Jr., has termed "the quest for coherent general theory in matters of the First Amendment."[3] However, if access obligations are sustained for the electronic media but constitutionally barred for the print media, the two types of media will be assigned fundamentally different statuses under the Constitution. The access controversy thus poses the very large question of whether our law should opt for a unified or a divergent conception of the First Amendment for the mass media.

The discussion of access to the media that follows is divided into four general parts. Part I introduces the subject by summarizing briefly the leading Supreme Court decisions dealing with access. Hopefully, an overview of this complex material will convey some sense of the types of access problems that have made their way to the Supreme Court, and of the Court's fluctuating response. The next chapters in Part I aim at providing general perspectives on the subject, first by suggesting the variety implicit in the idea of access, and the range of effects and purposes of different types of access obligations. There then follows an analysis of access in relation to the history of freedom of the press and the major strands of First Amendment theory, as reflected in the ideas of the framers and the fundamental premises of First Amendment case law. Part I concludes with chapters on the two characteristics of the media that have had the greatest impact in precipitating demands for access: the seemingly inexorable trend toward concentration and centralization in the communications industry, and the growth of a public perception of subjectivity and bias in the performance of the press.

Part II concerns recent developments in First Amendment law to which the access controversy is closely related. Particularly important are the major decisions concerning libel and the evolving conceptions of "the public forum," which concern various kinds of expressive activities in public and, occasionally, private places. Part II also treats early efforts to extend "public forum" principles to create a constitutional basis for access to various public and private newspapers, journals, and printed advertising media.

Part III examines the place of access obligations in the legal regulation of radio and television. The statutes governing radio and television impose specific requirements of access for political candidates. Moreover, the Federal Communications Commission (with support from the courts) has interpreted the mandate that broadcasters operate in the public interest as requiring stations to devote air time to different sides of controversial issues and, in some circumstances, to give access to specific persons or points of view. Radio and television thus constitute a segment of the press that has lived under extensive access rules, with consequent restraints on editorial autonomy. Controversy has focused not only on the wisdom and constitutionality of this scheme of regulation for broadcasting, but also on whether such a regulatory framework might be extended to newspapers, magazines, and other elements of the traditionally autonomous print media.

Part IV analyzes the Supreme Court's response to this prospect, when it reviewed a state statute that apparently imposed on newspapers an access obligation similar to one that has been applied to radio and television. The Court's rejection of this statute on First Amendment grounds poses the questions whether there is room under the Constitution for any access obligations for the print media, and whether the Court's decision suggests a rethinking of the place of access theory in the regulation of radio and television. The book concludes with some thoughts about the responsibilities of the press to provide a forum for the expression of views, whether or not under compulsion of law.

1

Access And The Supreme Court:
A Brief Overview

*It is the purpose of the First Amendment to preserve an un-
inhibited marketplace of ideas in which truth will ultimately
prevail, rather than to countenance monopolization of that
market, whether it be by the Government itself or a private
licensee.*

Opinion of the Supreme Court in
Red Lion Broadcasting Co. v. FCC (1969)[1]

*The choice of material to go into a newspaper, and the decisions
made as to limitations on the size of the paper, and content,
and treatment of public issues and public officials—whether fair
or unfair—constitutes the exercise of editorial control and
judgment. It has yet to be demonstrated how governmental
regulation of this crucial process can be exercised consistent
with First Amendment guarantees of a free press as they have
evolved to this time.*

Opinion of the Supreme Court in
Miami Herald Publishing Co. v. Tornillo (1974)[2]

Disputes about access to various forums and communications
media as a matter of legal right have come before the Supreme Court
in a number of important cases during the past two decades. During
the 1960s, the Court seemed to welcome access in three categories of
First Amendment decisions as an egalitarian advance in free speech
theory. These three categories included decisions involving access to
the electronic media, decisions concerning "public forums," and de-

cisions that limited libel action by public officials and figures. But the 1970s have seen a dramatic reversal of that trend. Although these decisions will be discussed in detail in later chapters, it may be helpful at the outset to provide a brief overview.

In 1969, in the landmark *Red Lion* decision, the Supreme Court unanimously upheld the validity of Federal Communications Commission regulations that obliged broadcasters to provide free reply time to persons whose honesty or integrity were attacked over the air during discussions of controversial public issues.[3] "It is the right of the viewers and listeners," concluded the Court, "not the right of the broadcasters, which is paramount." The enthusiasm with which the Court embraced reply rights in *Red Lion* reinforced demands for broader rights of access to radio and television. For a time, access obligations appeared ready to assume major significance on a number of fronts in the law governing electronic media. The Federal Communications Commission (FCC) and the courts experimented with the concept of free counter-commercials whenever product advertisements raised questions of public health and safety. Rights of reply for the political and Congressional opposition were proposed. In one case, such rights of reply were required by the FCC, as one answer to the dramatic increase in television appearances by the President. In another extraordinary case, the U.S. Court of Appeals for the District of Columbia, which exercises the bulk of judicial oversight of broadcast regulation, declared that the First Amendment prohibited broadcasters from flatly refusing to air advertisements about politics and public affairs.[4] In 1972, moreover, broad rights of access were established in the FCC's first effort at comprehensive regulation of cable television, as cable operators were required to set aside entire channels for use by the public, educational institutions, and local governments.

Beyond the access rights that *Red Lion* triggered for radio and television, the expansive rhetoric of the Court's opinion also seemed to imply that access obligations for the print media might survive constitutional review, at least in the case of media monopolies. In a decision that some regard as a foreshadowing of things to come, the Florida Supreme Court upheld the constitutionality of a state statute that granted a right of reply to political candidates attacked or criticized by newspapers.[5] "The First Amendment," said the state court, "did not create a privileged class which through a monopoly of instruments of the newspaper industry would be able to deny to the people the freedom of expression."[6]

During the 1960s the Supreme Court also handed down numerous decisions dealing with a problem that many viewed as analogous to access to the press. That was, when should expressive activities in public places (such as parks, streets, and the grounds around public buildings) be protected by the First Amendment? On the whole, the decade was marked by expansion of the rights of individuals and protest groups to use public places as forums for dramatic and sometimes unsettling public expression. Although most of the cases concerned public places rather than private communications enterprises, the courts characteristically extolled the virtue of providing outlets for effective expression by persons who lacked means of expression through conventional media. Moreover, a few holdings involved privately owned property, such as shopping centers, and imposed on private areas First Amendment rules applicable to expression in public places. As a result, some have urged that the principles developed to govern access to both publicly and privately owned "public forums" be applied by analogy to the press.

A third important group of cases during the 1960s sheds some indirect light on access to the press as an ingredient in First Amendment adjudication. The great libel decisions, which molded defamation law to fit modern conceptions of the First Amendment, were based in part on the assumption that certain victims of defamatory falsehoods in the press, particularly public officials, would as a practical matter have access to the press to vindicate their reputations through corrective statements. Partly on this account, the first of these important libel decisions, *New York Times* v. *Sullivan*,[7] limited the capacity of public officials to recover libel damages. In later decisions, the Court expanded the First Amendment's protection while limiting defamation actions by non-official "public figures," and, for a time at least, by private persons involved in newsworthy events, even if such victims of defamation did not have access to the press to vindicate themselves. In this process, the notion that access might serve the vindicatory functions of defamation law, without the harshness and chilling effects of that body of law, changed from an underlying assumption to hoped-for consequence. Thus, in the most expansive of these decisions, three justices virtually invited the states to create rights of reply for defamation victims denied libel recovery by the *Sullivan* rule. Politicians from President Nixon down have echoed this call. In this roundabout way, libel decisions have been a potent source of arguments in favor of access requirements. The diminished efficacy of libel laws to protect defamation victims and deter publication of damaging falsehoods has naturally led to interest in other legal mechanisms that might restore the constitutional equilibrium between individuals and the press. Access rights have been prominent among the suggestions advanced to correct the imbalance.

The decisions concerning expression in public forums, defamation, and access to the electronic media were among the most notable developments in constitutional law during the 1960s. Each of these areas of First Amendment adjudication seemed to promise constitutional approval for a right of access to the communications media. It is not surprising, then, that scholarly and popular writing in support of legal rights of access began in the late 1960s. For example, Jerome Barron, a professor of law at George Washington University, hammered away in favor of guaranteed access to communications media in several articles and a widely noted book.[8] Barron argued not only that statutes creating access rights ought to be upheld under the Constitution, but further that the courts should independently interpret the First Amendment as guaranteeing access to private publishing enterprises. Barron provided much forceful rhetoric in support of a new general access theory. He gave less attention to specifying the occasions when access rights should be exercised and how they should be administered. Yet, this indistinctness about scope and practical implementation tended to magnify, rather than lessen, the appeal of his arguments. Others sounded similar access themes and generated an outburst of largely supportive literature.[9]

Access devotees have found effective allies in public interest groups and law firms pursuing formal legal avenues to access, particularly to radio and television. These foundation- and church-supported enterprises provided litigation support for access claims whose intrinsic economic import often would not have generated sufficient means for expensive judicial or administrative proceedings.[10] Perhaps even more significant has been the growing interest of minority groups in rights of access as an important way of advancing their overall political and economic goals.[11]

By the end of the 1960s, then, court decisions, the writings of legal scholars, and the commitment of reformist lawyers and minority groups seemed likely to promote a widening acceptance of access to the press as a legal right. But the decade of the 1970s has been marked by an abrupt shift in the Supreme Court's attitude. Judicial hospitality to access rights has changed to hostility. Three cases directly concerning the right of guaranteed legal access to communications media have come before the Court during the 1970s and, in each of the cases, the Supreme Court rejected the claim of access.

In the first case, the Court dealt with claims that the First Amendment should guarantee to political parties or interest groups the right to air political advertisements on radio and television at the going rate for commercial advertisements. The Court directed its most elaborate judicial response to this case. A majority of the Court firmly rejected the First Amendment as a source of the right to advertise political messages over the electronic media.[12] However, the First Amendment was not regarded as a constitutional barrier to the creation of such rights by legislation or administrative rulemaking. Even so, the FCC won the majority's clear approval for having declined to establish such an access right.

Meanwhile, two dissenting members of the Court urged that the electronic media be treated as a government instrument since electronic media are licensed and regulated by the FCC. These dissenters argued that radio and television should be governed by constitutional doctrines developed to protect expressive activities in public places. They also maintained that a governmentally licensed broadcaster who accepts one sort of advertisement—for commercial products—must also constitutionally accept others, such as political announcements, on an equal basis.

The second case concerned the right to display political advertising in public transit buses that presented commercial advertising. As in the case concerning the electronic media, the claim of access for political advertising advanced here was based on notions of equality, as well as on the First Amendment right of free expression. Because the medium involved was operated by government, and because it accepted advertisements for commercial products, the argument was that it should not be allowed to refuse advertisements expressing political ideas. Although the Supreme Court, in June 1974, upheld the right of the public transit authority to accept only commercial advertising, it divided four to four on the First Amendment and equality issues raised.[13] The power to reject political advertising was approved by one vote because Justice Douglas regarded the transit authority's customers as a "captive audience," whose privacy rights should shield them from exposure to all advertising. Therefore, he rejected any right to advertise on public transit, even if other ads (impermissibly, as he believed) had been accepted. Combining with

Justice Douglas to form a majority for the judgment, four Justices concluded that the transit authority was constitutionally empowered to discriminate among different types of advertising on a reasonable basis. In their view, political advertisements were reasonably distinct from other types because they tend to be more controversial, they are more subject to sticky administrative problems of allocation, and they run for a short time only.

The four dissenters argued that the transit authority had elected to become a public forum for paid expression by accepting commercial advertisements, and, as a state instrument, could not constitutionally reject political messages. In a sense, then, the present Court stands virtually in equipoise on the right of political advertising in a government-owned forum that accepts commercial advertisements.

The third access case posed, for the first time, the question whether newspapers, consistently with the First Amendment, could be obligated by state statute to publish the replies of political candidates who had been attacked in the newspaper's editorials. This access case has received the widest public attention and is the most significant of the three. In this case, *Miami Herald Publishing Co.* v. *Tornillo*,[14] the Court held unanimously that the reply statute in question violated the First Amendment right of editorial autonomy for newspapers. Notwithstanding the Justices' unanimity, the Court's opinion seems almost apologetic, as it reviews sympathetically the arguments in favor of access rights before concluding that "[h]owever much validity may be found in these arguments,"[15] the reply statute nevertheless "fails to clear the barriers of the First Amendment because of its intrusion into the function of editors."[16] At another point, the opinion states: "A responsible press is an undoubtedly desirable goal, but press responsibility is not mandated by the Constitution and like many other virtues it cannot be legislated."[17] Apart from this platitude the opinion offers virtually no reasons for its result. None of the cases that the Court cited had decided a question remotely germane to the constitutionality of an access statute directed at newspapers. The opinion wove together a series of incidental remarks from opinions dealing with a variety of other First Amendment questions, and the Court pronounced its judgment on access as if the rule had been the verdict of settled precedents. The Court's disingenuous use of precedent seems almost capricious since the opinion does not even mention the five-year-old *Red Lion* decision, in which the Court upheld the constitutionality of access requirements as applied to the electronic media. In view of the absence of explicit justification, either from constitutional policy or from precedent, the Court's opinion can be expected to draw criticism, even from those unsympathetic to access claims.

There are grounds to wonder also about the constitutional principle announced in the *Miami Herald* case. At points in the opinion, the constitutional barrier to access requirements for print media seems absolute. However, the First Amendment has not been construed as an absolute bar to other types of government regulation that impinge upon freedom of the press. Criminal punishment for expression, and even prior restraints, are sustained in certain circumstances. Yet the Court's opinion in *Miami Herald* betrays no hint of relativity. No analysis of the nature of First Amendment restraint on access statutes is provided; no effort is made to relate the Amendment's principles on access to its principles in other areas.

Thus, the *Miami Herald* decision is something of a curiosity. The Court's opinion is almost devoid of reasoned support, its use of precedent is disingenuous, and the constitutional principle announced is not consistent with other rules grounded in the First Amendment. At a minimum, the decision means that access rights generally are perceived by the Court as counter to First Amendment principles, in the same sense that prior restraints or punishment for expression are generally counter to First Amendment principles. As such, *Miami Herald* stands as an important First Amendment decision, but only the beginning of analysis. Questions of the nature and scope of the print media's protection from access requirements remain open. These questions are one focus of this book.

The *Miami Herald* decision calls for comment for another reason. When Supreme Court decisions are not grounded in reason, they are fragile. A subsequent Court, when exposed to similar problems, is less likely to follow an earlier decision if the logic of that decision is not visible. It will be more difficult to persuade new personnel on the Court of the sanctity of the earlier result. Commentators will create doubts. If *Miami Herald* is not a reasoned treatment, political and popular pressures for guarantees of access will build up again. Paradoxically, the sweeping and conclusive fashion in which the Court rejected the constitutionality of access statutes may prove less durable than less categorical arguments against broad access requirements.

Miami Herald, of course, concerns only the print media. As mentioned before, one of the striking aspects of the opinion is its failure even to mention *Red Lion*. Accordingly, *Miami Herald* leaves access requirements in the regulation of radio and television in a puzzled state. Access to the electronic media and related issues of broadcast regulation are also a focus of this book.

The debate over access to the media has suffered from unrestrained rhetoric and abstract treatment of subtle legal questions. The literature of access rings with grandiose and indiscriminate calls for legal guarantees that the people have a voice, for equal sharing of the power of effective expression, for fairness and fullness in public debate, and similar manifestoes. Access proponents make much use of analogy. They argue that rules from public forum cases should govern private communications entities and would draw from television a regulatory system for newspapers. But this use of analogy has neglected serious questions of difference and degree. Considerations of whether access guarantees would work and how they might be implemented have been largely ignored. *Miami Herald* is, in a sense, a reply in kind. The opinion is about as undiscriminating in its rejection of access as the literature of access has been in inflating the concept.

2

Sorting Out the Concept of Access

If I may ride a hobby for an instant, I should say we need to think things instead of words.

Justice Oliver Wendell Holmes, Jr.[1]

Evaluation of access guarantees in terms of constitutional principles and public policy is a complex task. It is made more difficult because discussion of "access to the press" is necessary, but simplistic. "Access" is actually a collection of related conceptions, varied in function, in theoretical underpinning, in methods of administration, and in anticipated direct and incidental effects. To sort out each of the potential versions of access in every discussion would try the limits of patience. For convenience, therefore, this book will speak sometimes indiscriminately of "access to the media," but the variety implicit in the phrase should be appreciated.

Rights of access can be formulated in a number of ways, as the following examples may suggest. To work from the narrow to the broad, access rights might encompass:

1. The right of a defamed person to bring a court action for vindication, with the remedy being an obligation for the defamatory publication to publish the court's judgment.[2]

2. The right of certain political candidates to advertise (or appear at no expense) in certain media in which another candidate for the same office has been allowed to advertise (or appear at no expense).[3]

15

3. The right of a representative of some group or cause to present the viewpoint of that group or cause in a particular publication in response to an earlier opposition statement.

4. The right of a person who has been attacked as to honesty or integrity, criticized, put in a false (though not necessarily adverse) light, or mentioned in any fashion, to have published in the same medium a reply of his own composition.[4]

5. The right to advertise in any medium that exercises monopoly power over effective communication of the subject matter of that advertisement in a given market.

6. The right to advertise on a first-come, first-served basis in any medium that accepts advertisements for similar goods, services, or ideas, or that accepts advertising of any kind.[5]

7. The right of anyone to have views published at no cost concerning any matter; or any matter determined to be of substantial public importance as ruled by a court or public official; or any matter on which the medium sought has editorialized, covered as news, or published an advertisement about; or any matter of substantial public importance on which the medium has editorialized, covered as news, or advertised.

Obviously, the possibilities for access requirements are nearly inexhaustible. However, differences in access requirements cluster around three general issues. These are: differences in *operational scope*, differences among the *legal institutions* that declare and implement a given access rule, and differences in the *purposes* a given access requirement is designed to serve.

Operational Scope

The issue of operational scope raises a number of questions that can be posed in traditional terms. First, to whom does the right of access belong: to everyone who might put pen to paper or image on film, or to an objectively defined recipient (for example, a defamed person)? Second, what medium should be responsible for providing access when an access right is invoked: television, radio, cable T.V., newspapers, or journals of some degree of regular periodicity (daily, weekly, monthly, etc.) or level of circulation (as defined by number of readers or by level of saturation of some specific market)? And, should this responsibility also extend to books, pamphlets, advertisements on subways, movies, persons on soap-boxes, or the Government Printing Office? Third, is the bundle of rights and duties imposed by a particular access requirement contingent or affirmative? That is, are access rights and duties triggered by a prior publication such as a personal attack? Or are they independent, as in the case of a newspaper being obligated to print all letters to the editor, or to accept all advertisements that pay the going rate, or to provide space for political candidates?

Institutions That Implement Access

Besides questions of operational scope, another overall difference in various access requirements concerns what institution should promulgate a particular right of access, and what institution should make the factual findings and value determinations necessary to its implementation. Constitutional doctrine and sound political theory posit important distinctions between a right of access premised only on the First Amendment and imposed by the courts without regard to legislation, and a right of access created by legislation or administrative rulings. Limitations on judicial action, grounded in constitutional principle and political prudence, may not apply to legislation. A statute creating access might call for judicial deference to legislative acts, resting on democratic theory and legislative competence in such areas as broad fact-finding and line-drawing.

Aside from considerations of judicial review and constitutional survival, access legislation would face important institutional questions. As Professor Thomas I. Emerson has noted, one of the most common deficiencies of discussion and lawmaking dealing with expression is the "failure to take into consideration the realistic context in which such limitations are administered."[6]

Should a given access right be entrusted to an administrative agency, or enforced through criminal statutes, or implemented through judicial enforcement of a civil statute? If rights of access to the press are entrusted to an administrative agency, there are dangers of overzealous administration or "captivity" of the agency by the regulated entities, distorted application of standards, and possible political favoritism. On the other hand, there are obvious difficulties in placing an access right within the system of criminal law enforcement. Enforcement questions concerning access rights are likely to arise in circumstances of heated political controversy, which is not a promising context for disinterested law enforcement. Moreover, access statutes are likely to be vague, a common feature of laws regulating expression. Vagueness is especially troublesome in penal laws, because of due process requirements that a criminal statute provide fair notice to persons of their statutory duties.

The third method of implementation would be by judicial enforcement of a civil statute granting a right of access to any plaintiff meeting statutory requisites. There are difficulties here also. The delay characteristic of most judicial proceedings would often render judicially enforced access rights unseasonable. Moreover, litigation costs would be a problem. If each party bears his or her own legal fees, as is usual in American law, few plaintiffs would pursue such expensive vindication of their statutory rights. On the other hand, to impose the costs of both parties on the loser may discourage participation in litigation. This may result in broader or narrower obligations of access than were originally intended. The overall problem of what legal institutions might, individually or in combination, be given responsibility for developing and applying particular access rights raises vital questions of constitutional theory and public policy.

Purposes of Access Requirements

Differences in the operational scope of access rights and in the legal institutions that might implement them eventually depend on what purpose a particular access right is designed to serve. Most writing in support of access tends to cite broad purposes. These include granting everyone an equal right to effective communication, and ensuring that the public is fairly informed of all sides of issues that are of public importance or popular interest. More modest possible aims for access obligations have not received equal attention. However, they may be more sensible.

To begin with the broadest purpose, access rights might be designed to offer each citizen the capacity for effective communication to a large audience. Equality through access would attempt to offset capital investment, skill at communication or distribution, perceptivity, popular acceptance, organizational skills, continuing commitment, hereditary privilege, hard work, charisma, luck, and all other economic, social, and experience-based factors that tradition- ally determine who has the capability for effective communication in our society. For example, the owners and reporters of the *New York Times* would be required to share their power to communicate through that medium with the beneficiaries of access rules. This form of access would be a subsidy provided by newspapers, broadcasters, or whatever other publishers are covered, for those who wish to express themselves through these mass media.

Pursued to its end, such a broad aim would necessitate a centralized system of publication and distribution in which all citizens could claim equal shares. Resolute equality of access would end only in access to the Government Printing Office. Private publishing enterprises would be swamped. And the Government Printing Office would be converted by necessity to a free common carrier for all who wish to express themselves in the communications media. Furthermore, even this would not ensure equality in expression, for effective expression depends on the particular talents of the speaker, author, or producer. Equality could not be achieved, even by a centralized common carrier press, unless official editors and producers converted all expression, the exciting and the commonplace, into a common denominator of interest and persuasive power.*

Of course, no one has proposed anything so utterly absurd. But the absurd has its uses in law, as in literature. Here, it suggests the

---

*The spurious equality of access pure and simple was dramatically illustrated in one of our most famous instances of access: Senator McCarthy's 1954 broadcast on *See It Now*. Of the Murrow broadcast and the Senator's reply, Gilbert Seldes wrote:

> In a sense this formula of equal time is the only ground rule we have, and we are stuck with it until a better one is worked out. Unfortunately, it doesn't make sense, except mathematically, and Senator McCarthy's answer to Murrow was a brilliant demonstration of the fallacy involved. · . . . In the case of Murrow and McCarthy, we had on the original broadcast the product of some three years of experience in the handling of film clips, an art in which Murrow and his co-worker Fred Friendly have no peers. . . . . In reply Senator McCarthy came up with a feebly handled newsreel talk illustrated by two or three unanimated maps—about as weak a television program as you could devise.

The Murrow-McCarthy broadcasts are vividly recounted in FRIENDLY, DUE TO CIRCUMSTANCES BEYOND OUR CONTROL 23 *et seq.* (1967).

sweep of casually accepted values and focuses attention on the intervening principles and devices that keep certain values, such as equality, from overwhelming other values that call for differentiation. Holmes made the point trenchantly: "I used to say that equality between individuals, as a moral formula, was too rudimentary."[7]

The purpose of equal capability for effective expression can underlie limited access requirements that would not result in a totalitarian press. But other values must provide the limits. Equality, by itself, is leveling. And even a narrow access right, perhaps covering only political candidates, or business advertisers, or the objects of newspaper criticism, and designed to rectify inequalities in the practical power of expression, is likely to exhibit expansionist tendencies.*

Another broad purpose for rights of access, comparable to equality in its ubiquitous implications, is that of ensuring "fairness" in public debate. For example, suppose that an official is criticized in the press for unethical conduct. The public will be better informed, and the official can try to resurrect his reputation, if he can use the media to state his side of the question. This example suggests two notions of fairness. In one sense, fairness serves the public interest by exposing the public to relevant information that it needs to make an informed judgment. This is particularly true if democratic responsibilities for choice are involved. However, this public sense of fairness may be distinguished from a second concept of fairness: concern for fair treatment of individuals. If a person is assailed in the public press, that person should, in fairness, be allowed to present his or her side. These two purposes of fairness will often coalesce, as when a public official is charged with corruption of office. However, fairness to the public might support access when no particular individual's interests are at stake. Conversely, an individual's reputation might be protected by access in a dispute having no public interest. Access to serve specific *individual* interests can be placed among the more modest goals of access rights.

Like the goal of equality, creation of access rights to achieve *public* fairness would evolve, if unchecked, into exclusive sway for the Government Printing Office. Fairness requires that all sides of

---

*In the words of Tocqueville: "it is natural that the love of equality should constantly increase together with equality itself, and that it should grow by what it feeds upon." TOCQUEVILLE, 2 DEMOCRACY IN AMERICA 353-54 (Reeve ed. 1862).

matters discussed in the press be presented, and that significant issues not addressed at all be aired. Thus, every item published and every matter not covered would raise questions of fairness. Moreover, the effectiveness of communicating different points of view must be equalized if fairness is to be achieved. If James Reston or Eric Sevareid presents one point of view, fairness to the public is not achieved by airing the rejoinder of the first person who knocks at the *Times* or CBS door to respond. If fairness is taken seriously as a goal of access, an official "fairness editor" should have the last word on every publishing decision. The result would be, in effect, a conversion of all private publishing enterprises into branches of the Government Printing Office. *E pluribus unum* would be the motto for our books and newspapers as well as for our coinage.[8]

Access rights designed to achieve fairness in the public sense need not be pressed to the radical end of official responsibility for every editorial judgment. Limited access might seek justification under a public fairness rationale. For example, public fairness might underlie access rights only for candidates for certain political office. Or it might operate only on a contingent basis for candidates for the same office. Or perhaps, in either case, it might apply only to paid advertising. Yet, it is still useful to reduce the fairness purpose to a level of absurdity when thinking about access. Like equality, the goal of public fairness cannot be carried to its natural end without eradicating a free press.

The awareness that, in principle, the rationales of equality and public fairness are limitless must force attention to the real questions posed by such justifications. What values cut across fairness or equality and justify calling a halt to access at one point or another? If equality and fairness must be limited by other values in fashioning rights of access that stop short of the absurd, are these two seductive but sweeping purposes ever appropriate rationales for access rights?

Other purposes that might impel access rules are more modest. A frequent theme of those who favor access is the concern about counteracting the growing concentration and monopoly power of the communications media. Access requirements of various sorts are often suggested as a partial corrective for these worrisome trends. For example, it has been suggested that monopoly publications be treated as public utilites, available to all on a common carrier basis or subject to administrative rules designed to ensure fairness. Another version of access drawn from antitrust principles would establish a right to advertise in any publication that accepts similar advertisements. This extends somewhat the remedies already applied against monopoly newspapers and broadcasters found to have refused to deal with certain would-be advertisers for anti-competitive reasons.

Other sorts of limited access rules serving narrow purposes are easy to imagine. Political candidates might be afforded affirmative or contingent rights of access for the purposes of informing the electorate and maintaining fairness in elections. Another aim of a limited access right might be the vindication of individuals defamed by the press. This type of access right would not be designed as an egalitarian advance into the private preserves of the press, but would aim at redressing or preventing damage done to a specific individual. The range of purposes for which access rights might be sought is extensive.

The questions of operational scope, of institutional responsibility and competence, and of underlying purpose that the notion of access to the media raises should be respected. Evaluating access from the level of generalizations produces only a confrontation of abstractions. A distrust of generalization, appropriate in approaching so many First Amendment problems, is surely the suitable posture for dealing with access.[9]

3

Access In First Amendment History and Theory

Upon my arrival in the United States, the religious aspect of the country was the first thing that struck my attention; and the longer I stayed there, the more did I perceive the great political consequences resulting from this state of things, to which I was unaccustomed. In France I had almost always seen the spirit of religion and the spirit of freedom pursuing courses diametrically opposed to each other; but in America I found that they were intimately united, and that they reigned in common over the same country.

Alexis de Toqueville[1]

From a historical perspective, the controversy over rights of access to the press is a strange phenomenon: a basic First Amendment issue without parallel in the long history of Anglo-American law. It is difficult to find even strained historical analogies to any form of guaranteed access. And this novelty poses special problems in relating access issues to First Amendment principles, since First Amendment law has evolved on a case-by-case basis, with changing expositors on the Supreme Court. The constitutional principles involving freedom of expression have not emerged deductively from a central premise. Instead, these principles are the residue of a common law process that has tended to arrange First Amendment principles in diverse groupings, matching the problems that have cropped up in the important cases. Genuinely new controversies about freedom of speech or of the press do not fit easily into this pluralistic array. To relate access to "First Amendment theory" is, therefore, not a matter of measuring access in light of some comprehensive theory of freedom of expression. Rather, it is a matter of trying to draw relevance from the variety of First Amendment principles that have evolved pragmatically to govern different problems.

Access and the History of Freedom of the Press

History has special claims in constitutional law. Even cases that take the longest strides toward new doctrine often draw fresh insights from the legal experience of the past.[2] Complaints are voiced frequently that the Supreme Court makes instrumental use of history, shaping it to meet expedient ends or ignoring it when it will not easily bend. Even so, the Court's occasional failings in historical objectivity do not alter the habit of our common law tradition that the history of legal conceptions is the starting point of analysis.

For access, as for so many problems of freedom of the press and of speech, the dominant historical experience to contend with is the system of licensing and censorship that existed in England[3] and, very briefly, in several of the American colonies,[4] before the adoption of the First Amendment. The different lessons that have been drawn from this experience call to mind Carlyle's saying that "in every object there is inexhaustible meaning; the eye sees in it what the eye brings means of seeing."

Adamant opponents of access have compared access to licensing and censorship. If this likeness were real, access claims would be doomed in all but the most narrow and compelling cases. The system of wholesale prepublication licensing, existing in England from the rule of Henry VIII to the expiration of the Licensing Act in 1694, is the most repellent of all the historical symbols of government suppression of expression. It was the demise of the licensing system that led Blackstone, in 1765, to make his famous formulation of freedom of the press in English law: "The liberty of the press is indeed essential to the nature of a free state; but this consists in laying no previous restraints upon publication, and not in freedom from censure for criminal matter when published."[5] Abhorrence of government licensing or censorship is at the heart of our tradition of constitutional freedom. Anything that smacks of it must overcome the strongest historical aversion.

Access, however, does not fit into historical experience with prior restraints. An access right is not an official order that something not be printed without prior permission. Access obligations allow anything to be published in the first instance—they simply require publication in addition. Access requirements would be tantamount to censorship only if they were imposed discretionarily or if they submerged the autonomous content of unfavored publications in a sea of trivial access. Very burdensome conditional rights of access also could have the effect of inhibiting publication of whatever type of expression triggers the access guarantees.

Failing to achieve an exact likeness between licensing or censorship and access, historically minded opponents of access move to a level of abstraction: The essence of the reaction against licensing is that government must keep its hands off the prepublication editorial process. The media must be entirely free until some publication has occurred; the government can react, if at all, only after publication. Access requirements necessarily involve governmental intervention before publication. The ignominy associated with licensing thus should attach to access as well.

The force of this historical proposition is strictly rhetorical. It does not persuade on the levels of purpose, consequences, and administration. The purpose of government licensing was initially to secure for the Crown the economic advantages of the profitable printing business. In time, licensing also served as a convenient mechanism for preventing the publication of ideas considered dangerous to authority. But these purposes are quite different from those of any reasonable access requirement.[6]

The consequences of access rights, as well as the purposes, diverge from those of historical licensing. In Tudor England, the licensing system granted exclusive privileges to print in very broadly designated fields. For example, one individual printer was given an exclusive license to print "all manner of books concerning the common laws of the realm."[7] Moreover, nothing could be published even within the confines of the exclusive licenses without the imprimatur of the royally chartered Stationers Company.[8] The result was a suffocating system of licensing and blanket censorship. This system collapsed, not so much from the urge for free expression as from economic pressures for easier entry into the highly profitable printing business. Only an economically ruinous access requirement could approximate these grave consequences.

Finally, the means of implementing access requirements need not follow the pattern of historical licensing. To carry out its high

functions, the royally chartered Stationers Company fastened a
stranglehold on the English press. Very broad access requirements,
guaranteeing complete equality in public expression or ensuring
fairness in public debate, would produce a similar stifling official
supervision of the press. However, nothing remotely so intrusive
would be required to administer reasonable access obligations. In
light of these three differences, much imagination is required to see
in access requirements anything comparable to the English system of
"previous restraints." If access requirements should be regarded as
unconstitutional or as unwise legislative policy, it should be on
grounds other than historical reflex.

On the other hand, to draw arguments in favor of access from the
rejection of licensing is equally farfetched. It is true that economic
stultification of the licensing system led to its demise, not opposition
to its suppression of unapproved expression.[9] And in a sense, then,
the end of licensing was the result of dissatisfaction with monopolization of the means of expression and a demand for access to the
privilege of printing. However, it is mere semantics to enlist this
historical experience in the cause of access. The printers of the
seventeenth and eighteenth centuries in England and America wanted
government to stop interfering with their opportunity to engage in a
profitable business. They would have been equally outraged by a
government order to print in the service of some conception of the
public interest.

The only other historical analogy to access that comes to mind is
strained. The development of the party system in Parliamentary
politics led early eighteenth-century political leaders to use unofficial
mouthpieces for disseminating approved versions of governmental
affairs. Many of the leading literary figures of the day, including
Daniel Defoe, Jonathan Swift, and Joseph Addison, were employed
by either Whig or Tory leaders. Other writers, such as Henry Fielding
and Samuel Johnson, received valuable sinecures or pensions from
political leaders for presenting party views through ostensibly
uncommitted newspapers and pamphlets.[10] In a distant sense, the
press in the eighteenth century afforded access to officially mandated expression. But such voluntary, if mercenary, subsidization is a far
cry from the access obligations conceivable today.

Although history supplies no parallels to access obligations, this
absence does not necessarily mean that history is not significant to
the issue of access. Novelty in matters pertaining to the First
Amendment often triggers a Burkean impulse in constitutional law.

As Chief Justice Hughes expressed it in *Near* v. *Minnesota*:

> *The fact that for approximately one hundred and fifty years there has been almost an entire absence of attempts to impose previous restraints upon publications relating to the malfeasance of public officers is significant of the deep-seated conviction that such restraints would violate constitutional right.*[11]

But our constitutional law also has long recognized the dangers of falling into the habit of mind that Tocqueville ascribed to the defenders of the *ancien regime:*

> *[T]hey confound the abuses of civilization with its benefits, and the idea of evil is inseparable in their minds from that of novelty.*[12]

However, a deep-seated suspicion of access simply because it is new is not a convincing answer to its proponents. Some years ago, Morris Cohen wrote:

> *It is customary to have historical introductions to all sorts of practical discussions; but generally they are like the chaplain's prayer that opens a political convention, graceful and altogether unexceptionable, but hardly determinative of subsequent proceedings.*[13]

History's failings as a teacher in the access controversy are useful background to consideration of access requirements. The conclusion that our historical tradition of government and the press has little of significance to say on a problem is, in itself, a significant conclusion.[14] The boundaries of debate are therefore both compressed and expanded: Access may be neither justified as an extension of that which history has approved nor attacked as tantamount to something history has rejected. When history provides no mode of evaluation, we are put to the test of contemporary analysis.

Access and First Amendment Theory

The discussion that follows is intended to suggest the problems of First Amendment principle posed by the access controversy. Analysis of such a variegated problem as access, in terms of a body of diverse constitutional principles, is better deferred until after discussion of the areas of law bearing directly on it. Therefore, the issues introduced here will be treated in greater depth and in more concrete settings later in this book. Perhaps the most basic question is whether the First Amendment contains both principles of individual (or institutional) autonomy *and* social policies of diversity of expression—ideas that, in some circumstances, may conflict. Another basic question concerns the impact that the notion of equality might have on First Amendment freedoms. When one person's asserted First Amendment rights of expression conflict with another's asserted right of individual or editorial autonomy, should the courts look to the Constitution's guarantee of equal protection under the law for a mediating principle? Some see this conflict expressed in the First Amendment's dual prohibition on abridging "the freedom of speech, or of the press." Does the freedom "of the press" guarantee autonomy, with principles of equality and policies of diversity of expression guaranteed in the phrase "freedom of speech"?

Consideration of access poses other basic questions as well. What is the role of private property in the exercise of constitutional obligations? Guarantees of access for purposes of expression have been vigorously enforced in public places such as parks, streets, and government grounds. But should comparable constitutional guarantees of access also apply to private communications media? Constitutional guarantees, including those of the First Amendment, apply only to the conduct of government, or "state action," in the lawyer's phrase. However, ostensibly private conduct can functionally resemble or be implicated with official acts to such an extent that the courts will subject it to constitutional limitations. A major element of the access question, as a problem in constitutional law, is whether certain types of communications media are so intertwined with the state, or perform functions so similar or central to those of government, that they should be treated as state action. If so, what constitutional obligations of access should result? A moment's reflection about vast differences in publications in this respect—public school newspapers, federally licensed broadcast stations, advertisements in public buses, union newsletters, private newspapers—suggests that the state action question, like other elements of the access problem, is a matter for particularistic analysis rather than broad generalization.

But even when access questions involve private publications that are not state action, and therefore not subject to possible access obligations under the Constitution, the question still remains whether legislatures may impose access by statutes. In this setting, the Constitution becomes a shield rather than a sword. Whereas a finding that some publication should be regarded as state action is the predicate for possibly opening it as a public forum for expression under the compulsion of the Constitution, a statute imposing access obligations on a private publication must overcome possible First Amendment barriers against such legislative regulation of the press.

And what basic questions of First Amendment principle are posed by such statutory access obligations applicable to private publications? First Amendment theory has long been the preserve of *laissez-faire* thinking. The premise has been that "a multitude of tongues," protected by the First Amendment from governmental interference, would naturally tend to produce diversity of expression in which all shades of opinion could compete for political or cultural acceptance. The Bill of Rights generally reflects a conception of liberty as a collection of negative controls on official power. Consequently, the First Amendment has been viewed in negative terms: a constitutional prohibition on official interference with the free play of ideas. This prophylactic conception of the First Amendment has deep roots in the historical struggle for freedom of expression, a struggle in which government played the part of repression. Holmes and Brandeis captured this tradition in their metaphor of the "free marketplace of ideas," and in their pragmatic view of truth as the residue of competition in ideas.

Proponents of access requirements argue that guaranteed entry into modern mass communications media will increase diversity of expression, and that access obligations accordingly should be viewed as consistent with, and even supportive of, the First Amendment. However, some types of conditional access rights could actually discourage diversity of expression. For example, what if publishers were obligated to provide access whenever a publication was alleged to be a personal attack? Might they not decide to avoid the expense of providing free reply space, the hassle of suits over whether the circumstances required reply, and the infringement on their editorial autonomy by not publishing a critical item in the first place?

Although such "chilling effects" are a common issue in First Amendment adjudication, assessing them is very difficult, perhaps impossible, and estimating the potential effects of conditional access requirements is no exception. In some areas, such as libel, vague criminal statutes bearing on expression, and loyalty oaths, the Supreme Court has been willing to rest on intuition as to the amount of inhibition involved. On the other hand, the Court has refused to accept estimates of chilling effect in rejecting a journalist's privilege not to disclose information from confidential sources[15] and in upholding the application of conditional access rules to broadcasters.[16] One suspects that the Court's willingness to make such assumptions depends on the extent of its sympathy for the underlying claim. The nub of the issue is whether the Court will insist on an empirical showing of the chilling effects of access requirements when, in fact, they tend not to be demonstrable.

The constitutional status of advertising is also related to some types of access requirements. Many cases have held that commercial advertising is not protected by the First Amendment.[16] Regulation or prohibition of advertising is routine in connection with securities prospectuses,[17] deceptive product advertisements,[18] ads by legal or medical professionals,[19] racial preferences in real estate ads,[20] and a great variety of other commercial matters.[21] Furthermore, in 1973, a narrowly divided Supreme Court upheld a local ordinance that prohibited a newspaper from carrying "help-wanted" ads in sex-designated columns, except when gender was a genuine occupational qualification.[23] In contrast, the Court has given political advertising the same First Amendment protection granted to noncommercial political expression. *New York Times Co.* v. *Sullivan*, for example, significantly expanded First Amendment protection for political expression in a case involving a newspaper advertisement on behalf of civil rights activities in the South.[24]

Thus, a fundamental, though sometimes illusive, distinction has been drawn between commercial and political advertising. Since commercial advertising can be freely regulated or suppressed, and newspaper formats for commercial ads can be regulated, perhaps a newspaper's power to reject commercial ads does not necessarily involve the exercise of First Amendment freedoms. However, forcing publication of political ads might be a different matter.

Of the problems of First Amendment doctrine posed so far, one problem deserves more extended treatment at this point because it is central to reflection about the constitutional status of access to the media. This is the question of whether the First Amendment, in essence, states a constitutional policy in favor of the broadest diversity of expression, and nothing more, or whether the First Amendment guarantees individual (or institutional) autonomy from government regulation with respect to the content of expression.

Most discussion of access requirements takes as its premise the notion that the First Amendment favors diversity of expression.[25] Most writing in opposition to access also accepts this same constitutional premise, but argues that access obligations will produce chilling effects or have the effect of dangerously expanding official supervision of expression and that either of these effects, in the long run, will restrict diversity of expression.[26] But is the Constitution's goal of diversity of expression the only basis for analyzing access obligations?

When the First Amendment is considered generally, it is clear that instrumental policies favoring the broadest diversity of expression are not an adequate account of the religious freedoms guaranteed. No one would claim that a Jehovah's Witness who publishes an anticlerical pamphlet should be required to provide access to a Roman Catholic to state his defense of the priesthood. Such a demand, hardly even conceivable, would be met with the majestic principle of the Virginia Statute of Religious Liberty, drafted in 1786 by Thomas Jefferson, ushered through the legislature by James Madison, and an important part of the "generating background" of the First Amendment:

> . . . to compel a man to furnish contributions of money for the propagations of opinion which he disbelieves, is sinful and tyrannical.[27]

If an order to furnish money for alien religious views is tyrannical, how much more so, in Jefferson's and Madison's view, would be a requirement actually to propagate repugnant views?

Can First Amendment guarantees of autonomy with respect to religious belief also have some bearing on the question of access in nonreligious contexts? The insulation of religious expression from access obligations might be thought to rest on the distinct constitutional text of the religious guarantees; access obligations might be thought closer to "prohibiting the free exercise" of religion than to "abridging the freedom of speech, or of the press."

Some historical evidence suggests the founding fathers may have considered both freedom of expression and freedom of religious conscience—the two great individual liberties protected by the First Amendment—to be based on an integrated conception of individual autonomy in matters not appropriate for government regulation. J. B. Bury tells us that the earliest arguments in favor of free speech rested on the premise that a person should not be punished for opinions held and expressed as a matter of conviction, similar to faith, since one could not help having such beliefs.[28] Moreover, Jefferson's and Madison's concerns with political and religious freedom went hand in hand, and there are hints in their writings that constitutional protections of religious liberty have parallels with respect to political expression. In the *Memorial and Remonstrance against Religious Assessments*, Madison wrote in 1785:

> *[T]he equal rights of every citizen to the free exercise of his Religion according to the dictates of conscience is held by the same tenure with all our other rights. If we recur to its origin, it is equally the gift of nature.*[29]

Jefferson chose the Virginia Statute of Religious Freedom as the occasion to attack what was in the eighteenth century the central means of inhibiting political expression: the "bad-tendency" test of criminality that lay at the heart of the common law of seditious libel (the punishment of expression critical of political authorities):

> *[T]o restrain the profession or propagation of principles on supposition of their ill tendency is a dangerous falacy* [sic], *which at once destroys all religious liberty . . . it is time enough for the rightful purposes of civil government for its officers to interfere when principles break out into overt acts against peace and good order.*[30]

The leading historian of the First Amendment, Leonard Levy, tells us that Jefferson was indebted for this idea to the libertarian Reverend Philip Furneaux, who had proposed the same overt-acts test as the condition for official control of expression of any nature, political or religious, because, in Furneaux's words, "religious and civil liberty have a reciprocal influence in producing and supporting one another."[31]

Suggestions of parallelism between religious and political constitutional liberties also appear in Jefferson's reaction to the infamous Sedition Act of 1798. Jefferson's great biographer, Dumas Malone, notes that Jefferson apprehended that "since freedom of the press had been so successfully attacked, there had surely been grounds to fear for freedom of religion."[32] And there is the striking symmetry of Jefferson's most famous statement about the Sedition Act:

> I discharged every person under punishment or prosection under the sedition law, because I considered, and now consider, that law to be a nullity, as absolute and as palpable as if Congress had ordered us to fall down and worship a golden image.[33]

Despite the concerns of the founding fathers, federal repression of religious beliefs happily has not been as serious a problem in the United States as the repression of political freedom has been. American history shows no laws endangering religious freedoms to the extent that the Sedition Act of 1798 or the Espionage Act of 1918 endangered liberty of political expression. Compulsory oaths in the United States have aimed for political loyalty, not religious orthodoxy.[34] The First Amendment judicial tradition, entirely a product of the twentieth century, since no case raising First Amendment issues came to the Supreme Court before 1900, has accordingly centered on freedom of political expression. In building a rhetoric of freedom of political expression, the Supreme Court naturally has turned more to considerations of social utility than of freedom of conscience. Holmes and Brandeis sought to persuade their brethren on the Court to protect speech largely on pragmatic grounds of social value. The marketplace of ideas was the result, and it remains the dominant imagery in the rhetoric of freedom of expression. Individual speech must be protected because it brings diversity, competition, and therefore efficiency to the collective search for truth, not because it is a manifestation of personal autonomy on which the state may not impinge. Access, apart from conditional obligations that might produce chilling effects, fits comfortably within this instrumental tradition. However, demands for access to the media raise the question of whether the utilitarian way of looking at freedom of expression that we have inherited from Holmes and Brandeis does full honor to our tradition of freedom.

In at least one great First Amendment decision, *West Virginia State Board of Education* v. *Barnette*,[35] the Court integrated political and religious freedom in a unitary conception of personal autonomy. There the Court held that school children could not be compelled to salute the flag against their religious scruples. Interestingly, the majority opinion rested exclusively on freedom of speech, did not even mention the provisions of the First Amendment dealing with religious freedoms, and specifically stated that the issue did not turn on the possession of religious beliefs. Justice Jackson's language is suggestive: "... compelling the flag salute ... invades the sphere of intellect and spirit which it is the purpose of the First Amendment to our Constitution to reserve from all official control."[36] In order to sustain the compulsory flag salute, Jackson wrote, the Court would be "required to say that a Bill of Rights, which guards the individual's right to speak his own mind, left it open to public authorities to compel him to utter what is not in his mind."[37]

The flag-salute case might be considered of only minor relevance to the question of access to the media. Although the Court did not rely expressly on guarantees of religious liberty, it must still be conceded that the compelled expression at issue was closely related to religious autonomy. The flag salute ceremony may not seem comparable to access because the former implied affirmation of belief, while access can be given to expressions without representing the view of the publisher. But this distinction tends to be fuzzy. Indeed, in an earlier flag-salute case, Justice Frankfurter regarded the identical compelled ceremony as "not aimed at the promotion or restriction of religious beliefs."[38] Being forced to go through obnoxious motions, however, can infringe on personal autonomy.

The second reason *Barnette* may be of limited relevance to access to the mass media is that, even if *Barnette* can be read to affirm a right of political autonomy, it does so in the context of individual expression. Thus, while it might be the basis for a claim by Thomas Paine that he may not be forced to give access to Edmund Burke in one of his pamphlets, a guarantee of autonomy that protects personal expression against access obligations would not necessarily extend to the collective enterprises that now constitute the media of mass communications. A second decision of the Supreme Court, not concerned with access, may shed some light on this issue.

In *International Association of Machinists* v. *Street*, a member of a labor union (which the member had been compelled to join by virtue of a union-shop agreement) claimed that the union was spending his compulsory dues to support political candidates and doctrines with which he disagreed.[39] The Supreme Court's majority opinion concluded that the member's claim raised constitutional questions "of the utmost gravity."[40] But it ruled that these questions did not have to be decided because the Railway Labor Act, which controlled the power of that union to exact compulsory dues, did not authorize the union to spend the dues of members to advance political causes to which the members were opposed. However, Justice Black urged that the statute did authorize such spending and, so construed, should be held to violate the First Amendment:

> *Compelling a man by law to pay his money to elect candidates or advocate laws or doctrines he is against differs only in degree, if at all, from compelling him by law to speak for a candidate, a party, or a cause he is against. The very reason for the First Amendment is to make the people of this country free to think, speak, write and worship as they wish, not as the Government commands.*[41]

The *Street* decision suggests that a large organization's espousal of political causes can violate an individual's First Amendment rights. The decision demonstrates that the concept of autonomy under the First Amendment is not limited to matters of religious scruple, and that actions by large collective enterprises can raise questions of autonomy. *Street* does not indicate that a collective publishing enterprise, as such, could claim comparable autonomy. But it is a step in that direction.

The aim of this discussion has been to suggest the incompleteness of instrumental approaches to the meaning of the First Amendment. Certainly the marketplace of ideas is a powerful constitutional symbol. It is also a reminder that the First Amendment rests on a more pragmatic base than simple altruistic respect for individual autonomy. However, the tradition of the First Amendment, and important decisions related to this tradition, define a scope for the Amendment that is not instrumental, not designed to shape the political process, and not a policy of efficiency in democratic self-governance. Against a historical perspective of commitment to religious and political autonomy, required access assumes a more questionable theoretical posture.

If autonomy is a basic element of our tradition of free expression, deserving of respect in constitutional analysis along with the utilitarian goal of diversity of expression, then demands for access theoretically require us to reconcile the values of autonomy and diversity. The aim of analysis would be to determine which "publishers" should be protected from access so that the values of autonomy can be best preserved. And, conversely, analysis would have to determine which other "publishers" should be made accessible to serve the goal of diversity. Rights of access would have to be allocated to particular publishing units in such a way that the aim of diversity would be served to the maximum, but jeopardy to the values of autonomy would be kept to a minimum.

This sort of analysis is more easily described than executed. One of the more realistic aspects of First Amendment law, in libel and a number of other areas, is what Professor Harry Kalven, Jr., has termed "the distrust of the law's own capacity to make needed discriminations."[42] The necessity of generalization in drawing legal principles may argue for rather gross distinctions in reconciling autonomy and diversity. In fact, current rules of access to the communications media implement such a gross distinction. With regard to the electronic media, now subject to certain rights of access, the imposition of broader access guarantees is considered a purely administrative and legislative question, not enmeshed in First Amendment strictures. The print media, however, have not been subject to rights of access and recently have won a ringing endorsement of their autonomy. Accordingly, current law may reflect a rough accommodation of the policies of equality and diversity, and the principle of publisher autonomy. Is this divergent treatment of print and electronic media with respect to access a sound pattern for accommodating these dialectical First Amendment interests? We will return to this central question later, after exploring some of the characteristics of modern communications media that have led to demands for access rights.

Access as a Remedy for
Concentration of the Media

[Right] conclusions are more likely to be gathered out of a multitude of tongues, than through any kind of authoritative selection. To many this is, and always will be, folly; but we have staked upon it our all.

Judge Learned Hand[1]

... the American people should be made aware of the trend toward the monopolization of the great public information vehicles and the concentration of more and more power over public opinion in fewer and fewer hands.

Vice-President Spiro Agnew[2]

Nothing has raised greater doubts about traditional First Amendment precepts than the trend toward concentration and centralization of the communications media. First Amendment theory has long been grounded in *laissez-faire* thinking, as the durability of Holmes's free marketplace of ideas metaphor reflects. However, substantial economic and organizational barriers to entry into this competitive marketplace are challenging the assumptions of traditional First Amendment theory. If the nature, the structure, and the economics of modern communications are such that only a few can enter the marketplace, then the negative conception of the First Amendment as a protection against government interference no longer ensures diversity of expression. As communications media become ever more concentrated, centralized, and remote, many are searching

37

for an affirmative dimension to the First Amendment, whereby the constitutional mandate would be used to force open the marketplace of ideas. Access obligations have been prominent among the legal refo:ms proposed.

At first glance, an open and diverse communications marketplace seems like a far more realistic assumption today than at the time that the First Amendment was adopted. From the founding of the first regular newspaper in the American colonies in 1715, the number of papers grew slowly to 14 in 1750 and 23 by 1765.[3] By the eve of the Revolution, only 37 newspapers were regularly published in the thirteen colonies, with Boston, Philadelphia, and New York each having at least three competing papers. By the end of the Revolution, the number of papers had dropped to 20.[4] In 1790, the United States had only 8 daily newspapers, although there were 83 weeklies.[5] Thus, during the mid-eighteenth century, when Benjamin Franklin celebrated his editorial autonomy by remarking that his newspaper was not a stagecoach with seats for everyone, the number of periodicals in operation hardly gave promise of an open and pluralistic marketplace of ideas.

Compared to these early days, the present seems like an era of almost bewildering abundance and diversity in mass communications. In 1973, a total of 1,774 newspapers reached more than 60 million readers on a daily basis,[6] while 9,755 periodicals of various types catered to innumerable mass and specialized audiences.[7] Electronic mass media operating in the United States in 1973 totaled 704 television stations, 4,346 AM radio stations, and 2,307 FM stations.[8] And to this must be added an annual flood of books: in 1969, some 1,769 publishing houses produced over 200 million textbooks and almost 900 million trade books.[9]

These unrefined statistics suggest that we today have a freer and more open marketplace of ideas than did the founding fathers. If so, how can one account for the widespread belief that effective means of mass communication are far more remote and inaccessible to most persons today than in the formative years? Consider these representative statements from a 1969 staff report to the Violence Commission:

When the Constitution was adopted, 97 percent of the population lived in places so small that they were not even called towns. Of the remaining three percent, most lived in towns whose populations were under 25,000—most only a few thousand. Under these conditions, the individual could make his opinions known by giving a speech on Sunday outside the local church or by getting a printer to put up a broadside and by posting it in taverns and in other public gathering spots around town. With relative ease he could have an impact.

Today, unless the individual has access to formal channels of communication, it is almost impossible for him to have an impact. His ability to communicate widely is extremely limited. At a minimum, an effective marketplace requires access on approximately equal terms by all those with messages. Long ago, perhaps, a newspaper might have been started with relatively little capital by one whose views were strong enough to demand that they be aired. . . .

Yet, as we have said, the media today comprise institutions far different from the press of two centuries ago. The forms have changed. Circulation has increased beyond anything then dreamed of. Competitive pressures have increased and in response the media have learned from sheer necessity the art of manipulating vast audiences for economic gain. In the process of this growth and change, the ability of any single man to gain access to the "marketplace of ideas" has become all but extinct.[10]

Impressions of this kind underlie the arresting opening paragraph of Professor Barron's argument that the First Amendment be reshaped in an affirmative dimension to guarantee rights of access:

There is an anomaly in our constitutional law. While we protect expression once it has come to the fore, our law is indifferent to creating opportunities for expression. Our constitutional theory is in the grip of a romantic conception of free expression, a belief that the "marketplace of ideas" is freely accessible. But if ever there were a self-operating marketplace of ideas, it has long ceased to exist. The mass media's development of an antipathy to ideas requires legal intervention if novel and unpopular ideas are to be assured a forum.[11]

Thus, despite the seeming multitude of mass communications media, most citizens in the United States experience monopoly newspapers, a small number of television stations that are dominated by network programming, and a larger number of radio stations broadcasting largely interchangeable programs with a minimum of concern for public affairs. No wonder, then, that basic questions for constitutional law and the public's attitudes toward the press are

concerned with the trend toward media concentration and centralization. Because our law's traditional responses under the antitrust
statutes are widely perceived to be inadequate in countering this
trend, some contend that access guarantees are necessary to
reconstitute a free and open marketplace of ideas.

Concentration of the Media

The extent of media concentration can be measured in three
contexts: (1) concentration of outlets within a single geographic
area; (2) common ownerships (chains) of outlets in a number of
markets; and (3) conglomerate acquisition of news outlets. Some
statistics will give an impression of the problem.

Concentration within a single area. Local media concentration is
indicated by a decline in the number of competing newspapers and
by lack of competition between broadcast and print media in many
cities.

The number of cities with competing newspapers has shrunk
dramatically during this century. The percentage of American cities
that are served by newspapers and have more than one paper fell
from about 60 percent in 1910 to less than 4 percent in 1972.[12] In
1910, more than 600 cities had separately owned, competing, daily
newspapers. By 1945, this number had dropped to 117.[13] By 1968,
"[O]f the 1500 cities served by a daily newspaper, 85.6% were
one-newspaper towns. Although another 150 were served by two
dailies, these dailies were under single ownership. Thus, 95% of our
communities at the beginning of 1968 had newspapers that were
controlled by a single owner."[14] In 1975, only New York City has
more than two newspaper owners.[15]

A countervailing trend has been the growth of the suburban press.
In 1967, Donald Turner reported that, between 1945 and 1962, the
daily circulation of suburban papers in the ten largest metropolitan
areas rose 80 percent. During the same period, the aggregate
circulation of metropolitan dailies rose only 2 percent. "Just as
suburban merchants are taking business from downtown merchants,
suburban newspapers are effectively competing for areas of circulation growth that would otherwise go to the downtown papers by
default."[16] Within any given geographic area, however, there is likely
to be little competition among newspapers.

Additionally, in many markets there is little competition among various media in providing news. In 1967, local daily newspapers also controlled broadcast stations in 250 cities. Approximately 213 of these cities had only one newspaper.[17] And about 100 of those same newspapers controlled television stations as well.[18] Thirty of the largest fifty TV markets had at least one VHF station under common control with a daily newspaper.[19] Cross-ownership of newspapers and television stations is especially worrisome because surveys show that VHF television stations and newspapers are the public's dominant sources of information. Of persons questioned in a 1973 Roper poll, 64 percent said TV was their primary source of news, 50 percent named newspapers, 21 percent chose radio, and only 6 percent sought magazines. A similar poll found that 80 percent of the sample relied on TV and newspapers for news.[20] In 1974, 60 American cities were served by monopoly newspapers that also owned television stations in the same city. In 20 smaller cities, the only newspaper owns the only AM radio station.[21] The Federal Communications Commission has taken tentative steps to use its power of licensing radio and television broadcasters to reduce cross-media concentration in particular areas. But the FCC's actions have not had much effect. In rulemaking procedures in 1970 and 1971, the FCC adopted the so-called one-to-a-market rule, which prohibits common ownership or operation of a VHF television station and another television or radio station in the same service area.[22] However, the rule prohibited only new common ownership, and did not apply to existing licensees. Nor did the 1970 and 1971 rulemaking deal with cross-ownership of newspapers and broadcasting stations.

In 1975, the FCC issued important new rules concerning newspaper-broadcasting combinations.[23] The 1975 rules prohibit common ownership of daily newspapers and broadcast stations in the same service area. Here again, however, the prohibition operates prospectively only, and will not break up existing combinations. Because most newspaper-broadcasting common ownerships have existed for years, and tend to be very stable, the 1975 rules will not have much effect.[24] As to one type of common ownership, where the only newspaper in a community owns the only broadcasting station, the 1975 rules call for breaking up existing combinations by 1980. Even in these cases of required divestiture, however, the Commission has indicated that waivers will be granted where broadcast licenses cannot be sold to a satisfactory purchaser at a fair price.[25]

Apart from these rulemaking proceedings, the FCC has been reluctant to give cross-ownership and concentration issues significant weight in individual license renewal proceedings. In one 1969 decision, the Commission treated concentration as a key factor in refusing to renew the license of WHDH, Inc. to operate a VHF television station in Boston.[26] WHDH, Inc. also owned a newspaper, an AM radio station, and an FM station. The Court of Appeals for the District of Columbia affirmed the Commission's decision, and endorsed the policy of diversification of media ownership.[27] But later Commission decisions suggest that concentration issues will not be considered in individual license renewal proceedings (unless a licensee has engaged in a specific violation of the antitrust law), but rather left to rulemaking.[28] This in effect protects most existing cross-ownerships. Thus, *WHDH* appears to be an aberrational decision.

In short, despite the Federal Communications Commission's concern about media concentration, residents of an American town rarely have more than one newspaper to choose from, and that monopoly paper commonly controls one of the few broadcasting stations.

Chain concentration. Media outlets that are independent from other media within a particular market are still likely to be owned by chains of newspapers or broadcasting stations strung across the country.[29] The proportion of daily circulation held by newspaper chains rose from about 43 percent in 1950 to over 60 percent in 1972.[30] The ten largest daily newspaper chains account for one-fourth of the total annual revenues for the industry and one-third of the circulation.[31]

Chain ownership is also increasing in broadcasting. Under FCC regulations, no single interest may control more than seven television stations, only five of which may be VHF. But these regulations have little impact on the diversity of programming available to viewers. The most significant chains, having five stations each, belong to the three major networks—ABC, CBS, and NBC. Together these three networks and their total of 15 stations received 52 percent of the total revenue of all television stations in 1974, while the other 48 percent of this revenue was shared among 654 other stations. Moreover, these three networks largely control the programming even of those affiliates they do not own outright. The networks produce or control the licensing of 95 percent of all prime-time programming, as compared with 67 percent in 1957.[32] And, in

1973, over 95 percent of the VHF stations in the top ten markets were owned by groups, while over 75 percent of all commercial television stations in the top 100 markets were held by groups. Furthermore, the type of group that owns the largest proportion of VHF stations in the top 100 market is the newspaper-based group, which owns 25 percent of these strong signal channels.[33]

When both cross-ownership and group ownership are considered together, one finds that over four-fifths of commercial VHF television stations are owned either by a group or a daily newspaper. In 11 states and in the District of Columbia, all stations are thus owned.[34]

In addition to the problem of media power being concentrated in a few hands, it has been argued that the news disseminated by chains and groups is more concerned with national events than with local events. Moreover, as chains increase in economic efficiency, they tend to bar new voices from entering the media. Nevertheless, at least one economist has maintained that group ownership is not undesirable given the present structure of the television industry.[35] Group ownership provides potentially a competitive alternative to the three television networks, whose horizontal integration through nationwide affiliation contracts and whose vertical integration through extensive holdings in all stages of programming production creates enormous economic power.

Conglomerates. The acquisition of media by conglomerates is a direct challenge to the ideal of a press that covers public affairs without fear or bias. Conglomeration is a problem about which many are concerned, but about which nobody seems to know much. The problem is complicated both by the difficulty of deciding what a conglomerate is and by the novelty of conglomerate mergers as an antitrust and regulatory concern. But impressionistic data are a useful indicator of trends.

Conglomeration probably has gone farthest in broadcasting. ITT's recent attempt to purchase ABC would have brought the last of the networks under conglomerate control, and the vast empire of that would-be purchaser has focused attention on potential conflicts-of-interest in news reporting. Meanwhile, NBC is owned by RCA, which "has substantial foreign investments . . . , is the leading international telegraph company, owns RCA Victor Records, Random House Books, a drug company (Hoffman-La Roche), and a car rental firm (Hertz)."[36] CBS has 39 major subsidiaries, including Holt, Rinehart, and Winston, Creative Playthings, and Columbia Records. (For a time, it owned the New York Yankees.) CBS also has substantial space and defense interests, and it has invested heavily in the credit affiliates of Chrysler, Ford, and General Motors.[37]

Newspapers also are parts of conglomerate empires. The Mormon Church has pervasive newspaper holdings in Utah and in the Southwest, as well as a 50 percent interest in the Utah-Idaho Sugar Co., a major investment in the *Los Angeles Times,* an insurance company, a trucking company, numerous farms, and other interests, all of which solidify an important influence in Utah and Idaho politics.[38] A similar situation exists in Delaware, where the du Ponts' influence on state politics is enhanced by their ownership of both Wilmington daily newspapers. Moreover, the Christiana Securities Company, a holding company associated with the du Ponts, owns all but one of the dailies in the state. That one exception has a circulation of only 13,000.[39]

The exact proportion of media outlets owned by conglomerates is difficult to determine. Hard data is lacking, but enough is known to warrant serious concern. "The combined holdings of groups, cross-media owners, conglomerates, and firms related to the mass media encompass 58 percent of daily newspapers, 77 percent of TV stations, 27 percent of AM and 29 percent of FM stations."[40]

Moreover, in assessing the significance of these indications of media concentration, one must also add the influence of the two national wire news wire services, Associated Press and United Press International. Although a few large metropolitan newspapers subscribe to several wire services (the *Washington Post,* for example, receives teletyped information from 8 services), most smaller newspapers subscribe to only one, either AP or UPI.[41] On most papers, about 80 percent of what comes in on the wire services is not used, and a single editor (usually termed the "gatekeeper") decides what should be published and what should be discarded. These persons operate at incredible speed. Ben Bagdikian's excellent study *The Information Machines* found that gatekeepers take an average of two seconds deciding to discard a story, and about six seconds per story selected for use.[42] Furthermore, he found in studying 23 Wisconsin dailies that the single most important factor in the decision to use wire service stories or discard them was the time of their delivery on the teletype.[43] The later a story arrived, the less chance it had of being published. The extent of reliance on wire services for published news varies substantially from paper to paper, but one study suggests that reliance increases with monopoly characteristics. A newspaper that was initially a local monopoly, then had a vigorous competitor for a time, and then was a monopoly again, devoted 40 percent of its nonadvertising space to local news during its first monopoly period. When it had a strong competitor, the amount of local news increased to 50 percent. When it reverted back to a monopoly, local news fell back to 43 percent.[44] The explanation for this pattern is probably that local news is roughly 90 percent more expensive for newspapers to gather and publish, since it does not come from the wire services.*

Reliance on the national wire services is even stronger in broadcast journalism. Edward Jay Epstein's study of NBC national news in 1968 and 1969 found that 70 percent of the stories broadcast were based on either AP or UPI, and less than 15 percent were based on in-house sources.[45] Local broadcasting stations are even more dependent on AP and UPI. Thus, as Bagdikian has written, "in both the small radio and the large television station, the national news is substantially the leading item in the standard wire service menu for the day—a headline service." On the other hand, broadcasters' reporting of local news "is a reaction to the initiative of others: free information from official sources, press conferences called by those wishing publicity, or plagiarizing headlines and first paragraphs of a local paper."[46]

The impressionistic data collected in this chapter suggest the impact of media concentration and centralization on that important segment of the marketplace of ideas comprised of newspapers and broadcast stations. The typical American lives in a city served by a newspaper that is a local monopoly and is owned by the same interests that control one of the local television stations. Both the newspaper and TV stations are, in turn, likely to be either part of a centrally controlled chain that holds numerous other broadcasting stations or newspapers, or part of a conglomerate corporation with numerous interests that are potentially in conflict with unbiased reporting. Moreover, the TV station is almost certain to rely on a centrally controlled network for most of its programming, including news and public affairs. Two of the existing three networks are themselves conglomerates. And most of the news conveyed by the local paper, and even more of the news that is broadcast in the area, will have emanated from one of two national wire services. The result

---

*Another difference was that under competition, the newspaper increased its coverage of dramatic and sensational news, while as a monopoly it included more articles on long-range developments.

is that the typical American's main sources of news simply do not conform to the ideal of a wide variety of competing, locally controlled and oriented, independent organizations.

Former Vice-President Spiro Agnew thus was acute enough to choose a vulnerable target for his assault on the nation's communications media. The trend toward local monopoly, cross-ownership, and conglomeration of media directly challenges the *laissez-faire* premises of the First Amendment. No other tendency so endangers the press's traditional freedom from government control.

Is Access an Appropriate Remedy for Media Concentration?

American law has two ways of dealing with economic concentration. First, the antitrust statutes seek to protect markets made up of diverse, independent competitors from becoming dominated by monopolies, and they attempt to prevent unduly concentrated economic enterprises from taking certain actions that would increase their shares of the market. However, some goods and services are characterized by economies of scale to such an extent that one firm can serve a market more efficiently and, therefore, more cheaply than can two or more competing firms. It is not within the power, nor is it the aim, of antitrust law to prevent such "natural monopolies." Moreover, with respect to certain types of economic activity, our law makes a conscious choice to prefer monopoly, as in the case of telephone communication or electric power companies, because necessary public regulation is easier to impose on a single enterprise than on separate competitors. The law's second answer to economic concentration, in cases of "natural" or "preferred" monopolies, is ordinarily public utility regulation or, occasionally, government ownership and operation.

Analysis of whether access obligations are a necessary or appropriate response to media concentration and monopoly can be pursued by reference to these two bodies of law: antitrust law, which attempts to prevent monopoly, and public utility regulation, which accepts the inevitability or desirability of monopolies and imposes comprehensive legal controls to protect society from the economic power that monopolies could wield in the absence of regulation. The initial question is whether either body of law is, or should be, applicable to the communications media. If so, are the rules and remedies characteristic of that body of law analogous to, or do they suggest the desirability of, imposing access obligations on the press?

Antitrust Remedies and Access Rights

The First Amendment does not prevent antitrust law from being applied to the communications media. In fact, the concerns of antitrust law are harmonious with the premises of the First Amendment. In the words of the Supreme Court in the seminal *Associated Press* decision of 1945:

> *It would be strange indeed, however, if the grave concern for freedom of the press which prompted adoption of the First Amendment should be read as a command that the government was without power to protect that freedom. The First Amendment, far from providing an argument against application of the Sherman Act, here provides powerful reasons to the contrary. That Amendment rests on the assumption that the widest possible dissemination of information from diverse and antagonistic sources is essential to the welfare of the public, that a free press is a condition of a free society. Surely a command that the government itself shall not impede the free flow of ideas does not afford non-governmental combinations a refuge if they impose restraints upon that constitutionally guaranteed freedom. Freedom to publish means freedom for all and not for some. Freedom to publish is guaranteed by the Constitution, but freedom to combine to keep others from publishing is not. Freedom of the press from governmental interference under the First Amendment does not sanction repression of that freedom by private interests. The First Amendment affords not the slightest support for the contention that a combination to restrain trade in news and views had any constitutional immunity.*[47]

But, if antitrust law applies to the press, do any accepted antitrust remedies support access rights by analogy? Of the traditional concerns of antitrust law—price-fixing or similar cartel arrangements restricting competitive activities, mergers tending to produce monopolies or oligopolies, and predatory practices designed to drive competitors out of business—the concern closest to access problems occurs when an entity refuses to deal with a buyer or seller in order to consolidate or extend its monopolistic position. Antitrust law responds to such refusals to deal in a manner suggesting the appropriateness of a right to advertise in communications media under certain circumstances. Although authorities have stated that the decisions concerning refusals to deal are "hopelessly irreconcilable"[48] and "foster a caricatured view of the law,"[49] nevertheless some simple principles can be drawn. If a newspaper enjoying monopoly power in a given area refuses to accept advertisements, with the aim of protecting or extending its dominant market power, it may be required by law to accept those ads. The *Lorain Journal,* which enjoyed a substantial monopoly of news and advertising in Lorain, Ohio, refused to deal with any advertisers that advertised over a radio station in a nearby town. The District Court determined that the *Journal*'s refusals were designed to eliminate the threatened competition in advertising by destroying the broadcaster. The court, therefore, issued an injunction directing the *Journal* not to refuse advertisers for this reason,[50] and the Supreme Court affirmed:

> *The publisher claims a right as a private business concern to select its customers and to refuse to accept advertisements from whomever it pleases. . . . The right claimed by the publisher is neither absolute nor exempt from regulation. Its exercise as a purposeful means of monopolizing interstate commerce is prohibited by the Sherman Act. . . . The publisher suggests that the injunction amounts to a prior restraint upon what it may publish. We find in it no restriction upon any guaranteed freedom of the press. The injunction applies to a publisher what the law applies to others. The publisher may not accept or deny advertisements in an "attempt to monopolize . . . any part of the trade or commerce among the several States. . . . Injunctive relief under Section 4 of the Sherman Act is as appropriate a means of enforcing the Act against newspapers as it is against others.[51]*

A similar judicial order to publish an ad can be expected when the refusal to deal stems not from the newspaper's desire to monopolize but from pressure by another advertiser. For example, if a supermarket that advertised in a newspaper pressured that paper not to accept advertising from a competing food cooperative, the resulting refusal to deal would be a violation of the antitrust laws.[52] Presumably, in these circumstances, a court might order the newspaper to carry the cooperative's ad. Under the present antitrust statutes, however, the food cooperative would face the heavy burden of proving that there was a "contract, combination, or conspiracy" between the newspaper and the supermarket to effect the boycott. Of course, if the supermarket's contract with the newspaper contained an express prohibition on the newspaper's dealing with the food cooperative, there would be no difficulty in proving a violation of the Sherman Act. Otherwise, the excluded competitor must show that the newspaper was party to an agreement. In the absence of such proof or other evidence of an intention to monopolize, the newspaper is free under present law to refuse any advertiser.[53]

If such judicial orders present no difficulty under antitrust precedents, the same rationale might underlie legislation prohibiting refusals to deal that are motivated by anti-competitive purposes. Guidelines for such legislation might be that if a publication accepts advertising from enterprises in a given business, it must accept advertising from all persons or entities in the same business. The statute could contain exceptions to allow refusals in cases of fraud or criminality. Such a statute would not interfere with the right of a publication to refuse ads dealing with specified activities, such as astrology, X-rated movies, guns, or whatever, of which the publisher disapproves. This sort of legislation would bring refusals by the media to accept advertising in line with Professor Turner's suggestions covering refusals to deal in general:

> [W]hile there may well be merit in protecting the right of the trader to deal with those whom he chooses as a general rule, there is also merit in not letting him refuse to deal for any reason that suits him in those situations where refusal induces compliance in a course of action that offends public policy.[54]

Accepted principles of antitrust law thus lend support to the idea of an access obligation designed to assure advertisers some measure of equal treatment from media that deal with competitors. The constitutionality of such a statutory obligation has not been tested in the Supreme Court, but related precedents suggest that a statute of this kind would be upheld. The *Lorain Journal* decision indicates that court orders directing newspapers to run ads are a constitutional remedy for antitrust violations. Such narrow orders, enforceable through the judicial process, do not seriously threaten the economic or political independence of the newspaper. Broadening the principle of the *Lorain Journal* into legislative form does not call for a different constitutional result. Where comparable ads have been published previously, a publisher cannot persuasively advance concern for the "tone" of his publication. On the other hand, the ability to advertise can be vital to a business enterprise, and competitors with large advertising budgets can exert considerable economic leverage over access to advertising. For this reason, statutory access to advertising space would protect the smaller competitor.

A long line of decisions has generally depreciated First Amendment interests in advertising, whether the claim involves the right to advertise at all[55] or the right to advertise in a given form.[56] Access obligations as applied to advertising are, therefore, least vulnerable to constitutional challenge. A publication is not forced to donate its property and skills to a position that is not its own.

Whether such a narrow access requirement is desirable as a matter of public policy depends on two variables. First, to what extent are advertisers actually discriminated against in a manner adverse to the policies of the antitrust laws? Second, in situations where anti-competitive forces have not caused refusal to deal, is a general statute that would require acceptance of advertising justified by the number of truly anti-competitive refusals that would be corrected?

Antitrust laws do not prohibit refusals to deal motivated by other than anti-competitive purposes, and thus do not support by analogy the wisdom of general access obligation applicable to all commercial advertising, even if similar ads have not been accepted. A publisher may wish to exclude information about certain disapproved activities, or may wish to accept ads only for products that it has found acceptable or accurately described, such as those bearing the "*Good Housekeeping* Seal of Approval." Refusals to accept ads for these reasons reflect the general right of the newspaper to deal with whom it chooses. This right is not, nor should it be, a concern of the antitrust laws.

Although an obligation to publish all commercial ads would be undesirable, whether such a statute should be held unconstitutional is another matter. The vision of *Readers' Digest* being required to advertise a risque movie suggests that an appealing case could be made for the unconstitutionality of a statute requiring publication of all lawful advertisements. Certainly any access statute applicable to advertising would run considerable constitutional risks unless it respected reasonable publisher discretion about the general sorts of activities deemed appropriate for publication.

Access obligations dealing with political advertising are far afield from traditional antitrust concerns and would present more substantial First Amendment problems. The Supreme Court's latest statement on the application of First Amendment protections to advertising distinguishes sharply between commercial and political advertising.[57] The degree of publisher autonomy that the Court would uphold is probably different for commercial ads and for political ads. In any event, the constitutionality of obliging publishers to accept political ads involves analysis of the regulations governing radio and television[58] and careful consideration of a number of recent First Amendment decisions. Thus, it is best left for later discussion.

The Press as a Public Utility

Advocates of access rights are not satisfied with the sort of narrow right to advertise designed to protect competition which the antitrust laws would support. Indeed, the usual claim is that the antitrust laws are ineffective in bringing about a free and open marketplace of ideas in mass communications. Access guarantees, advocates contend, should not be patterned on the inadequate antitrust laws, but on the much broader laws pertaining to regulated industries and public utilities.

In assessing antitrust law's ability to deal with media concentration, one must start by recognizing that antitrust law does not, by reason of its own internal logic, hope to prevent natural monopolies, although it does control certain types of behavior by natural monopolies. A natural monopoly tends to arise when an enterprise's fixed costs are very high in relation to those costs which vary with the level of production. In such a situation, economies of scale are possible since a larger output allows lower costs per unit of production. If fixed costs can be spread over the entire output for a market, a monopolist supplying the entire output for that market will have lower unit production costs than would a greater number of entities, each with substantially the same fixed costs but with a smaller output over which to spread them.[59]

As high fixed production costs have increasingly characterized the newspaper business, and as mass advertising has rewarded newspapers with the largest audiences, economies of scale and advertising revenues, which tend to reinforce market dominance, have made the newspaper industry a classic example of local natural monopolies. The courts have recognized this fact. In *Union Leader Corp. v. Newspapers of New England, Inc.,*[60] the U.S. Court of Appeals for the First Circuit reviewed the antitrust implications of a fight between two newspapers for dominance in Haverhill, Massachusetts. The fact that the natural outcome was a monopoly, the court held, made the acts of either paper designed to dominate that market not "monopolizing" in violation of the Sherman Act. The court noted that "cities of the size in which [the newspapers] operate cannot support two good daily newspapers under present-day conditions."[61]

In the controversial Newspaper Preservation Act,[62] Congress also has recognized that newspapers tend to be natural monopolies. This statute is designed to allow separate newspapers operating in the same market to enter into joint arrangements with respect to printing and other elements of production, distribution, advertising, circulation, and other business operations. Such joint operations would ordinarily violate the antitrust laws. There are two conditions to the statute's application. First, the newspapers that participate in such joint arrangements may not pool editorial or reportorial staffs, and editorial policies must be separately and independently determined. The second requirement is that no more than one of the newspapers participating in the joint arrangement is "likely to remain or become a financially sound publication"[63] if the merger is prohibited.

The Newspaper Preservation Act seeks to enable competing newspapers to enjoy some of the economies of scale of a single enterprise, but without losing the social benefits of separate editorial policies. The Act broadens a judicially created exception to the antitrust laws concerning "failing companies," whereby mergers and certain cartel agreements that would otherwise be prohibited are allowed if one of the parties faced the probability of business failure. In a 1969 decision, the Supreme Court had held that the "failing company" exemption did not authorize joint operating agreements between competing newspapers unless it were shown that not only did one of the papers face business failure but also that there was no prospective purchaser of the failing paper other than the other paper with which the joint agreement was made.[64] The Act appears to enlarge significantly the Supreme Court's definition of the "failing company" by eliminating the requirement of no other prospective purchaser and liberalizing the Supreme Court's requirement of "grave probability of financial failure" and "dim or nonexistent" prospects for reorganization under the bankruptcy laws.

Because newspapers in most localities are classic examples of natural monopolies—as attested by the predominance of one-newspaper cities in America—antitrust law is largely impotent to prevent newspaper monopolies from developing.[65] This inadequacy has led to suggestions that the mass communications media should be regarded as public utilities, with the usual legal obligations that are imposed on public utilities in connection with their dealings with the public. If public utility treatment is a sound legal prescription for mass communications media, broad access guarantees would be supportable.

Public utility regulation is American law's usual response to natural or desired monopolies. Regulation is normally quite extensive. Often, the prices that regulated industries may charge for their products are determined by administrative rule. Moreover, it is common for a regulated enterprise to be prevented from discriminating among potential customers. Some are required to be common carriers. For example, the telegraph company and railroads are obliged to accept customers who will pay the established rates on a first-come, first-served basis. If the mass communications media are conceived to be public utilities, then access obligations might closely parallel the nondiscrimination and public service requirements that have traditionally been imposed on public utilities.

Analysis of whether mass communications media may be regulated in the manner of public utilities or other regulated industries need not be pursued on a level of speculation. We can look to radio and television for specific and lengthy experience in the treatment of communications media as a regulated industry. Since 1927, entry into the field of broadcasting has been conditioned on government licensing, and radio and television stations have been required to operate in the public interest, subject to periodic administrative review. Certain access obligations have been imposed on broadcasters as an aspect of their obligation to perform in the public interest.

Part three of this book devotes five chapters to the general subject of broadcast regulation, with specific attention to access requirements that have evolved. Assessment of whether access obligations should be imposed on the mass media because they resemble regulated industries in certain economic aspects is premature at this point. Likewise premature is consideration of the major First Amendment principles that stand in the way of treating the print media as public utilities. The purpose of this chapter has been to examine the extent of media concentration, the law's response to this problem, and how media concentration has raised demands for access rights. That this discussion should lead to exploration of the notion of public utility status for the mass communications media demonstrates the powerful and disruptive effect that concentration has had on traditional First Amendment assumptions about the press in the United States.

5

Access and Current Perceptions of the Press

The American people do not seem at all happy with their press. The fact itself . . . is beyond dispute and the nation's publishers are acutely aware of the general indictment. . . . It would be easy—and I think it would be foolish—to try to minimize the importance of this critical clamor. . . . All . . . in so large a chorus are hardly likely to be wrong.

Katherine Graham[1]

Along with concern over scarcity and concentration of the mass communications media, many have doubts as to whether new attitudes and practices by journalists have made access obligations an advisable means of counteracting journalistic bias and unfairness. Recent years have seen unparalleled changes in the nature of the press and in its relationship with government. Deep divisions in American society over a range of important issues have forced the press and the government into bitter confrontation. In this atmosphere of social tension, many journalists have become activists or advocates on matters of public policy. Meanwhile, most Americans now choose television as their primary source of information about public affairs. Television has compressed and personalized the news, further reducing the possibilities of diversity and tarnishing the image of journalistic "objectivity."

During the Nixon years, the press and the government assumed attitudes of truculence bordering on caricature. William Safire, President Nixon's former speechwriter, has recalled: "I must have

heard Richard Nixon say 'the press is the enemy' a dozen times."[2]
And the statement was not meant figuratively. Nixon saw the press
as committed to his political ruin, and he reciprocated. "This really
flicks the scab off, doesn't it?" he commented in approving Vice
President Agnew's attack on the national news media made during
the famous 1969 Des Moines speech.[3] Safire also quotes a Nixon
memorandum to an aide, written during the McGovern campaign:

> . . . [T]he Eastern Establishment media finally has a candidate
> who almost totally shares their views. Here again, if you con-
> sider the real ideological bent of The New York Times, The
> Washington Post, Time, Newsweek, and the three television
> networks, you will find overwhelmingly that their editorial bias
> comes down on the side of amnesty, pot, abortion, confiscation
> of wealth (unless it is theirs), massive increases in welfare, uni-
> lateral disarmament, reduction of their defenses, and surrender
> in Vietnam. Now they have a candidate within sight of the
> nomination who shares all these views. Now the country will
> find out whether what the media has been standing for during
> these last five years really represents the majority thinking of
> the country or is, in fact, a minority view.[4]

And the memo concluded, ironically it appears in retrospect, "The
Liberal Establishment Media May Have Had It."

The press tended to return this attitude in kind. Many persons
within the press thought they detected a campaign organized by the
Nixon Administration to intimidate the press. They pointed to the
administration's suggestions that public concern about media bias
would lead to demands for antitrust action, its repeated complaints
about news distortion, its wiretapping of journalists,[5] the wave of
subpoenas commanding journalists to testify about news sources,[6]
the thinly veiled threats to make political use of the FCC's power of
licensing broadcasters, and the FBI investigation of CBS news
correspondent Daniel Schorr.[7] While Nixon and his aides fulminated
against the Eastern elitist press, reporters and editors of The
Washington Post were engaged in a dramatic cloak-and-dagger effort
to peel away the lies and hypocrisies about Watergate and related
misdeeds by President Nixon and his associates.

Thus, two caricatured images of the press grappled until the Nixon
White House collapsed in disgrace. These polarized views of the press
that emerged in the Nixon years were not simply the products of
eccentric attitudes and events. Each is true and valid in significant

aspects, and they both represent, in exaggerated relief to be sure, tendencies in journalistic self-image and outside perceptions that have been gathering momentum for years. These attitudes have survived the end of the Vietnam War and the purging of the executive branch after Watergate. A notable dissenter from government policies during the Vietnam and Watergate period, former Senator J. William Fulbright, decried the press' new iconoclasm in 1975: "If once the press showed excessive deference to government and its leaders, it has now become excessively mistrustful and even hostile." He sees "a new inquisitorial style" in the press following Watergate and Vietnam, as new scandals are dredged up "for the delectation of an increasingly cynical and disillusioned public."[8]

The Traditional View of American Journalism

American journalism has traditionally carried an image of objectivity, neutrality, and practicality. Familiar exemplars might be Walter Lippmann and James Reston, persons of facts and occasionally of judgment, but never of ideology. On the cruder side of the image, one thinks of the reporters in the press room at the Chicago police headquarters in *The Front Page*, who care about nothing but an entertaining story. As journalist Richard Reeves wrote recently when he reviewed the 1975 movie version of this classic: "We're in the only business where lack of commitment and absence of conviction are considered high virtues."[9]

Paul Weaver has labeled this traditional stance "liberal journalism."[10] Liberal journalism's method of operation is objective presentation of information and opinion supplied by high-level official sources. News about public affairs is acquired from persons who are deeply involved in events, rather than from outside observers, and is presented to the public in an objective, noncritical manner. The viewpoint is "practical rather than ideological or theoretical."[11] Of course, even the most objective reporter or publication is more than just a neutral conduit of information. The necessity and power of selection create a degree of journalistic independence, as Douglass Cater emphasized:

Communications media have a vast power to shape government —both its policies and its leaders. This is not an editorial-page power. It is the power to select—out of the tens of thousands of words spoken in Washington each day and the tens of dozens of events—which words and events are projected for mankind to see. Equally powerful is the media's capacity to ignore; those words and events that fail to get projected might as well not have occurred.[12]

Because the objective tradition is based on information provided voluntarily by officials, reporters should be generally sympathetic with official perspectives on public events, and they should not publish embarrassing information or undermine public policy initiatives by premature disclosure.[13] On the other hand, officials should not deceive reporters or be unduly secretive. Each side of this symbiotic relationship has the tools to police the other side. Officials can discipline reporters by withholding information, by denying opportunities for a sophisticated "inside" view of unfolding events, and even by excluding reporters from newsworthy occasions. Reporters can put pressure on duplicitous or uncooperative officials by employing a combination of embarrassing publicity and withering lack of attention.

The Shift toward "Adversary Journalism"

Observers of the press noted a shift in basic journalistic attitudes and practices during the 1960s. The label commonly affixed to this new style is "adversary journalism." Liberal journalism's reliance on official sources of information had already produced not only a concrete, practical, and reasonably thorough version of public events, but also a vulnerability to cooptation. To ward off this danger, Paul Weaver argued, the liberal tradition included a self-image of independence and, indeed, a fiction of antagonism toward government.[14] But events in the 1950s and 1960s, Weaver believes, led more and more journalists to take seriously this fiction of "a journalism that is autonomous instead of interdependent, original instead of derivative, and in an adversary instead of cooperative relationship with government and officialdom."[15]

Three events are usually cited as initiating this shift from liberal to adversary journalism: McCarthyism, the U-2 incident, and the Bay of Pigs invasion.[16] Many journalists have concluded in retrospect that objectively rendering the official versions of these complex events added up to unwitting journalistic cooperation with official irresponsibility and demagoguery, outright deceit, and secretive foreign military machinations which were not in the national interest. Of course, it took more than three instances in which the press felt duped and victimized to bring about a new stance for journalism.

The Vietnam War was critical in changing the attitude of journalists toward their government. The extent of radical change in the relationship between government and press can be seen in the problem of maintaining military and foreign policy secrets. This nation has operated, throughout its history, with no clear laws governing publication of defense secrets, other than a few quite specific prohibitions pertaining to such narrow kinds of information as communications intelligence data, including codes, interception devices, and code-breaking techniques.[17] In fact, the United States was the only country to fight World War II without a general censorship law. This absence of clear legal prohibitions was tolerable only because the limits of the right to publish were so rarely tested. Generally, secrets were kept because persons in and out of government concerned with foreign and defense policy, including the press, shared basic premises about national aims.[18] But the unspoken rules of the defense and journalism establishment were violated under the pressures of the Vietnam War. The radical perspective of journalist I.F. Stone ("Every government is run by liars and nothing they say should be believed") became an accepted premise of reporting about the war.[19]

In the post-Pentagon Papers period, reporters and publications can no longer be relied upon to maintain defense and foreign policy secrets. Willingness to keep secrets tends to depend on sympathy for the underlying substantive policies that the secrecy serves. In recent years, American foreign and military policies have been sufficiently unpalatable that many journalists now actively attempt to thwart government secrecy.

The growth of serious radical, minority, and countercultural movements has also had a profound effect on relations between press and government. As numerous groups became disenchanted with cultural and political norms during the 1960s, and even committed themselves to legal disobedience to achieve their ends, the press increasingly found itself reporting on matters of immediate interest to law enforcement authorities. In covering these alienated groups, some journalists made extensive use of confidential informers. Law enforcement officials found journalists with information about militant groups to be tempting sources of information, and a spate of subpoenas aimed at journalists were issued in the late 1960s and early 1970s.[20] Over a four-year period, beginning in 1968, the *Chicago Tribune* staff alone received over 400 subpoenas.[21] This wave of subpoenas generated a feeling among many journalists that the government wished to cut off the flow of news from militant political, racial, and counterculture groups. As a result, many journalists viewed cooperation with law enforcement authorities in any matter having political overtones—campus demonstrations, urban riots, bombings, ingesting or selling drugs, official corruption, breach of secrecy investigations, and the like—as a threat to their ability to investigate and report on such matters. Law enforcement thus joined foreign policy and defense strategy as an area in which journalists perceived their own interests as adverse to the government.

In 1972, University of Michigan Law Professor Vince Blasi conducted a nationwide, empirical study of journalists' attitudes toward cooperation with law enforcement authorities in matters that might compromise assurances of confidentiality made to news sources. Even as a study of abstract attitudes, rather than of willingness to cooperate in real situations, the results show "a stance of jealous independence." Blasi found that only 26 percent of his sample of 1,000 journalists would be willing to inform the police of a likely bombing by a radical group before the bombing took place.[22] After such a bombing, only 38 percent said they would tell the police of the radical group's discussion of the bombing possibility. And, even if the journalists had strong reason to doubt that the person indicted for the bombing was responsible, only 60 percent expressed a willingess to testify in the defendant's behalf.[23]

Some observers, particularly those in government, believe that new patterns of recruitment have inculcated an adversary consciousness in journalists. Daniel Moynihan, an important member of the administrations of Presidents Kennedy, Johnson, Nixon, and Ford, decried in a widely read article what he regarded as the systematic hostility of journalists in the national media to the institution of the presidency.[24] He ascribed much of this hostility to the fact that the national media "thought to improve itself by recruiting more and more persons from middle- and upper-class backgrounds and trained at the universities associated with such groups." Moynihan contended that these recruits from the "adversary culture" infused their elitist, anti-Establishment attitudes into the national media. The muckracking heritage of American journalism, which in the past had been a small part of the overall tradition, has been inflated by dramatic instances of government deceit into a general attitude that exposing the seamy side of official acts is the optimum in successful reporting. Moynihan claimed that the result was a decline in journalistic objectivity, a harmful condition that is worsened by the absence of any tradition of self-correction in the American press.

An interesting response to Moynihan's charges was that of Max Frankel of *The New York Times*. Frankel argued that the growing spirit of skepticism in the press was mainly attributable to "the conduct of the government itself":

> *[Y]ou must begin by noting not the power for occasional deception in the White House, but the* habit *of regular deception in our politics and administration. . . . It is the damnable tendency toward manipulation that forces us so often into the posture of apparent adversaries.*[25]

However, Frankel conceded that "some of the newest recruits to our business":

> *. . .are impatient with the objective, or, more accurately, 'neutral' standards of journalism to which their elders aspired. . . . A few of them are impatient with any standard that would prevent them from placing their own views before the public. It is an important subject and an interesting debate.*[26]

But, in any event, Frankel argued, "opportunity for correction is rarely denied to the White House." Corrective mechanisms are not needed for "men of power." "It is the ordinary citizens, sometimes including the editors of the Eastern press, who require an outlet."[27]

Other critics attribute the press' adversary stance not to recruitment, but to the geographical milieu within which the leading mass media operate. Kevin Phillips points an accusing finger at the "New York-Washington media axis," which includes the *New York Times*, the *Washington Post* (owner of *Newsweek*), *Time*, *U.S. News and World Report*, the three television networks, the major book publishers, and the leading opinion magazines (*Harper's Magazine*, *The New Republic*, *National Review*). Phillips quotes columnist Robert Novak: "The national media is a melting pot where the journalists, regardless of background, are welded into a homogeneous ideological mold, joined to the liberal establishment and alienated from the masses of the country."[28]

Government officials are not alone in pointing to bias and to the absence of corrective mechanisms within the press. Ben Bagdikian, one of very few outstanding journalists who has taken the perform- ance of the press as his beat, has named systematic conflict of interest, commercialism, and general unresponsiveness to social change as dominant characteristics of American journalism. Bag- dikian has argued that "the most immediate threat to a free press in this country is [the press'] own conflict of interest."[29] These interlocking economic and political interests of publishers result in suppression of news in many cities, as Bagdikian demonstrated in his studies of the Delaware and Houston press.[30] A great amount of the "news" in newspapers, perhaps as much as 33 percent, is directly inspired by public relations agents.[31] The small-town press receives stories without charge from news syndicates that make a profit by charging propagandists a fee for distribution of their views, often in the form of ready-to-insert editorials. Moreover, the amount of news coverage supplied by newspapers is on the decline. In 1940, the average daily paper had 27 pages. By 1965, the number of pages had grown to 50; but 20 of these additional 23 pages were devoted to advertising. During this same period, enlarged type size, more liberal use of blank space, and increases in the size and number of photographs, comics, and syndicated features have all diminished the coverage of "hard news" by more than three pages.

The Impact of Television As a News Medium

The subjectivity, bias, antagonism to government, and absence of diversity that disturbed journalism's traditional image during the 1960s coincided with, and were partly the result of, the emergence of television as a leading news medium. In 1963, CBS and NBC expanded their nightly network news programs from fifteen minutes to half an hour. ABC followed in 1967. Today these three evening news shows draw a combined audience of more than 50 million persons each night. By comparison, the *New York Times* sells about 2 million copies each day, while a best-selling book reaches only 100,000 to 500,000 homes. As David Littlejohn has written: "The systems of television in leading Western countries have developed into a mass medium so unparalleled in the extent of its audience as virtually to require a redefinition of the adjective *mass*."[32] Besides attracting the largest audience of any news medium, television has with regularity strengthened its position over competing news media as the primary source of information about public affairs for most Americans.[33]

The characteristics of television news have contributed much to the public's concern over trends in American journalism. The typical city newspaper presents vastly more stories, both because space constraints are not so severe and because a newspaper can publish many stories that any particular reader will skip. In contrast, television, by its nature, offers an extremely compressed version of the news. A television news program is designed to be viewed in its entirety by all its viewers.

This difference also applies to individual stories. Newspaper stories typically present a focal event at the outset and follow that with background information, additional facts, elaborations of significance—all generally arranged in descending order of importance. This "inverted pyramid" organization allows the reader to either stop part way along or read just the first paragraph and scan the remainder. It also enables the editor to shorten a story by simply lopping off from the end.[34] Thus, the structure of the newspaper story allows for a looser, more discursive presentation of the facts. By contrast, a television news story must be tightly integrated.

Paul Weaver has noted that these structural differences, both in format and in individual stories, between newspapers and network news programs tend to make television news more thematic, more interpretive, and generally more unified and monolithic.[35] Furthermore, these tendencies are reinforced by the most obvious difference between television news and newspapers: the fact that, whereas newspapers typically employ an impersonal narrative style, television relies on the personalized narrator:

> [T]he reporter, in writing his story, never speaks in the first
> person, but the matter goes far beyond that. The reporter also
> never makes reference to his own actions in observing events
> and finding facts; there is never any explicit allusion to the
> reporter's own awareness of the motives of sources, the proba-
> ble validity of quoted statements, the extent to which the story
> at hand confirms or falsifies previous stories, and so forth.
> Moreover, the news story is couched in the extremely narrow

and stylized vocabulary which has become standard for all modern news writing; it too helps to expunge any intimation of the reporter's identity and consciousness.[36]

Television news is the opposite:

[I]t is, above all, a personal voice that tells the day's news on the tube. One actually hears the voice; one sees the face, body, and manner of the person who speaks. This individual is constantly on view, intruding his person and personality almost continuously into the narrative.[37]

A third important characteristic of television as a news medium is its preoccupation with spectacle and melodrama. Television focuses literally on the surface of selected dramatic events that involve action, conflict, or ritual. This propensity to spectacular news furthers the compression that is the essence of television news.

Moreover, television news also tends to have a narrow geographic focus. Networks rely on a limited number of camera crews in major cities for the bulk of their news. For example, in 1969, NBC had camera crews stationed in just five major cities.[38] Only a minute fraction of network news comes from affiliated stations.[39]

Weaver has brilliantly summed up the differences between newspapers and television as news media. Newspaper news provides abundant precise information "within a cognitive framework that is crude and nearly chaotic." It requires each reader to choose what to read and how to interpret the information presented. Television news, on the other hand,

. . . seems utterly to lack the liberal, privatizing characteristics of print journalism—the discontinuities, the randomness, the ambiguities, and the diversity which give the ideal of individualism real substance. The television news emphasis on spectacle, its reliance on the single omniscient observer, and its commitment to the notion of a unified, thematic depiction of events, all make TV an extraordinarily powerful mobilizer of public attention and public opinion. The mobilization is organized around a single vision of public affairs promulgated by a single journalistic organization. . . .

Television news, in other words, is perhaps the most powerful centralizing-democratizing machine ever let loose in American society, a machine which, in its commitment to social unity

*and intellectual coherence, can scarcely avoid riding roughshod
over the historic aspirations of liberalism—pluralism, diversity,
localism, privacy, individualism, and untrammeled freedom for
what is personal and idiosyncratic.*[40]

The implications of television's vast, national audience for a
compressed and geographically focused body of news are hard to
exaggerate. To mention a single, suggestive possibility: Is it a
coincidence that, since the emergence of television network news,
the path to the presidency has become centered in the District of
Columbia rather than in the states? Between 1900 and 1956, only 7
percent of the nominees for president or vice president were
senators. Since 1956, every person nominated for these offices has
been either an incumbent or former senator, with the exception of
Spiro Agnew.[41]

Access and the New Journalism

Demands for guaranteed access to the press are one response to
journalistic antagonism toward government, conflicts of interest and
suppression of important news, and general inadequacy of news
coverage. When government cannot get its version of events to the
people without having its secrets made public or its policies put in an
unsympathetic light, one predictable result will be official pressure
for a means of direct access to the public. The dramatic increase in
use that presidents have made of simultaneous, prime-time, television
and radio broadcasts is partly an adaptation to adversary journalism.[42] Certainly there is reason to applaud direct presidential access
to television as a "unifying national forum."[43] However, one might
also question the impact of such one-sided access on separation of
powers and on the political system.[44] Other predictable responses to
deficiences in the press include proposals for a right of reply to
criticism[45] and statutes giving political candidates equal opportunities for media coverage.[46] But politicians are not the only ones who
feel victimized by their inability to penetrate the mass communications media. Minority groups, feminists, the *avant-garde* of communications, and groups of people who lack specialized interests have all
sought the creation of access rights. Many Americans now doubt the
traditional assumption that the American press is self-correcting, fair

and objective, and diverse in its coverage.

The controversy over legal guarantees of access is also the cutting edge of a debate about the general position of mass communications media under American law. A significant body of academic opinion holds that America currently represents a "post-industrial society," to use sociologist Daniel Bell's term for an economy which is increasingly organized around the production, dissemination, and consumption of knowledge rather than manufactured products.[47] Politicians reflect this post-industrialism, Kevin Phillips argues, in their awareness that "politics increasingly becomes a struggle for influence through, and control of, the media."[48] Indeed, Phillips contends that, in all aspects of American life, the mass media play a dominant role. Controversy about the power of the media, particularly questions of access, will be a central aspect of post-industrialism, Phillips predicts:

> [T]he media represent an emerging new concentration of power akin to the railroads, trusts, and monopolies of the late-nineteenth century. . . . Bear in mind that, one hundred years ago, railroads, utilities, and trusts were also claiming the protection of the Bill of Rights. . . If the Fourteenth Amendment could mean something different in 1938—in recognition of changing circumstances—from what it did in 1888, then perhaps the First Amendment may undergo a shifting interpretation of its own to reflect the new status of the communications industry. The media may be forced into the status of utilities regulated to provide access.[49]

Taken together with growing anxiety about media concentration, conglomeration, and monopolization, the nature and practices of American journalism have raised fundamental questions about the extent of First Amendment rights. And, simultaneous developments in First Amendment law have, in turn, further fueled demands for access to the press.

PART II

ACCESS AND
FIRST AMENDMENT DEVELOPMENTS
IN LIBEL AND
THE "PUBLIC FORUM"

Prodigious change in perceptions of history, the basic theories, and the social impact of First Amendment principles has come during the 1960s and 1970s. Much of the current impetus for a legal right of access to the media stems from the two most significant of these recent First Amendment developments: the constitutionalization of defamation law, and the broadened application of the concepts of equality and "public forum." Many assert that legal access is a necessary counter to the first development and a logical extension of the second.

The landmark 1964 decision in *New York Times Co.* v. *Sullivan* substantially revamped the traditional law of defamation in libel actions by public officials. Successive decisions made further inroads on defamation law, proceeding in more or less orderly fashion and extending the basic *Sullivan* principle beyond the prototypical situation that gave it birth. No recent constitutional development has had greater impact on basic First Amendment theory than *Sullivan* and its successor decisions.

One of *Sullivan*'s many significant consequences is the variety of arguments it has generated for a right of access to the media. The strongest of these arguments stems from the belief that *Sullivan* has made it virtually impossible to recover damages for defamation by the print media. Accordingly, a search has begun for a mechanism, other than the traditional libel action, that would protect an individual's reputation against defamation and encourage responsibility by the press. Many commentators feel that a right of reply to criticism or personal attacks is such a mechanism.

The other recent First Amendment development that approaches the libel decisions in importance is likewise a major source of arguments favoring access guarantees. Numerous decisions during the 1960s expanded the concept of the "public forum" to accommodate such forms of expression as parades, public meetings, protest marches, and sit-ins. This line of cases, more than any other, forged the theoretical links between First Amendment principles and the egalitarian thrust that dominated constitutional theory during the 1950s and 1960s. Recognition of equal rights to expression in public places has been a principal feature of the modern public forum decisions. The rhetoric of these decisions has fed demands that equality also be guaranteed to traditional forms of expression through the press.

Demands for media access have deep roots in the recent developments in constitutional law relating to defamation and expression in public forums. An effort to measure these existing bodies of law is critical in evaluating the constitutionality and wisdom of various rights of access to the media.

Defamation and Access:
The Claims of Equilibrium

But unfortunately, some libel lawyers have interpreted recent Supreme Court decisions, particularly the decision in Sullivan v. New York Times, *as being virtually a license to lie where a political candidate, a member of his family, or one of his supporters or friends is involved. This is wrong. It is necessary that a change be made.*

President Richard M. Nixon[1].

*It [*Sullivan*] is an occasion for dancing in the streets.*

Alexander Meiklejohn[2]

As sober an observer of First Amendment law as Harry Kalven, Jr., has said that the Court's opinion in *New York Times Co.* v. *Sullivan* "may prove to be the best and most important it has ever produced in the realm of freedom of speech."[3] Professor Kalven's judgment was addressed mainly to the theoretical underpinnings of the decision and to the Court's important resolution of the knottiest ambiguity in the meaning of First Amendment history. On these levels, *Sullivan* well deserves a preeminent rank in First Amendment adjudication.

The impact of this decision on defamation law commonly is accorded similar weight. However, on this particular level, *Sullivan* deserves a more measured assessment than it usually receives. Overblown concern for the demise of defamation law has been a prime motivation for imposing access obligations on the press. Proponents of access requirements have exaggerated *Sullivan*'s impact on defamation law. They have also failed to narrow sufficiently the precise access obligations that would counteract the effects of *Sullivan.*

Has narrowing the defamation remedy so altered the relative standing of the press and the individual as to warrant corrective action in the form of a right of reply? This is the main issue to consider when evaluating the relevance of *Sullivan* to demands for access. *Sullivan* must also be assessed in terms of its general contributions to First Amendment theory. A departure from First Amendment principles then in existence, *Sullivan* offered a new constitutional perspective: that the First Amendment protects "robust, uninhibited, and wide-open" public debate, and that criticism and uninhibited discussion of government is "the central meaning of the First Amendment." If "public debate" is taken to mean "effective public expression," then the idea that it should be "wide-open" and free from all inhibitions leads naturally to access obligations.

The Traditional Law of Defamation

When a body of law that has evolved in slow and variegated fashion at the state level is brought under the sway of some august constitutional principle, initial enthusiasm for the constitutionalizing reform often gives way, after a few years, to a yearning for the good old days. Constitutionalization of an area of law means nationalization.[4] Local diversity of doctrine and practice is forced into a uniform mold. Moreover, because constitutional reform must be justified and administered by reference to explicit principle, it tends to impose simplicity in place of prior doctrinal complications. Conversion of a sprawling melange of state laws to uniform and relatively simple constitutional doctrine is likely to win praise at first. Reform of law by constitutional adjudication, like law reform through political action, does not usually go forward unless existing law is widely perceived to be unsound. However, as experience with the once-unsatisfactory body of law recedes into the past, and is displaced by nostalgic recollection, the uniformity and generality of constitutionally based doctrine may begin to chafe against the attractions of variety, experimentation, and discrimination in dealing with complicated legal issues.

The law of defamation follows this pattern. Constitutional reform at first was hailed widely as an improvement over an antiquated body of state law. Now it has been criticized increasingly by those who have forgotten how wretched the law of defamation was when it was the preserve of the states.

Under the traditional law of defamation, before *Sullivan*, a publication was considered libelous if the words tended to injure a person's reputation or bring that person into public contempt. Recovery of damages followed unless the publisher could show that the statement was true. Thus, traditional defamation rules imposed liability without fault for damaging statements of fact not proved to be true. Many jurisdictions awarded damages without proof of actual harm. In every state, however, these basic rules of defamation were subject to a confusing myriad of exceptions and privileges, occasions to which defamation liability did not apply. The complexity of libel law ensured prolonged and expensive litigation, certain delay, and haphazard results. For these reasons, among others, only a minute portion of the libel suits initiated were actually pushed to a litigated conclusion. As one expert on tort law has said of traditional defamation: "no other formula of the law promises so much and delivers so little."[5]

Of the many qualifications to the general rules of defamation law, two were most common. These were the conditional privilege of reporting about government processes and official acts, and the privilege of fair comment—a concept that criticism and inference if based on true fact should be liberally privileged when the matter under discussion is of public concern. In some states, under the conditional privilege for publication about official acts, a false and damaging statement of alleged fact made about a public official in connection with his official duties was privileged, unless it could be shown that the publisher of that statement had acted with malice.[6] The elements of malice varied from state to state: Some jurisdictions required intent to injure, while others insisted merely on knowledge of falsity. In virtually all states, the question of malice was for the jury to decide.[7] Although these conditional privileges were designed to provide legal breathing room for expression dealing with public affairs, these protections were subject to haphazard interpretation and even circumvention by a judge or jury if a publication happened to be unpopular.

Zachariah Chafee, our first great First Amendment scholar, wrote in 1947 that the law of libel was "confused, archaic, with no relation to modern life."[8] This harsh view he based on the confusing variety of "subsidiary rules," the "intangible nature" of the chief issues in a libel suit (such as truth and falsity, injury to reputation, and amount of damages), and, above all, "the jury's predominance." Libel litigation, wrote Chafee, resembles a "free-for-all," and he subscribed to the conclusion of a leading libel lawyer: "the result in a libel case depends upon whether or not the jury likes the plaintiff. If they do, he gets a verdict, otherwise not."[9]

Not only was the law of libel unsatisfactory, it was also entrenched. As one law professor wrote in 1948: "The anomalies and absurdities of this branch of the law have been exposed time and time again by able legal writers but an almost incredible judicial and legislative inertia have preserved a mausoleum of antiquities peculiar to the common law and unknown elsewhere in the civilized world."[10] Thus, the law of libel was largely inert, various from state to state, absurdly complex, expensive as well as speculative to coax through litigation, and an invitation to the whimsicality of juries. A dreadful mess, perhaps, but was libel law a systematic threat to freedom of the press? Not really. As Professor Thomas Emerson has put it, "on the whole the role of libel law in the system of freedom of expression has been relatively minor and essentially erratic."[11]

The Constitutionalization of Defamation Law

During the 1960s, the furious sectional resentments of the civil rights struggle revealed the chilling potential of the traditional law of defamation. An advertisement placed by supporters of Martin Luther King in *The New York Times*, in March 1960, recited the repressive activities of Alabama authorities, with several essentially minor inaccuracies and exaggerations. An Alabama jury awarded a local official $500,000 damages against the *Times*. Similar suits against the *Times* and CBS in Alabama sought damages totaling millions of dollars.

The Supreme Court responded to this intolerable situation with sweeping changes in the constitutional status of defamation law. The first doctrinal casualty was the notion that defamation was beyond the reach of First Amendment protection. "[L]ibel," stated Justice William Brennan's opinion for the Court, "can claim no talismanic immunity from constitutional limitations. It must be measured by standards that satisfy the First Amendment."[12] Where alleged defamation involved criticism of public officials and governmental acts, the Court held that the First Amendment did not allow recovery of damages merely upon the showing of factual error that had sufficed under traditional defamation law:

> *A rule compelling the critic of official conduct to guarantee the truth of all his factual assertions . . . leads to . . . "self-censorship." . . . [W]ould-be critics of official conduct may be deterred from voicing their criticism, even though it is believed to be true and even though it is in fact true, because of doubt whether it can be proved in court or fear of the expense of having to do so.*[13]

In place of factual falsity as a basis for liability, the Court imposed a new standard to govern defamation actions brought by public officials:

> *The constitutional guarantees require, we think, a federal rule that prohibits a public official from recovering damages for a defamatory falsehood relating to his official conduct unless he proves that the statement was made with "actual malice"—that is, with knowledge that it was false or with reckless disregard of whether it was false or not.*[14]

The Court did not remand the *Sullivan* case for a jury determination of malice. Instead, the Court performed an "independent examination of the whole record," and concluded that the facts did not support a finding of actual malice, as defined by the decision.

With respect to substantive doctrine, the *Sullivan* decision was not a radical departure. The "actual malice" rule, a common-sense extrapolation of both the traditional conditional privilege for reporting public affairs and the fair comment doctrine, was patterned after the rules applicable to libels of public figures in Kansas and a sizeable minority of other states.[15] Moreover, it was virtually identical to the rule that Professors Fowler Harper and Fleming James advocated in 1956 as the progressive direction of reform grounded in common law evolution. Measured against traditional defamation law, *Sullivan* was an advance, not a revolution.[16]

On the level of constitutional dynamics, however, *Sullivan* did effect important changes. Defamation law had been left to the states, subject to gradual common law evolution in state courts not often exposed to First Amendment issues. *Sullivan* federalized this diversity of local rules into a single national body of doctrine overseen by a Court peculiarly sensitive to First Amendment problems. Furthermore, the intangibility of defamation law had left a wide range of discretion in trial court juries; *Sullivan* imposed independent appellate court review of the facts in defamation actions as a First Amendment guarantee. And, in place of the complexity of overlapping liabilities, offsetting privileges, and jurisdictional diversity, *Sullivan* instituted a simple national rule that put a stringent burden of proof on plaintiffs.

Decisions that followed *Sullivan* extended the "actual malice" limitation on the law of defamation beyond the case of criticism of high public officials. These cases included lower officials,[17] non-official "public figures ... involved in issues in which the public has a justified and important interest,"[18] and businessmen whose activities become of interest to the police, though without leading to ultimate criminal liability.[19] The *Sullivan* principle appeared to encompass virtually anyone the media decided was worthy of broadcast time or newsprint.

Following these expansive decisions, many assumed that the showing of malice required by the *Sullivan* rule would be an almost insurmountable obstacle to the recovery of damages for defamation. Politicians at all levels seemed persuaded that the media had been accorded a constitutional license to lie. From President Nixon down, many called for corrective action. Thus, *Sullivan*'s impact on traditional defamation law led to demands for a right of reply as a means of protecting the reputation of those who became the objects of false criticism but who no longer had practical means of vindication through libel judgments.

A right of reply was also seen as countering the untoward effects of *Sullivan* in a second sense. Many thought that the balance of journalistic responsibility had been upset. They believed that the press had little compunction in disseminating unfounded and damaging misinformation about public personalities and also about the reticent who, through no fault or intention, found themselves the momentary objects of journalistic interest. An access requirement appeared well-suited to counter this ill effect. The feeling was that, even though a journalist was no longer bound by traditional libel and invasion of privacy constraints, he might have greater concern for initial accuracy if he knew that the subjects of his stories also had access to his audience.

Access demands were triggered by the defamation decisions for a third, and more complex, reason. The Court had explicitly assumed that public officials enjoyed access to communications media as a practical matter. It had partly justified its freeing public discussion from the chilling effect of defamation law by relying on this assumed access. Yet, some asked: if assumed access is thought to enhance robust public discussion, why not assure access by legal guarantees, and for all persons discussed in the media?

Defamation and Access:
The Supreme Court's View from *Sullivan* to *Gertz*

Assumptions about access to the media have played a changing but significant role in the Supreme Court's effort to shape defamation law in line with the guarantees of the First Amendment. Assumed access had a hesitant beginning in *Sullivan*. Only two Justices expressly relied on assumptions about public officials' access to the media. Justice Arthur Goldberg, also joined by Justice William O. Douglas, pointed out that a constitutional privilege to criticize public officials

> *does not leave the public official without defenses against unsubstantiated opinions or deliberate misstatements. . . . The public official certainly has equal if not greater access than most private citizens to media of communication.*[20]

Justice Goldberg went on to say, however, that even if access were unavailable to correct press abuses, the press should be protected from libel actions by public officials. He saw support for this view in another perspective on access. Liability for defamation of public officials, Justice Goldberg argued, would reduce the willingness of newspapers to accept controversial ads. The consequence would be "that the ability of minority groups to secure publication of their views on public affairs and to seek support for their causes will be greatly diminished."[21]

As the Court extended the reach of the *Sullivan* principle to protect discussion of "public figures" as well as officials, assumptions about access as a justification for limiting defamation recoveries played an increasingly important role. In the *Walker* and *Butts* decisions,[22] all members of the Court referred to access considerations. Justice John Harlan, writing a minority opinion for himself and Justices Tom Clark, Potter Stewart, and Abe Fortas, contended that public figures should not recover libel damages unless a publication had departed substantially from ordinary standards of investigation and reporting adhered to by responsible publishers. They argued for this narrowing of traditionally strict defamation liability because, in their opinion, public figures are comparable to government officials. That is, "both command sufficient continuing interest and had sufficient access to the means of counterargument to be able to 'expose through discussion the falsehood and fallacies' of the defamatory statements."[23] Similarly, Chief Justice Earl Warren, writing the majority opinion for himself and Justices Hugo Black, William O. Douglas, William Brennan, and Byron White, stated that "surely as a class these 'public figures' have as ready access as 'public officials' to mass media of communication, both to influence policy and to counter criticism of their views and activities."[24]

The Court's substantial reliance on access, in *Walker* and *Butts*, was a departure from the casual reference of two Justices in *Sullivan*. Professor Kalven, the most astute commentator on this line of First Amendment cases, noted and criticized this departure:

> It is a doubtful reading of New York Times to see it resting so heavily on a concern with counterargument. Indeed the whole discussion of competition of ideas and counterargument seems to me misplaced in this context. These are, to be sure, key principles when we are talking about doctrines and ideas. Here, with Mr. Justice Brandeis, we look to counterargument as the correct remedy for the mischief of false and pernicious ideas and doctrine. And we grant an absolute privilege to false doctrine. All this is well understood, widely shared, and invaluable.
>
> But these notions sound only the faintest echo when we turn to false statements of fact about individuals. For centuries it has been the experience of Anglo-American law that the truth never catches up with the lie, and it is because it does not that there has been a law of defamation. I simply do not see how the constitutional protection in this area can be rested on the assurance that counterargument will take the sting out of the falsehoods the law is thereby permitting.[25]

Consistent with Kalven's skepticism, the Court soon took the position that assumptions about access should not be used to justify accommodating defamation law to First Amendment principles. In *Rosenbloom* v. *Metromedia*,[26] a plaintiff who was neither an official nor a public figure argued that his defamation recovery should not be conditioned on proof of actual malice under *Sullivan* because, unlike public figures, a private citizen does not have access to the media to counter the defamatory material. Justice Brennan's opinion, joined by Chief Justice Warren Burger and Justice Harry Blackmun, responded that such a distinction between private and public figures "makes no sense in terms of the First Amendment guarantees":[27]

> *While the argument that public figures need less protection because they can command media attention to counter criticism may be true for some very prominent people, even then it is the rare case where the denial overtakes the original charge. Denials, retractions, and corrections are not "hot" news, and rarely receive the prominence of the original story. When the public official or public figure is a minor functionary, or has left the position that put him in the public eye . . . the argument loses all of its force. In the vast majority of libels involving public officials or public figures, the ability to respond through the media will depend on the same complex factor on which the ability of a private individual depends: the unpredictable event of the media's continuing interest in the story. Thus the unproved, and highly improbable, generalization that an as yet undefined class of "public figures" involved in matters of public concern will be better able to respond through the media than private individuals also involved in such matters seems too insubstantial a reed on which to rest a constitutional distinction.*[28]

Having disclaimed access assumptions as a ground for constitutional limits on defamation law, Justice Brennan's plurality opinion virtually invited the creation of access rights:

> *If the States fear that private citizens will not be able to respond adequately to publicity involving them, the solution lies in the direction of ensuring their ability to respond, rather than in stifling public discussion of matters of public concern.*[29]

The footnote to this provocative statement went even further toward approving the right of reply to defamation:

Some States have adopted retraction statutes or right-of-reply statutes. See Donnelly, The Right of Reply: An Alternative to an Action for Libel, 34 Va. L. Rev. 867 (1948); Note, Vindication of the Reputation of a Public Official, 80 Harv. L. Rev. 1730 (1967). Cf. Red Lion Broadcasting Co. v. FCC, 395 U.S. 367, 89 S. Ct. 1794, 23 L. Ed. 2d 371 (1969).

One writer, in arguing that the First Amendment itself should be read to guarantee a right of access to the media not limited to a right to respond to defamatory falsehoods, has suggested several ways the law might encourage public discussion. Barron, Access to the Press—A New First Amendment Right, 80 Harv. L. Rev. 1641, 1666-1678 (1967). It is important to recognize that the private individual often desires press exposure either for himself, his ideas, or his causes. Constitutional adjudication must take into account the individual's interest in access to the press as well as the individual's interest in preserving his reputation, even though libel actions by their nature encourage a narrow view of the individual's interest since they focus only on situations where the individual has been harmed by undesired press attention. A constitutional rule that deters the press from covering the ideas or activities of the private individual thus conceives the individual's interest too narrowly.[30]

Thus, in the *Rosenbloom* plurality opinion, access takes on a reverse theoretical relation to defamation. In *Sullivan, Walker,* and *Butts,* assumptions of access were treated as one justification for limiting defamation; in *Rosenbloom,* limiting defamation remedies became a justification for creating rights of access.

Other members of the Court who concurred in the judgment in *Rosenbloom* did not express concern about access. Justice Black reiterated his view that the First Amendment leaves no room for the law of libel. He made no mention of access. Likewise, Justice White's narrow concurring opinion ignored the question. And Justice Thurgood Marshall's dissent, joined by Justice Stewart, did not refer to the difficulty of access in arguing that the *Sullivan* malice principle should not be applied in cases of defamation of private persons.[31] In fact, only Justice Harlan, in dissent, urged that the constitutional limits of defamation recoveries be geared to the probability of access, with *Sullivan* applicable only to public officials and public figures:

For me, it does seem quite clear that the public person has a greater likelihood of securing access to channels of communi-

cation sufficient to rebut falsehoods concerning him than do private individuals in this country who do not toil in the public spotlight.[32]

However, in the *Gertz* decision, handed down in June 1974, the Court again relied on access assumptions when it determined that the actual malice requirement of *Sullivan* should not apply to defamation actions by private persons. This latest effort by the Court to reconcile protection of private persons from defamation with the First Amendment returned to the thrust of Justice Harlan's position in *Rosenbloom*. After voicing a warning about the inevitable tendency of general rules to ignore differences in particular cases, Justice Louis Powell's opinion for the Court pointed out:

> *The first remedy of any victim of defamation is self-help—using available opportunities to contradict the lie or correct the error and thereby to minimize its adverse impact on reputation. Public officials and public figures usually enjoy significantly greater access to the channels of effective communication and hence have a more realistic opportunity to counteract false statements than private individuals normally enjoy. Private individuals are therefore more vulnerable to injury, and the state interest in protecting them is correspondingly greater.*[33]

A footnote to this paragraph referred in passing to Professor Kalven's doubts about the existence of an underlying access rationale in *Sullivan*:

> *Of course, an opportunity for rebuttal seldom suffices to undo harm of defamatory falsehood. Indeed, the law of defamation is rooted in our experience that the truth rarely catches up with a lie. But the fact that the self-help remedy of rebuttal, standing alone, is inadequate to its task does not mean that it is irrelevant to our inquiry.*[34]

Justice Powell added a second justification for limiting the scope of the actual malice rule to defamation actions by public figures:

> *An individual who decides to seek governmental office must accept certain necessary consequences of that involvement in public affairs. He runs the risk of closer public scrutiny than might otherwise be the case. . . . Those classed as public figures*

stand in a similar position. . . . [T]he instances of truly involuntary public figures must be exceedingly rare. . . . [T]hose classed as public figures have thrust themselves to the forefront of particular public controversies. . . . [T]hey invite attention and comment.[35]

Gertz thus offered a double rationale for limiting the *Sullivan* rule to public officials and public figures. Such persons were presumed to have access to the media for self-protection, and, in any event, they could be regarded as having assumed "increased risk of injury from defamatory falsehoods concerning them."[36]

Although *Gertz* refused to apply the *Sullivan* rule to defamation actions by private persons, it did not leave the traditional law of defamation intact in such cases. The Court held that liability for defamation of private persons must rest on a determination that the publisher was "at fault." However, it did not define what standards should govern this determination. Presumably, it would be sufficient if a jury found that a publisher had been negligent in the general sense of having failed to take reasonable care under all the circumstances. Or, perhaps, "fault" might be satisfied by a departure from the customary standards of investigation and reporting ordinarily adhered to by responsible publishers, along the lines suggested by Justice Harlan in his minority opinion in the *Butts* case.[37] In either event, *Gertz'* insistence on fault as a constitutional requisite for private defamation actions departs from traditional defamation liability without fault for damaging statements of fact that are not proven to be true.

The Court also cut back the rule of common law defamation that allowed awards of presumed and punitive damages without a showing of actual loss. It held that when actual malice (in the *Sullivan* sense) is not established, damages may not exceed actual injury.

The constitutional standards for defamation of private persons announced in *Gertz* still leave questions open. For example, who is a "public figure" governed by *Sullivan*? *Gertz* suggests that the question is not simply a matter of who is a public figure for purposes of any and all defamation. Rather, the question will be put in a particular context "by looking to the nature and extent of an individual's participation in the particular controversy giving rise to the defamation."[38] In a sense, this approach is a counterpart to the suggestion in *Sullivan*, not developed in subsequent decisions, that defamation concerning the *private* affairs of public officials would not be governed by the requirement of actual malice. Just as public officials may have private areas of conduct not subject to the *Sullivan* standard, so private persons may have public areas of conduct that are subject to *Sullivan*. Although this notion is easy enough to state, it remains to be seen how it will be administered by the courts as a constitutional principle of decision.

There are also questions under *Gertz* of what the limitation to "actual damages" will mean in practice. This is especially true since the jury may include mental anguish and impairment of reputation and community standing as elements of actual harm. Nor does *Gertz* answer the vital questions of what degree of judicial control over jury discretion will exist and what sort of appellate review of private defamation verdicts will be held guaranteed by the First Amendment.

However interesting, these problems are secondary to the overall question of how access theory relates to developments in the constitutional law of defamation. From their modest beginnings in *Sullivan*, assumptions about what types of defamation plaintiffs enjoy access to the communications media have played an increasingly significant part in the constitutionalization of defamation law. In the critical effort to accommodate competing values of freedom of the press and protection of individual reputation, the Supreme Court has tended to view defamation law and access (either by right or as a practical matter) as a complex equilibrium. The more access, the less need for defamation remedies. The Court's treatment has promoted the view that access and defamation recoveries are roughly interchangeable protections for victims of libel by the press.

Defamation and Access: The Functional Connection

The widespread assumption that *Sullivan* has made defamation recoveries impossible is difficult to evaluate. No empirical study has compared the number of defamation recoveries before and after *Sullivan*.[39] In fact, such a study may be virtually impossible. Reported cases would not tell the entire story. It would also be pertinent to consider libel settlements and even pre-publication textual changes made in an attempt to avoid libel problems.[40] Accordingly, one can only guess at *Sullivan*'s actual impact on the capacity of a defamed person to vindicate his reputation by winning a libel action. However, one may certainly suppose that the erection of additional and substantial evidentiary barriers to recovery will reduce the individual's chances of success in defamation actions.

The recent *Gertz* decision indicates that, for private persons, the law of defamation has not been seriously weakened. And even for public figures, substantial defamation verdicts have been upheld in several cases. The two best known defamation recoveries since the *Sullivan* decision were in favor of Wally Butts and Barry Goldwater.

In the *Butts* case, a splintered and closely divided Supreme Court upheld a recovery of $460,000 against the *Saturday Evening Post*. A *Post* story claimed that Butts, athletic director at the University of Georgia, had given Georgia's secret plays to Paul "Bear" Bryant, football coach at the University of Alabama, before a game between the two schools.[41] The jury found the story to be false, despite considerable evidence that, in essence, the story might be accurate. However, the record showed that the *Post* had made little effort to check the accuracy of the story, even though its source had been a questionable character with a criminal record who claimed to have overheard a telephone conversation between Butts and Bryant through an electronic mix-up.

Although the case had been tried before the *Sullivan* decision, Chief Justice Warren concluded that the judge's instruction to the jury, which allowed punitive damages on finding "wanton or reckless indifference or culpable negligence with regard to the rights of others," was close enough to the *Sullivan* formula not to require remand for a new trial. Justices Harlan, Clark, Stewart, and Fortas also upheld Butts' recovery, but on an entirely different ground. They asserted, as a minority position, that the *Sullivan* requirement of actual malice should not apply to defamation actions brought by public figures, as opposed to public officials. Public figures should be permitted to recover on a showing that the defendant publication had engaged in "highly unreasonable conduct constituting an extreme departure from the standards of investigation and reporting ordinarily adhered to by responsible publishers."[42] The four dissenters did join Chief Justice Warren's view that the *Sullivan* malice standard should govern defamation suits by public figures. However, they dissented on the ground that the jury instruction did not satisfy the standard.

Butts was thus an unusual recovery. The fact remains, however, that a substantial defamation recovery was based on a story that may have been true, that the *Post* believed to be true, but that the *Post* had not verified to the satisfaction of a Georgia jury and a narrow majority of the Supreme Court.

The defamation recovery in the *Goldwater* case[43] is easier to justify under the "actual malice" standard of *Sullivan*. Yet, *Goldwater* shows that post-*Sullivan* defamation law still has some teeth. Senator Barry Goldwater sued Ralph Ginzburg, the publisher of a magazine titled (wryly) *Fact*, for alleged defamation through a story purporting that an extensive polling of psychiatrists showed Senator Goldwater to be psychologically unfit for the presidency. *Fact's* story was a strident attack on Senator Goldwater's psyche, replete with inaccuracies, significant omissions, and fantasies, and rather more revealing of Ginzburg's pathology than Senator Goldwater's. Beyond the numerous incredible lies, the story was simply a vicious subjective attack. Yet, if anyone is open to such puerile rantings, it should be a candidate for the presidency. Psychological speculation is at the heart of the current style in uninhibited, robust debate about public officials, and this is the very sort of expression that *Sullivan* sought to protect from defamation actions. Even so, the First Amendment did allow a sizeable defamation recovery when the publication involved, though sprinkled with lies and half-truths, seemed better characterized as pathological fantasy than calculated falsehood.

Both *Goldwater* and *Butts* involved recoveries against magazines, which have time deadlines less pressing than newspapers or broadcasters. A finding of malice against these magazine defendants does not necessarily mean that newspapers could be tested by similar standards of journalistic responsibility. It may well be substantially more difficult to establish actual malice in the case of a newspaper.

Nevertheless, *Butts* and *Goldwater* demonstrate that malicious or reckless libels can lead to recoveries under the *Sullivan* doctrine. In addition to *Butts* and *Goldwater*, several post-*Sullivan* state cases have upheld defamation recoveries.[44] In 1975, the Supreme Court denied review of a series of cases in which libel judgments and damages were imposed on various publications. Even before *Gertz*, there was little basis for the view that *Sullivan* and its successor decisions left defamation law virtually useless as a means of vindicating individual reputation or restraining abuses by the media.

Gertz is cause for further skepticism toward the claim that the traditional equilibrium between the press and the individual has been so upset in the area of defamation that required access is necessary to right the balance. Private individuals still have as much protection against negligent defamations as they did before *Sullivan*, except that presumed and punitive damages no longer may be recovered. However, when one considers that actual damages may include damage to reputation, impaired standing in the community, and mental anguish, it is obvious that *Gertz'* restrictions should not significantly discourage deserving private plaintiffs from seeking litigation.

Furthermore, *Gertz* may well signal a more flexible approach to the problem of negligent defamations of government officials and public figures. *Gertz* adopted a discriminating test to determine which plaintiffs will be considered private with respect to which defamations. The plaintiff in *Gertz* was a prominent lawyer, the author of several books and articles, and a present or former officer of various civic and professional groups. Though he easily might have been considered a public figure under the *Sullivan* rules, the Court was careful not to apply the *Sullivan* rules to defamatory statements about matters not directly touching on his public activities.

Similar discrimination is likely to be applied to publications about the private activities of officials and public figures. The original *Sullivan* formulation concerned only defamations touching on the "official conduct" of government officials. *Gertz* suggests that this limitation on the reach of *Sullivan*'s malice rule may be sympathetically elaborated in future cases.

Summing Up Defamation and Access

On a functional level, *Sullivan* and later libel decisions offer support for a legal right of access to the media that is narrower and less weighty than is usually supposed. If access rights were designed to counteract *Sullivan* and *Gertz*'s restrictions on libel law, the role of access would modestly extend only to nonmalicious defamations about the public activities of public officials and public figures, and innocent defamations about private persons. Such a right of access would follow a judgment of defamation based on a finding that a publication had made a false statement that resulted in damage to reputation. The individual damaged by a false statement would bring an action for vindication, and the remedy would be a court order requiring the publication to publish the Court's judgment.[45] In short, defamation decisions support, at most, only a narrow right of reply, premised on prior judicial determination of the traditional elements of defamation.

The general First Amendment theory reflected in the *Sullivan* decision also has contributed to the demand for a legalized right of access to the media, though in ways more subtle and less frequently articulated. *Sullivan* embraces a dynamic approach to history in formulating the constitutional principles that govern the mass media of today. When the court accepted Professor Herbert Wechsler's invitation (as the principal lawyer for the *New York Times* in the case) to conceive of the political rejection of the Sedition Act of 1798 as the crystallized historical meaning of the First Amendment, it showed a willingness to bend First Amendment history to fit modern judicial notions. Such flexibility in assessing how First Amendment history relates to the constitutional issues of the day would be essential to the acceptance of any broad right of access to the print media.

Supporters of access also can find hope in *Sullivan*'s creative approach to First Amendment theory. Though dealing with the deeply rooted and complicated doctrine of defamation law, the Supreme Court departed from traditional First Amendment methodologies. Instead of the clear-and-present-danger test, the "two-level" theory of libel, or the balancing approach, it embraced a newly minted "central meaning of the First Amendment," deciding that a right to criticize government and public officials is at the heart of freedom of speech and of the press. As a result, the court gave hope to those who support First Amendment theories having negligible roots in constitutional precedents. Only such a novel approach could provide support for access rights to the media.

Moreover, in *Sullivan* and many later decisions, the rhetoric that public debate should be "robust, uninhibited, and wide-open" is significant. Rather than being just a barrier against government interference with expression, such rhetoric may be easily transformed into a justification for positive action designed to break down private barriers to expression. Therefore, although access requirements can claim only narrow support in countering the actual effects of *Sullivan* and its progeny, the rhetorical encouragement is much broader.

7

Access and "Public Forum" Cases:
The Power of Analogy

*The problem for the law is: When will it be just to treat differ-
ent cases as though they were the same?*

Edward Levi[1]

Freedom of expression in the United States has never relied on the
communications media alone for a vital marketplace of ideas. From
the Stamp Act crisis throughout the Revolutionary period, popular
marches, rallies, and even riots were quite as important, at least in
the cities, as the newspapers and pamphlets of the day in
communicating, coalescing, and sometimes coercing political
sentiments. The First Amendment summoned the more civil aspects
of this practice into constitutional principle, and explicitly recognized "the right of the people peaceably to assemble." The notion
that gatherings in streets, parks, and other "public forums" can serve
as "the poor man's printing press" has deep roots in both our
political experience and our constitutional theory.

The Supreme Court has given us a rich variety of judicial decisions
dealing with assembling, distributing handbills, parading, picketing,
and other sorts of expressive activity in public, and occasionally in
private, places. This body of public forum law is an abundant store
of arguments about access to the media. In Chapter 5, we explored
the notion that media failure to give voice to racial and political
minorities pushed such groups into dramatic, public manifestations
of their political positions in order to attract attention. Some
newspapers ignored the interests of blacks or the poor in their regular

reporting. They refused to cover press conferences or releases by representatives of such groups, and they maintained advertising rates that were out of reach. However, these same newspapers could be induced to put protest marches, sit-ins, or boycotts on the front page. As a result, a relationship of sorts developed between access and use of the public forum. Professor Barron even suggested that opening up legal avenues of access to the media would reduce much of the unsettling activity that increasingly dominated the public forum during the 1960s.[2]

No doubt some correlation does exist. However, one should not rest an argument for access rights simply on the hope that creation of such rights will reduce noisome public protests. To do so ignores the reasons, other than inaccessible media, that account for activity in the public forum. Advertising is no substitute for coverage in news columns or broadcasts. Groups with easy access to advertising or leaflet presses often find their messages more effective if conveyed through news coverage of events. This is particularly true if the message concerns a particular entity, for example a public library that follows practices of segregation in its booklending. In a case such as this, news coverage of a form of expressive activity tied to that place may have greater impact than disembodied publication in any medium. Moreover, assemblages and other joint activities bring cohesion and commitment to groups more readily than statements of purpose in the mass media. And, finally, protests and demonstrations register the intensity of political feeling more effectively than letters to the editor, ads, or op-ed page articles. For minorities especially, the political scientists tell us, communicating depth of commitment is critical to effective brokering in the political process.

However, although this practical notion that access rights might reduce political action in public places is both interesting and a good subject for debate, it is not the central significance of the public forum cases in the controversy over media access. Primarily, the public forum decisions are viewed as offering analogies to questions of access to the media. The argument proposed by Barron and others is that constitutional principles conferring the right of expression in streets, parks, municipal buildings, and occasionally private places should be extended to the mass communications media.[3]

A number of principles developed in the public forum cases are relevant to access demands. Of central significance are those principles that determine what places—public or private—will be treated as public forums—that is, places in which expressive activities can find some degree of protection under the First Amendment. If a public park must be open to expressive activities in some circumstances, should the same principles governing access to a park also be applied to such publicly owned media as public school newspapers or state bar association journals? Equally basic questions are raised by decisions that privately owned property may be treated, in certain circumstances, as if it were owned and operated by the state. Thus, expressive activities within a "company town" or a private shopping center may be protected under the First Amendment, just as if these activities had occurred in the streets or sidewalks of municipalities. But are the principles controlling these cases applicable, by analogy, to privately owned communications media?

This question of whether private entities should be subjected to constitutional obligations, which are applicable to official conduct, is one of the most perplexing and significant issues in constitutional law. Whether private conduct should be treated as "state action"—the term coined by courts to designate that conduct to which constitutional limitations adhere—has arisen most frequently in cases involving racial discrimination. The question, however, cuts across the range of constitutional guarantees, including the First Amendment. It is the central problem for claims of a First Amendment right of access to privately owned newspapers and broadcasting stations.

The law of the First Amendment tends naturally toward ambiguity rather than clarity in seeking to deflect collisions between the values of free expression and legitimate social policies calling for control. "Nothing is more characteristic of the law of the First Amendment," Professor Alexander M. Bickel has reminded us, "—not the rhetoric, but the actual law of it—than the Supreme Court's resourceful efforts to cushion rather than resolve clashes between the First Amendment and interests conflicting with it."[4] There is no better illustration of this condition than the public forum cases. Thus, it seems surprising, but isn't really, that the Supreme Court has not established an answer to the most basic question posed by the cases. It is not clear whether the government must *guarantee* *access* for expression to some types of public property, or, alternatively, whether the First Amendment obligation merely means that *if* a public forum is opened to some expression, then it must be open on an *equal access* basis.[5] The Court tends to avoid this and other similar questions by resorting to a variety of narrow procedural and substantive accommodations.

The Supreme Court's reluctance to paint with a broad brush in public forum cases has generated a narrow particularity in judicial approach. As Professor Harry Kalven has noted, "The flavor of these cases depends so much on nuances in the facts that there is no tidy way to compare them."[6] The ambivalence and particularity of the public forum cases presents special difficulties for analysis.

Analogical reasoning is the most characteristic and creative type of reasoning used in common law systems such as constitutional law.[7] It is not a mechanical process. To determine whether certain principles, developed over time to govern one set of problems, ought to apply to a different context calls for careful attention to the natures of the two situations. Factual similarities and differences must be weighed in light of the purposes and values embodied in those principles. Much discussion of access to the media has been marked by bald assertions that principles from public forum cases should be extended to cover the private communications media. Such propositions, however, rest on analogical assumptions that are complex and debatable. Their force can be measured only after careful assessment of public forum precedents.

Accordingly, this chapter will treat decisions concerning expressive activities in physical places, public and private. It will focus on the related issues of what a public forum is, when private activity is regarded as state action subject to constitutional restraints, and the role of the principle of equality in governing rights of access to public forums. The following chapter will deal with the precedents directly concerning constitutional claims of access to print media, such as public school newspapers and journals, private newspapers, and advertising media in public and private places.

Public forum cases have come in waves. During the 1930s and 1940s most of the cases involving expression in public places arose from prosyletizing by Jehovah's Witnesses.[8] During the 1950s, other First Amendment issues involving loyalty and subversive advocacy preoccupied the Supreme Court, and as Professor Kalven put it, "the story of the streets became a bit quaint."[9] In the 1960s, the civil rights movement generated a fresh influx of decisions to this branch of First Amendment law. By the late 1960s, anti-Vietnam War protest moved into the public forum. At present, a bewildering variety of social and political movements are active in the public forum.

The Jehovah's Witnesses
and the Early Expansion of State Action

Constitutional judgments are inexorably affected by the immediate social settings of the cases, often more so than can rest comfortably with the ideal of neutral and general principles in constitutional law.[10] Public forum cases over the years show the strains. The early cases dealt primarily with the public proselytizing of Jehovah's Witnesses. Although a sect "distinguished by . . . astonishing powers of annoyance,"[11] it is equally true that, as vociferous minorities go, the Witnesses were "small and eccentric."[12] Because they were isolated zealots of small significance, it is not surprising that in the various cases involving Witnesses who distributed handbills on the streets, harangued on street-corners, or rang doorbells to solicit contributions and distribute their literature, the Supreme Court in the 1930s and 1940s laid a libertarian foundation for the constitutional right of expression in public places. Compared to the Court's more dubious reaction to the explosive public forum controversies of the past two decades, the breadth of these early decisions is remarkable.

In upholding the Witnesses' rights of public expression, the Court did not narrowly relate its grounds for decision to religious liberty. Instead, it posed the issue as the general right of political expression in public forums. Thus, in the formative *Lovell* v. *Griffin* decision, which involved official permission as a condition to the distribution of religious literature, Chief Justice Charles Evans Hughes conceived of the permit ordinance in question as striking "at the very foundation of freedom of the press by subjecting it to license and censorship."[13] The historic symbol of freedom who enlivened the Chief Justice's powerful opinion was the secular propagandist Thomas Paine.[14]

In another case from this period, dealing with the playing of a strident anti-Catholic phonograph record door-to-door in a predominantly Catholic neighborhood, Justice Owen J. Roberts responded in the same expansive vein:

> In the realm of religious faith, and in that of political belief,
> sharp differences arise. . . . But the people of this nation have
> ordained in the light of history, that, in spite of the probability
> of excesses and abuses, these liberties are, in the long view,

*essential to enlightened opinion and right conduct on the part
of the citizens of a democracy.*[15]

Thus, sectarian diatribe was amalgamated to speech about public
affairs appropriate to a democracy.

The Jehovah's Witnesses decisions of the '30s and '40s left a
lasting imprint on First Amendment law. Integration of the
principles of religious liberty with those of political liberty in dealing
with expressive activity in public places gave force to the perspectives
of the First Amendment's framers. And measured more narrowly, in
terms of public forum doctrine, these decisions were strikingly
tolerant in subordinating to free expression such public interests as
avoidance of littering, prevention of public hostilities, or protection
of religious sensibilities. They firmly constrained official disapproval
of the content of expression through enforcement of permit systems,
parade regulations, or other forms of official oversight. They
established broad First Amendment guarantees of access for purposes
of expression to public places.

The Court during the 1940s also laid the groundwork for the claim
that First Amendment rights might limit the prerogatives of private
property and private organizations. Once again, in *Marsh* v. *Alabama*,[16] a Jehovah's Witness triggered the formative holding that
private property could be subject to the constitutional obligations of
a public forum. The case was generated in Chickasaw, Alabama (a
suburb of Mobile), which was owned by the Gulf Shipbuilding
Corporation. Chickasaw included residential areas, streets, a "business block," a post office, and a system of sewers. In the words of
the Court's opinion by Justice Hugo Black, "the town and its
shopping district are accessible to and freely used by the public in
general and there is nothing to distinguish them from any other town
and shopping center except the fact that the title to the property
belongs to a private corporation."[17] Here a Witness had sought to
distribute religious literature on the sidewalks of the business block,
and was asked to leave. When she refused, she was arrested and
eventually convicted of trespass.

The Supreme Court held that the Witness had a First Amendment
right to distribute religious literature in Chickasaw, even though the
town was privately owned. Had Chickasaw been a typical municipality, the right to distribute literature would have been clear under
Lovell. But the fact that Chickasaw was privately owned did not
support a different result:

We do not agree that the corporation's property interests settle the question. The State urges in effect that the corporation's right to control the inhabitants of Chickasaw is coextensive with the right of a homeowner to regulate the conduct of his guests. We cannot accept that contention. Ownership does not always mean absolute dominion. The more an owner, for his advantage, opens up his property for use by the public in general, the more do his rights become circumscribed by the statutory and constitutional rights of those who use it.[18]

The majority opinion pointed to the need of inhabitants of company towns to be informed through a "freely accessible" community shopping area.[19] It concluded: "When we balance the Constitutional rights of owners of property against those of the people to enjoy freedom of press and religion, as we must here, we remain mindful of the fact that the latter occupy a preferred position."[20]

The opinion in *Marsh* suggests various reasons why First Amendment obligations were imposed on this particular private entity. The simplest and narrowest basis would be that Chickasaw was virtually a replica of a public municipality. As such, this particular private property should be treated as a government instrument for all constitutional purposes, including (but not limited to) First Amendment constraints. A second rationale suggested by the opinion might be the need of the inhabitants of Chickasaw for information through public debate, and for some control over the effective monopoly exercised by Chickasaw's private owner, concerning the sort of public debate that takes place on the streets and sidewalks of any typical town's business center. The third, and broadest, possible approach would be to view *Marsh* as an exercise in balancing property rights against First Amendment rights. This kind of analysis could extend, presumably, not only to company towns or other private property that replicated governmental entities, but to private property of all descriptions that might be regarded as a barrier to "the rights . . . of the people to enjoy freedom of press."[21] These different rationales would have markedly different significance in terms of First Amendment claims of access to the private press.

During the same period that *Marsh* was decided, the question of applying to private entities the constitutional obligations applicable to state instruments arose in a second line of cases involving constitutional rights of access of a different sort. In this line of cases, rights of access to the electoral process were joined with issues of race discrimination through the stubborn efforts of some southern political parties to exclude blacks from voting in candidate selection processes before the general elections.

In 1927, the Supreme Court had, without difficulty in finding state action, held unconstitutional a Texas statute that provided "in no event shall a negro be eligible to participate in a Democratic party primary election held in the State of Texas."[22] Five years later, in 1932, the exclusion of blacks from a Democratic primary in Texas was again before the Court. However, this time the exclusion was not mandated by state statute, but rather by the party's executive committee, which the legislature had authorized to prescribe qualifications for party membership. Under this arrangement, both the state and the party contended, discrimination was the private act of a voluntary and exclusive political association. But they could not persuade a majority of the Justices. With some niceness of analysis, the Court decided that the statutory delegation of power to the party executive committee to set membership qualifications produced discrimination by state action in violation of the Fourteenth Amendment.[23]

Texas persevered in its effort to disentangle the state from racial exclusions in primary elections, and was temporarily successful in a third case that made its way to the Supreme Court in 1935.[24] In response to the two earlier rulings, Texas repealed all statutes limiting the freedom of political parties to determine membership qualifications as they pleased, and the Texas Democratic party resolved to restrict its membership to white voters only. This time the Court found no state action under the Fourteenth Amendment. However, the authority of the Texas Democratic party to exclude blacks from its primary elections was short-lived. Nine years later, in 1944, and after the Court had ruled in another case that primaries were an integral part of the overall state electoral machinery, the state's acquiescence in the Democratic party's exclusion of blacks was held to be "a delegation of a state function that may make the party's action the action of the State."[25]

The final decision of this dismal sequence was handed down in 1953, in *Terry v. Adams*.[26] In this case, the state of Texas had disclaimed every trace of control over the private primaries run by a county "Jaybird party." The winners of the Jaybird party primary almost invariably entered and won the Democratic primaries and the subsequent general elections. For opaque reasons, the Supreme Court construed this arrangement as state action subject to the limitations of the Fourteenth and Fifteenth Amendments. The various opinions of the majority of the Court concluded that the Jaybird party was, in reality, part of the Democratic party, and that its purpose was to exclude blacks from an effective electoral voice. According to the Court, whenever the state allows its electoral apparatus to be used by a political party that effectively controls the outcome of elections, that party "takes on those attributes of government which draw the Constitution's safeguards into play."[27]

The "white primary" cases, although decided in the same constitutional period as *Marsh* v. *Alabama*, presented state action questions in a different setting from the First Amendment right of access to public forums for purposes of expression. Instead of the right to expression, the effective right to vote was at issue. And, in contrast to *Marsh*, the issue of race discrimination was a vital ingredient of the decisions. However, the white primary cases did expand on the notion, suggested in *Marsh*, that when a private entity controls a state function, it should be regarded as state action in order to maintain practical constitutional guarantees. The guarantee protected in the white primary decisions is, in a sense, the right to participate in the "public" activities of private parties. These decisions might be seen as supporting a constitutional claim of access to private communications media, on the contention that the media carry out, or even control, certain vital public functions.

Furthermore, the white primary cases may be relevant to our concern with access in a second sense. A right of access to primaries operated by "private" political parties arguably infringes on rights of free association for political purposes.[28] One view of these cases is that claims of equal access to electoral activities conducted by private groups won out over group claims of privacy, autonomy, and exclusivity, resting on freedom of association. Thus, the white primary cases might be thought to support the proposition that constitutional claims of equality and access should be given preeminence generally over claims of privacy and autonomy. Such an undifferentiated statement needs testing, of course, and we will return to it after examining more recent public forum and state action decisions.

The Modern Cases

Looking back on the early public forum decisions in 1941, Zechariah Chafee sounded a cautionary note:

And yet, much as I like this broad language, there is something about the handbill and phonograph cases that makes me uncomfortable. The limitations they impose on governmental control of expression in the streets look a bit fragile for a rough and tumble world.[29]

Although the results of the public forum cases of the 1960s and 1970s generally uphold rights of expression in public forums, the Court is increasingly dubious. The modern decisions are closely reasoned and particularistic. In contrast to earlier decisions, the Supreme Court seems reluctant to build any broad principles of access to the public forum, although considerable imagination is expended to find narrow and, in some cases, singular grounds for reversing convictions. Many of the decisions upholding expression are grounded on vagueness or overbreadth attacks on statutes. Furthermore, these decisions often issue amid suggestions that narrowly drawn statutes might well have prohibited the same expression in the same place and yet survived judicial review.

Modern public forum cases exist in a kind of doctrinal no man's land between two antithetical principles.[30] One of these principles is identified with Justice Holmes, then a member of the Massachusetts Supreme Court, when he sustained a minister's conviction for speaking in a public park without a permit:

For the Legislature absolutely or conditionally to forbid public speaking in a highway or public park is no more an infringement of the rights of a member of the public than for the owner of a private house to forbid it in his house.[31]

The United States Supreme Court affirmed the conviction off-handedly.[32] However, it must be remembered that when this decision was made in 1897, the First Amendment had not yet been held applicable to the states under the Fourteenth Amendment.[33]

The other antithetical principle is drawn from the 1937 *Hague* v. *C.I.O.* opinion by Justice Roberts, rejecting a claim of full permit power:

Wherever the title of streets or parks may rest, they have immemorially been held in trust for the use of the public and, time out of mind, have been used for purposes of assembly, communicating thoughts between citizens, and discussing public questions. Such use of the streets and public places has, from ancient times, been a part of the privileges, immunities, rights, and liberties of citizens.[34]

Within a few years after the *Hague* decision, the Supreme Court seemed determined to ensure broad rights of expression in the streets and parks, subject only to reasonable and nondiscriminatory regulation of the time, place, and manner of public assemblages. The principles of the Jehovah's Witnesses cases were elaborated into a broad First Amendment theory of guaranteed access to the streets and parks.[35]

The Court's generous invitation to the public forum was issued in a time when individuals or small groups were the primary users. It did not survive the civil rights movement of the 1960s, when crowds of hundreds and sometimes thousands took their cause into the streets. The turning point came in 1965 as the Court reviewed the legal consequences of a peaceful demonstration by some two thousand black students across the street from a Louisiana courthouse. *Cox v. Louisiana* involved convictions under several different statutes, each raising somewhat different First Amendment problems.[36] Convictions for violating a statute that prohibited obstructing public sidewalks were reversed, but on the narrow ground that the statute had not been applied even-handedly to all assemblies and parades in the streets and sidewalks, and with a statement that retreated from the broad public forum position of *Hague*:

We emphatically reject the notion urged by appellant that the First and Fourteenth Amendments afford the same kind of freedom to those who would communicate ideas by conduct such as patrolling, marching, and picketing on streets and highways, as these amendments afford to those who communicate ideas by pure speech. . . .

We have no occasion in this case to consider the constitutionality of the uniform, consistent, and nondiscriminatory application of a statute forbidding all access to streets and other public facilities for parades and meetings.[37]

Cox also involved convictions under a statute that prohibited parading or picketing near a courthouse with intent to obstruct or influence judicial proceedings. Although the Court also reversed these convictions, its attitude toward this statute was sympathetic. A majority of the Court found that the local police chief had given demonstrators permission to parade across the street from the courthouse. This, in effect, immunized the demonstration. But the majority noted that this narrowly drawn statute was a "valid law dealing with conduct subject to regulation."

The *Cox* opinion appears to mark a definite shift by the Court, both on the status of the streets and on the status of public places other than the streets and parks. As to the streets, *Cox* seems to turn away from the early cases' notion of guaranteed access. Its concern with discriminatory enforcement and abuse of official discretion suggests that equal access is the essence of public forum rights in the streets. Moreover, approval in principle of the prohibition on parading near a courthouse suggests that the Court will be reluctant to recognize public forum rights in places other than the streets and parks.

On the whole, public forum decisions since *Cox* tend to confirm its narrow approach to the streets and its skepticism toward public places other than the streets and parks. The Court continued to reverse convictions of persons who engaged in expressive activities in streets and parks, but found narrow grounds for decision in the vagueness, unequal application, or overbreadth of the statutes involved.[38]

When places other than the streets and parks have been pressed into service as public forums, the Supreme Court's response has been increasingly doubtful in tone and mixed in result. In 1966, the Court by a 5-4 margin narrowly protected under the First Amendment the action of several blacks who had stood in the reading room of the Clinton, Louisiana, public library in mute protest against its policies of segregation.[39] However, later in the same year, the Court by a 5-4 vote sustained trespass convictions of persons who had gathered on the grounds of the county jail to protest the arrest of sit-in demonstrators and the jail's policies of racial discrimination.[40] With respect to academic environments, the Court, in 1969, upheld the First Amendment right of public high school students to wear black armbands in school to protest the Vietnam War.[41] The Court found no disruption in this activity. On the other hand, in 1972, the Court upheld the constitutionality of convictions for school-related demonstrating on the sidewalks surrounding a public high school.[42] The convictions had been obtained under a statute that prohibited any noise or diversion which tends to disturb the peace or good order of any school in session.

If any generalization can be drawn from these cases, it is that the Supreme Court is increasingly inclined to protect the functions of the public place from potentially disruptive expressive activity. Judgments depend not so much on balancing the value of expression against the impairment of public function, as on determining whether there is significant disruption. If there is disruption, the expressive activity is not protected.

The Court's reluctance to generalize in the public forum cases has caused it to look with favor on rationales for decision that do not pit the value of expression directly against legitimate social interests in regulating public places. The favorite of these intermediate premises is the doctrine of equality. This doctrine is shown in operation in a case in which an individual picketed a Chicago public high school to protest alleged policies of racial discrimination. He was convicted under an ordinance that prohibited picketing within 150 feet of any school, but which also contained an exception for "peaceful picketing of any school involved in a labor dispute." The Supreme Court reversed the conviction on equal protection grounds, "closely intertwined with First Amendment interests. . . . If peaceful labor picketing is permitted, there is no justification for prohibiting all nonlabor picketing."[43] When this decision is contrasted with the judgment upholding the conviction under the noise or diversion statute mentioned above, which was decided on the same day, it is clear that a city may constitutionally insulate its schools from the diversions of adjacent expressive activities. But it must implement its policy evenhandedly. A city cannot allow some forms of expressive activity and prohibit others that have a comparable impact on the legitimate interest the city is trying to protect—in these examples, an interest in preventing distractions and maintaining an atmosphere of repose around schools.

Nor is the principle of equality limited to instances in which the operative ordinance contains an inequality on its face. Often a municipality that prevents public expression will be found to have allowed other expressive activity that had similar effects on traffic, noise, littering, necessity of police supervision, or other social interests.[44]

The doctrine of equality within the context of the public forum is a favorite source of arguments for access to the media. The rule that proponents of access draw from these public forum cases is roughly this: If a forum is available for certain kinds of expression, it must not discriminate according to the content or source of expression.[45] Thus, newspapers or broadcast stations that open their media as forums for certain contributors or advertisers must respond to demands for access consistent with the principle of equality. It is ironic that the notion of equality, which assumed an important role in modern public forum decisions because the Supreme Court wished to avoid broad principles of guaranteed access, should give support to such a broad and radical extension of First Amendment guarantees. "Once loosed," Professor Archibald Cox has remarked, "the idea of Equality is not easily cabined."[46] However, it is questionable whether broad claims of equal access are appropriate in the cases of private newspapers or broadcast stations.

Public Forums and Private Property

To what extent are doctrines protecting expressive activities in public places also applicable to similar activities involving private property? This is the primary conceptual problem in access arguments resting solely on the First Amendment. The issue is central to the implementation of all individual liberties guaranteed by the Bill of Rights and the Fourteenth Amendment. Constitutional rights of individuals are rights that are good against the state. They do not constrain private persons or entities unless, for some reason, a private person or entity is treated as "state action" for purposes of applying a particular right. Although the distinction between private conduct and state action is simple in theory, it is sometimes exceedingly difficult to administer in practice.

After *Marsh* v. *Alabama*, in which the Supreme Court held that a company town owned by the Gulf Shipbuilding Company was "essentially a public function," and therefore subject to the constitutional rules applicable to a public municipality, the question of state action in the application of constitutional principles arose mainly in connection with racial discrimination. As in the "white primary" cases, the issue repeatedly was whether various forms of arguably private racial discrimination were to be immunized either from judicial control under the Equal Protection Clause of the Fourteenth Amendment or from Congressional regulation under the

Enforcement Clause of the Fourteenth Amendment. In these cases the Supreme Court has been pressured to clear away doctrinal barriers to national control of racial discrimination, whatever its local form.

In dealing with discrimination not covered by federal legislation, and therefore subject to equal protection doctrines only if construed as a state action, the Supreme Court developed a scope for state action that was at once expansive and quite amorphous, lacking any coherent doctrinal core. The Court rarely explicated the competing values at stake in any particular case. Instead, it tended to count up the ways in which private property resembled public property or was connected to the government. A decision mechanically and often mysteriously followed.[47] In the words of Professor Wechsler, "[t]he modern Court has, indeed, turned handsprings to find state involvement in discriminatory practices, going much further ... than it really has been able to explain."[48]

The second result in the race discrimination field was the substantial erosion of the doctrine of state action as a limitation on Congressional power to legislate against certain acts of private discrimination, such as violent reprisals against civil rights workers.[49] It is uncertain how far this new-found Congressional power extends, but it surely would support federal legislation against private conduct that seeks to deny someone's enjoyment of a federal right or benefit.[50]

Because the Supreme Court has treated the state action concept so expansively in laying the foundation for national control over race discrimination, some observers believe the concept can be treated in accordion-like fashion in the application of all constitutional guarantees whenever relationships exist between the private and public sectors. However, when racial discrimination has not been involved, the Court has been quite reluctant to embrace broad state action concepts that would subject private choice to constitutional restraints. For example, in 1974, the Court ruled that termination of electric services by a public utility, privately owned but subject to extensive state regulation, was not state action and did not require that customers be afforded procedural due process rights.[51]

Moreover, the present Court appears reluctant to treat private property as a public forum, even when the property is wide-open to public use. The issue has arisen twice in recent years in connection with expressive activities in shopping centers. In 1969, the Supreme Court extended the principle of *Marsh* to protect labor picketing of a supermarket in a privately owned shopping center.[52] This decision, however, was sharply cut back in a second shopping center case in 1972, in which the Court upheld the exclusion from a shopping center mall of anti-war protesters who wished to distribute leaflets.[53] The 1972 decision indicated that First Amendment principles apply to private property only when that property is both wide-open to the public by invitation, and also serves as a community center. Such private property is rare indeed.

The race discrimination cases have not given the Court much occasion to point up the good in state action limitations on the reach of constitutional principles. These limitations seal off certain areas of private choice and conduct from judicial control. The Constitution does not ordain a society in which "[t]he First Amendment empowers anyone to invade the home for the purpose of edifying, with a speech, its owners against their will."[54] State action is the concept that protects us against such authoritarian extensions of constitutional principle. It achieves a rough accommodation between such constitutional values as racial equality and personal privacy. In most race discrimination cases presented to the Court, the privacy interest has been minimal, and the reach of state action has expanded accordingly. But when the constitutional question involves access to the private print media, the principle of equal access is opposed by a stronger and more legitimate countervailing interest: the right to independence from authoritative controls over political and social expression. The Court's expansive attitude toward state action in the race cases cannot be automatically applied to the different constitutional context of access to the media.

Nonstatutory Access to the Print Media

---

*"State action" again? Yes, because the "state action" problem
is the most important problem in American law.*

Charles L. Black, Jr.[1]

Before the 1974 decision of the Supreme Court in *Miami Herald
Publishing Co.* v. *Tornillo*,[2] which will be discussed in the concluding
part of this book, no effort to win judicial recognition of access
rights to the print media had relied on statutes designed to confer
access. The First Amendment alone, supplemented by the guarantee
of equal protection of the laws under the Fourteenth Amendment,
has been the legal basis for access claims. Reliance on constitutional
guarantees applicable only to government has put the issue of state
action at the fore.

The decisions, only one of which reached the Supreme Court, fall
into several categories. One series of cases concerns access to
publications that are actually government-supported, such as public
high school or state university newspapers, an official journal of a
state bar association, and, in one intriguing case, a law review
sponsored by a state university law school. Vindication of access
claims in some of these cases has given rise to arguments that the
First Amendment should also guarantee broad access rights to
privately owned media. However, in a second group of cases, courts
have refused to impose access obligations on private publications.
Claims of access have failed in these cases because the courts did not
find sufficient connections between private newspapers and govern-

ment necessary to constitute state action in the constitutional sense. Several courts have gone farther than simply pointing to an absence of state action. They have concluded that the First Amendment is a barrier to finding state action in the operations of the private press, because one aim of the Amendment is to protect the press from official supervision, including judicial oversight in the application of constitutional principles. Thus, in a couple of cases in which federal statutes dealing with union elections or civil rights have been asserted to support access to publications as appropriate statutory remedies, courts have rejected the arguments by finding in the First Amendment a wall of separation between government and the press.

A final line of cases worth looking at deals with access to a print medium of a much more limited kind. A number of state courts and lower federal courts have upheld equal access to advertising in public places and facilities. Operative principles in these cases were borrowed from the public forum cases discussed in the preceding chapter. However, the Supreme Court's 1974 decision in *Lehman* v. *City of Shaker Heights*[3] appears to undermine the force of the equal access principle as applied to advertising in public facilities. Although the question of a right to advertise on public buses and subways may seem rather distant from issues of access to the press, the Supreme Court's approach in *Lehman* is suggestive across a broad range of First Amendment issues concerning the rights of individuals to gain access to forums for expression.

Access to State-Owned Print Media

Four decisions, involving a high school paper, a college paper, a law review, and a state bar journal, deal with the right of access to print media infused with "state action."

In *Zucker* v. *Panitz*,[4] a group of students at New Rochelle (New York) High School sought to place an anti-war advertisement in the school newspaper, at the standard student rate. The student editorial board accepted the ad, but the principal directed that it not be published.* School officials argued that the paper was intended as an educational device and should not concern itself with matters

---

*The ad read, in its entirety: "The United States government is pursuing a policy in Viet Nam which is both repugnant to moral and international law and dangerous to the future of humanity. We can stop it. We must stop it."

unrelated to the school. However, the paper had already published articles about national student opinion on the Vietnam War, draft board procedures, drug use, manner of selection to the school board, and a number of other political subjects. The District Court held that, in view of the paper's coverage of political topics, "[i]t is patently unfair in light of the free speech doctrine to close to the students the forum they deem effective to present their ideas."[5] The fact that only commercial advertisements had previously been published did not dissuade the court from ordering the political ad to be published. The decision left unclear whether the high school students had an affirmative right of access to the school newspaper, or whether an equality principle governed, with the right to advertise stemming from the paper's publications on other political subjects.

The second case upheld a right to advertise in a college newspaper. *Lee v. Board of Regents of State Colleges*[6] involved the college newspaper of Wisconsin State University—Whitewater, which refused political ads on three different subjects in accordance with a general policy of refusing noncommercial ads. Federal courts ordered acceptance of the ads, notwithstanding the fact that the plaintiffs could have had identical views published in the newspaper in the form of letters to the editor. Paid advertisements, the courts reasoned, could be arranged so as to command greater attention, and therefore create more effective expression, than letters to the editor. Although the District Court opinion spoke of an unrestricted right of expression for political ads, the Court of Appeals expressly premised its affirmance on the fact that the newspaper was "a state facility."[7] Both courts in *Lee* followed the reasoning of *Zucker*, maintaining that a right of political advertising in a school paper would further educational goals and would not be disruptive.

The third case, *Avins v. Rutgers*,[8] dealt with a state university publication and introduced an important qualification on the access theories of *Zucker* and *Lee*. This suggestive case arose from the refusal of the *Rutgers Law Review* to publish an article by Alfred Avins[9] arguing that the Supreme Court should have followed the "original understanding" of the framers of the Fourteenth Amendment in *Brown v. Board of Education*.[10] The student articles editor rejected the article for the reason that "approaching the problem from the point of view of legislative history alone is insufficient." In response, Avins asserted that the *Rutgers Law Review* had adopted a discriminatory policy of publishing only "liberal" views, and that the rejection of his "conservative" approach to constitutional law denied him freedom of speech. The Court of Appeals affirmed the District Court's judgment against Avins on the ground that the *Law Review* must have discretion over what it prints:

> [n]o one doubts that [Avins] may freely at his own expense print his article and distribute it to all who wish to read it. However, he does not have the right, constitutional or otherwise, to commandeer the press and columns of the Rutgers Law Review for the publication of his article, at the expense of the subscribers to the Review and the New Jersey taxpayers, to the exclusion of other articles deemed by the editors to be more suitable for publication. On the contrary, the acceptance or rejection of articles submitted for publication in a law school law review necessarily involves the exercise of editorial judgment and this is in no wise lessened by the fact that the law review is supported, at least in part by the State.
>
> The plaintiff's contention that the student editors of the Rutgers Law Review have been so indoctrinated in a liberal ideology by the faculty of the law school as to be unable to evaluate his article objectively is so frivolous as to require no discussion.[11]

The fourth access case, *Radical Lawyers Caucus* v. *Pool*,[12] involved the *Texas Bar Journal*, the publication of the Texas state bar, which is a state agency. A group called the Radical Lawyers Caucus sought to place in the *Journal* an ad announcing a caucus during the annual Texas bar convention at which various national issues would be discussed. The *Journal* refused the ad, in accordance with a general policy of refusing political advertisements. However, it had printed editorials and resolutions in the past condemning anti-war demonstrators and supporting President Nixon's handling of the Vietnam war. Thus, the District Court held, without much elaboration, that the *Journal* could not discriminate against ads because of their political content.[13]

Of the four decisions involving access to print media directly financed by state governments, three found a right of access for political advertisements in situations where similar topics had appeared in the medium's nonadvertising copy. The fourth case found no right of access for the author of an article, but the medium involved, a law review, is one that traditionally has been selective in accepting articles for publication.

Although four decisions are too few, and the opinions too cryptic, to provide a basis for confident synthesis, one can point to some common features. The three cases declaring a right of access did so at no economic cost to the publication. Only the right to advertise was approved. No right of access was found when access would have resulted in a subsidy of the author by the publication to which access was sought.

A similar point can be made about editorial discretion. The three findings of access for political advertising did not really impinge on editorial discretion, since advertising copy is not generally considered a reflection of the publisher's views. And, in a narrow sense, the *Zucker* case upheld editorial discretion by means of an access right, because the high school's student editors had wanted to run the anti-war ad. The law review case, on the other hand, upheld editorial discretion where it would have been seriously infringed by an access right. Of course, the primary common feature of the cases is the fact that each publication was an instrument of a state agency.

Access to Private Print Media

With one early exception, decisions concerning constitutional claims of access to private owned print media have denied access for both ads and articles. This one exception occurred in 1919, when an Ohio trial court ordered an ad printed in a newspaper because it judged that the paper in question was a "*quasi*-public corporation," analogous to a railroad company or a grain elevator, and must enter into contracts for use of its facilities on a nondiscriminatory basis:[14]

> We believe that the growth and extent of the newspaper business, the public favors and general patronage received by the publishers from the public, and the general dependence, interest and concern of the public in their home papers, has clothed this particuar [sic] business with a public interest and rendered them amenable to reasonable regulations and demands of the public.[15]

The First Amendment was not mentioned in this decision. But this is not surprising since it had not as yet been held applicable to the states.[16] Nor was mention made of any value of freedom of the press.

Aside from this ruling, all other decisions concerning refusals to advertise by private newspapers have denied the claim of access. One series of decisions has involved refusals to run ads for movies.[17] A typical decision of this series is that of the Ninth Circuit Court of Appeals, in *Associates & Aldrich Co. v. Times Mirror Co.*[18] In this case, a newspaper had altered a movie ad in both text and illustration. The advertiser contended that, because of the newspaper's monopoly status,* it occupied a "quasi-public position" and, accordingly, should be "subject to control for the public good." But the Court restricted this notion, under accepted principles of state action, to media "clothed with the power of the state and ... purporting to act thereunder."

Likewise, courts confronting claims of access for political advertisements have been unimpressed by the argument that a newspaper's monopoly over news dissemination or its beneficial treatment by the government should lead to a finding of state action. For example, in *Chicago Joint Board, Amalgamated Clothing Workers v. Chicago Tribune Co.*,[19] a union sought to place an ad that urged reduction in the importation of foreign clothing, and indicated that it was picketing the Marshall Field department store because the store sold imported clothing. All four major Chicago newspapers, two of which were owned by Field Enterprises, turned down the ad for various stated reasons, although Marshall Field's heavy use of newspaper advertising may have been the reason for rejecting the union ad. The union sued the *Tribune* in an attempt to force publication of the ad, claiming that the *Tribune* should be characterized as state action because of numerous privileges conferred on newspapers by Illinois statutes. These privileges exempted newspaper employees from jury service, required that legal notices be published in a newspaper, exempted printer's ink and newsprint from various taxes, restricted newsstands on public streets to the sale of newspapers published in the city (this is clearly unconstitutional), and provided free spaces in public buildings for reporters. However, both the Federal District Court and the Court of Appeals responded that "the traditional concept of the role of the press in our society" made a finding of state action especially inappropriate. The Court of Appeals was careful to conclude that the limited connections between the state and the *Tribune* would not justify a finding of state action in any event. But it went beyond this to declare that the press was insulated

---

*The paper accounted for 80 percent of all morning daily circulations in 1964.

from a finding of state action, quoting with approval this statement from the District Court opinion:

> *In sum, the function of the press from the days the Constitution was written to the present time has never been conceived as anything but a private enterprise, free and independent of government control and supervision. Rather than state power and participation pervading the operation of the press, the news media and the government have had a history of disassociation.*[20]

Unlike the unreflective counting up of state connections characteristic of the race discrimination decisions, the *Chicago Tribune* case presents a positive conception of constitutional interest in preserving the privacy of the press from obligatory publication.

The other access decision involving a political ad adopts the same rationale, although it embraces the judgment somewhat less enthusiastically. *Resident Participation of Denver, Inc.* v. *Love*[21] arose from the refusal of the *Denver Post* and the *Rocky Mountain News* to publish an ad calling for a boycott of the products of a company planning to establish a redolent animal rendering plant near a residential area. The three-judge District Court reviewed the various statutory benefits conferred upon newspapers by Colorado and concluded that, in view of the constitutional status of the press, these statutory benefits fell far short of the connections necessary to establish state action:

> *Whatever may be the reach of these imprecise ideas, we find them peculiarly inappropriate for describing the relationship between defendant newspapers and the State. . . . [T]he historic function of newspapers, like the pamphlets of a prior day, has been to oppose government, to be its critic not its accomplice.*[22]

However, the court suggested some sympathy for the access claim as a matter of public policy:

> *We are aware that lack of access to those media which reach large audiences has, some believe, given birth to a frustration which compels otherwise peaceful citizens to engage in violence to get their views to the nation. A cause of this frustration, one critic maintains, is that, although the courts have been vigorous*

in protecting free speech, they have been indifferent to creating
opportunities for expression. Barron, Access to the Press—A
New First Amendment Right, 80 Harv. L. Rev. 1641 (1967).
We note, however, that while Professor Barron spends consider-
able space exploring a statutory solution to this problem, he
devotes much less attention to constitutional arguments and but
one paragraph to the problem of state action, which we find
insurmountable. Professor Barron simply concludes, without
noticeable explanation, that newspapers can be subjected to the
"constitutional restrictions which quasi-public status invites."
Id. at 1669. As desirable as this result might be, we are unable
in good faith to reach it.[23]

Judicial reluctance to rule that private publications should be
treated as state action is most apparent in two cases in which federal
statutes were asserted to confer access rights. The more interesting
decision concerned not political or commercial ads, but rather a
private newspaper's handling of a routine story. Both Montgomery,
Alabama, daily newspapers were sued under certain civil rights
statutes[24] for relegating stories about black weddings to a separate
black society section. The papers followed a policy of segregated
publication of all wedding announcements and pictures. Initially, the
District Court held in *Cook* v. *Advertiser Company*[25] that the civil
rights statutes could only be violated by "state action," which did
not encompass private newspapers. Moreover, after a holding in
another case that private discrimination could violate the civil rights
statutes, the District Court adhered to its position:

Assuming that the plaintiffs have a statutory right under Sec-
tion 1981 to have their bridal announcements published and
that the defendant newspaper has a constitutional right to a
"free press," this Court reaches the firm conclusion that said
defendant's constitutional right to be free from judicial inter-
ference in the selection of announcements for publication far
outweighs the Section 1981 right plaintiffs are attempting to
assert. It is for this same reason that plaintiffs cannot prevail
against defendants upon a First Amendment theory.[26]

Though the Court of Appeals based its affirmance on a statutory
ground unrelated to the First Amendment question, Judge John
Minor Wisdom addressed the First Amendment issue extensively in
his concurring opinion:

*. . . a determination of newsworthiness—however warped—
underlies the* Advertiser's *decision to print more white wedding
announcements than black ones. . . . I think the First Amendment protects that editorial discretion, however perverse may
be the manner of its exercise.*
*It is true that commercial advertising, once accepted for
printing, is subject to Congressional regulation. . . . But that
does not mean that routine news stories, such as wedding
announcements, are to be subject to Congressional
regulation.*[27]

The second case in which a private publication was asserted to be
subject to statutory duties requiring access arose from the challenge
by Joseph Yablonski to W. A. Boyle's leadership of the United Mine
Workers Union. Yablonski charged that the *United Mine Workers
Journal*, the official union publication, had advanced Boyle's
candidacy for the presidency of the union and had not given
Yablonski's candidacy sufficient coverage. Yablonski argued that the
Landrum-Griffin Act[28] prohibited such use of union funds and
membership lists to promote or discriminate against any candidate
for union office. The remedy that he sought was a court order to the
Journal, forcing it to provide equal space for him until the election
and to print copy that he would supply to constitute the first half of
specified issues of the *Journal*. The Federal District Court in
Yablonski v. *United Mine Workers*[29] agreed with Yablonski's
assertion of statutory violations by the *Journal*, but refused the
remedy of mandatory access:

*The relief requested would in effect require defendants to print
certain material supplied by plaintiff. As desirable as this might
be from a public interest and union viewpoint, such requirement would be a clear violation of the First Amendment insofar
as it relates to the freedom of the press. Citation of cases should
be unnecessary.*[30]

The Court did order the *Journal* to provide "fair and comparable
treatment of both candidates." However, when Yablonski subse-
quently protested the *Journal*'s substantially greater coverage of
Boyle, the Court declined to find a violation of its previous order,
and noted:

This Court should refrain from taking control of a news publica-

*tion or its editorship by instructing an editor as to what he can
and cannot print.*[31]

Thus, even where a statute provides considerable justification for
imposing access obligations on a private publication, the courts have
resisted on First Amendment grounds.

Although these cases concerning rights of access to privately
owned print media rose before various lower courts, a general pattern
of judicial response emerges. Beyond the situation of a refusal to deal
with an advertiser in violation of the antitrust laws, as in *Lorain
Journal*, discussed in Chapter 4, the cases seeking access for
advertisements elicited a two-pronged rationale. First, the courts
emphatically maintained that the connections between the newspapers and the state fell far short of the governmental involvement in
private activity necessary to a finding of state action. This important
conclusion is consistent with existing state action precedents, which
have held that merely conferring statutory benefits on private
entities is not enough to warrant a finding of state action.* The
second proposition of these cases is more creative: that private
newspapers are positively insulated from characterization as state
action because of the constitutional values inherent in a free press.
This explicit restriction of state action principles in relation to the
press is a significant departure from the state action precedents
dealing with racial discrimination by private enterprises having
connections to the state.

Access to Advertising in Public Forums

The third group of precedents deals with constitutionally guaranteed access to a much narrower print medium. During the 1960s, a
number of lower federal and state court decisions began to establish
a right of equality in access to advertising in various public forums.
In one case, the New York City subway system was required to
accept an anti-war ad from the Students for a Democratic Society for
display on subway platforms.[32] The advertising agency representing
the Transit Authority had turned down the ad because it was "too
controversial" and would be objectionable to a portion of the public.

---

*Unless the statutory benefit bears directly on and promotes the asserted
constitutional infringement. *Cf., Moose Lodge No. 127 v. Irvis*, 407 U.S. 163
(1972).

The District Court held that once the public system accepted some ads, it could refuse others only if they raised a "clear and present danger" of some unspecified kind. Similarly, in California, Alameda-Contra Costa Transit District buses were required to accept an anti-war ad because they had accepted others ads.[33] The California Supreme Court was careful to limit the basis of this ruling to the principle of equality. A third case required an anti-war ad to be exhibited in the buses of Tacoma, Washington. Like the California court, the Washington Supreme Court also emphasized the equality rationale in allowing access.[34]

However, the Supreme Court has recently undercut these rulings. Its decision in *Lehman* v. *City of Shaker Heights*, handed down in June 1974, is a curious latest serial in the evolution of First Amendment doctrine in the public forum.[35] This case concerned the Shaker Heights, Ohio, Rapid Transit System, owned by the city of Shaker Heights. Although the system displayed commercial and public service advertisements in its buses, it refused to accept a political ad in behalf of a candidate for the State Assembly. In turn, the candidate sued the city, asserting that the system's refusal of his political ad infringed upon his freedom of speech and denied him equal protection of the laws.

The Supreme Court considered the doctrines involved in this case and divided four-one-four. Justices Blackmun, White, and Rehnquist, as well as Chief Justice Burger, upheld the city. Their view was that the city was permitted to draw reasonable distinctions in the ads it accepted for its public buses, and that political ads were sufficiently different from commercial and public service ads to warrant refusal. Taking the opposite view, Justices Brennan, Stewart, Marshall, and Powell concluded that the transit system had elected to become a public forum, and therefore could not constitutionally discriminate against ads on the basis of political content. Justice Douglas also voted to uphold the city's refusal, providing the critical fifth vote for that position. However, he adopted an entirely different rationale. He viewed bus riders as a captive audience whose right to privacy was more important than any right of expression the candidate might otherwise have. Thus, the *Lehman* decision narrowly sustained the transit authority's power to refuse political ads while taking commercial ads.

However, the Court was equally divided on the general doctrinal questions at stake in the broad issue of the public forum. Justice Blackmun's opinion, upholding the city, was largely oblivious to the approaches developed in other cases involving advertising in public facilities. It implies that free expression questions in such situations are not to be taken very seriously. Perhaps he is right. However, since this attitude undercuts much of the public forum law that has been a significant portion of the Court's First Amendment work over the years, this case deserved a more candid and explicit statement than it received from Justice Blackmun.

Justice Blackmun began his analysis by pointing to the particularistic tendency in public forum adjudication:

> Although American constitutional jurisprudence . . . has been jealous to preserve access to public places for purposes of free speech, the nature of the forum and the conflicting interests involved have remained important in determining the degree of protection afforded by the Amendment to the speech in question.[36]

Public transportation, Justice Blackmun continued, is not a meeting hall or a public thoroughfare—"[i]nstead, the city is engaged in commerce."

> In much the same way that a newspaper or periodical, or even a radio or television station, need not accept every proffer of advertising from the general public, a city transit system has discretion to develop and make reasonable choices concerning the type of advertising that may be displayed in its vehicles.[37]

This rationale stands typical state action reasoning on its head. According to Blackmun, when a state instrument regularly engages in "commerce," meaning an activity that is carried on by private entities, it then has the same freedom from constitutional constraints that a private business enjoys. However, Justice Blackmun recognized that the existence of state action required some measure of judicial oversight. But the requisite oversight was couched in language that has become a symbol to lawyers of virtually total judicial abnegation from serious review:

> Because state action exists, however, the policies and practices governing access to the transit system's advertising space must not be arbitrary, capricious, or invidious. . . . This decision [to exclude political advertising] is little different from deciding to

impose a 10-, 25-, or 35-cent fare, or from changing schedules or the location of bus stops.[38]

With this attitude, it is not surprising that Justice Blackmun supported the city's rejection of political advertising on its buses:

Revenue earned from long-term commercial advertising could be jeopardized by a requirement that short term candidacy or issue-oriented advertisements be displayed on car cards. Users would be subjected to the blare of political propaganda. There could be lurking doubts about favoritism, and sticky administrative problems might arise in parceling out limited space to eager politicians. In these circumstances, the managerial decision to limit car card space to innocuous and less controversial commercial and service oriented advertising does not rise to the dignity of a First Amendment violation . . . No First Amendment forum is here to be found.[39]

The countervailing nuances of this opinion are puzzling. In relation to the public forum precedents, it is clear that Justices Blackmun, White, and Rehnquist and Chief Justice Burger intend that the state should have considerable freedom to pick and choose allowable expression in public facilities that are not traditional public forums. However, Justice Blackmun did not speak for a majority, and his opinion may have limited applicability in other public forum cases. It is difficult to say whether this denial of the principle of equality in access to public forum advertising signals a general retreat from access to public forums.

Justice Douglas' captive audience rationale suggests very limited impact on public forum doctrine generally. He agreed with Justice Blackmun that buses, unlike streets and parks, should not be classified as public forums: "It is only a way to get to work or back home." Moreover, Justice Douglas stated that the city should not attempt to transform its buses into public forums at the expense of its commuters' rights:

In my view the right of the commuters to be free from forced intrusions on their privacy precludes the city from transforming its vehicles of public transportation into forums for the dissemination of ideas upon this captive audience.[40]

On the other hand, Justices Brennan, Stewart, Marshall, and

Powell, who held the dissenting opinion, took an approach to the case that was consistent with the public forum precedents of lower federal and state courts. They found it unnecessary to decide whether buses should be treated as open public forums because, in their opinion, the city had already voluntarily established its buses as public forums by accepting advertising. Consequently, the city could not now constitutionally discriminate against political advertising on the basis of content. Furthermore, these dissenters rejected Justice Douglas' captive audience rationale as inappropriate to a case such as this in which a forum has already been open to some expression.

Summing Up: The Public Forum Cases and Access

The public forum cases offer little support for access claims to private media. The public forum cases concern the state's constitutional obligation to open its public places and certain other facilities to expressive activities on an impartial basis. Here the notion of equality is central. There are no counterclaims of autonomy in these decisions. The state cannot claim any legitimate interest in limiting access in parks and streets only to expression of which it approves. However, the state action principle restrains the constitutional doctrine of equality from reaching into the realm of private expression.

Even when forums of expression are clearly state action, courts have not required equal access uniformly under the First Amendment and the Equal Protection Clause. The *Avins* case and the *Lehman* case reveal that the courts may reject claims of access when they perceive more important interests of autonomy, administrative convenience, and privacy. Furthermore, these two recent decisions seem likely to exert considerable influence in the field.

In the *Avins* case, the *Rutgers Law Review* was allowed to bar access to its pages in order to pursue its editorial notions of excellence, topicality, thoroughness of research, or even "bias" about the appropriate ingredients of constitutional analysis. Equality does not govern access to expression in the *Rutgers Law Review*. The *Avins* case indicates what is likely to happen when one takes the principles of access developed to govern public places and attempts to apply them to state-owned media that can claim a legitimate interest in selectivity of publication. The public forum cases do not support access even to all publications that satisfy the stringent tests of state action used to classify media of expression. The Government Printing Office has not become a public platform because of the First Amendment and the Equal Protection Clause.

The *Lehman* decision may represent a more significant restriction on the principle of equality as it is applied to state-owned means of communication. In this case, a medium of communication that was open to all members of the public who wished to advertise goods and services was closed to paid political announcements. And, despite the absence of any plausible claim of editorial autonomy, the closure won judicial approval. The decision is difficult to understand, and the Court was evenly divided with respect to public forum doctrine. But the result was that equality of access was subordinated to administrative convenience and the privacy rights of bus riders. *Lehman* and *Avins* warrant caution in assessing the impact of constitutional principles of equal access on state-owned means of communication.

As for private media, the public forum decisions give no support whatever to access claims based on the Constitution. The courts view state action as requisite to consideration of constitutional access claims. In cases involving private newspapers, the uniform denial of state action rests on a positive conception of the constitutional values of separation between the government and communications media. When all the cases are viewed together, it is apparent that the courts see state action as a necessary, but not sufficient, condition for the application of constitutional principles of equal access.

The positive conception of state action developed in these cases also has implications for statutory rights of access. The contrast between these access cases and the race discrimination cases is instructive. When it comes to distinguishing between governmental and private acts of discrimination, in terms of corrective federal intervention to protect rights of equality, it must be remembered that judicial action under the Fourteenth Amendment reaches only state action, while federal legislation can deal with either. However, the *Cook* and *Yablonski* decisions, involving claims of access under federal statutes, suggest that the pattern of the race cases will not apply to discrimination in publications by privately owned communications media. The *Cook* decision rejected application of the civil rights statutes to gain access to a newspaper's white society pages. The Court's decision rested not only on statutory construction, but also on the fact that the First Amendment guarantees a newspaper's control over access to its pages. *Yablonski* follows the same line of thought. These decisions suggest that the courts would be much more skeptical of federal legislation designed to guarantee equality of access to private newspapers than they have been of its legislative counterpart concerning race discrimination in employment, housing, and private violence. However, the constitutionality of statutory requirements of access of access cannot be analyzed before considering the legal regulation of radio and television, in which statutory and administrative access obligations have played a central role.

PART III

ACCESS TO
TELEVISION AND RADIO

The moving picture screen, the radio, the newspaper, the hand-bill, the sound truck and the street corner orator have differing natures, values, abuses and dangers. Each, in my view, is a law unto itself . . . .

Justice Robert H. Jackson[1]

First Amendment principles have long been rooted in a *laissez-faire* relationship between government and the media, and institutional tendencies have fit comfortably with this tradition. With respect to the print media, the fact that legal constraints must emanate from legislation or judicial decisions tends to foster a hands-off approach. The inertia of the legislative process, the inability of legislatures to scrutinize the general performance of enterprises, and the limited, prohibitory character of most statutes all reinforce the First Amendment presumption of government non-interference with communications media. Furthermore, judicial lawmaking, anchored in discrete cases rather than general problems, is even more clearly interstitial in character.

Radio and television operate in a legal milieu that is totally different, indeed opposite, in its regulatory tendencies. Almost from the beginning, broadcasting has fallen under the aegis of an administrative agency, the Federal Communications Commission. An astute student of administrative law, Professor Kenneth Davis, has pointed out: "the administrative process is always a took for *positive government*, never a tool for *laissez faire.*"[2] The natural tendency to posi-

119

tive government of an administrative agency, charged with overseeing communications media under both constitutional and statutory mandates to honor principles of free expression, has produced the fascinating spectacle of affirmative efforts to guarantee by law the goals of the First Amendment while wrenching it from its traditional *laissez-faire* moorings.

The special nature of this administrative process is not all that has set the legal status of broadcasting apart from that of the print media. Society's perceptions of television have also tended toward legal differentiation. Television has become the symbol of the media's mammoth power in the post-industrial age. It is the focus of late twentieth-century anxieties about the adequacy of an eighteenth-century First Amendment to govern the relationship between government and the media, not only because of its technical novelty, but also because its social force is vastly greater than that of any other communications medium in history.

According to an assessment by Daniel Boorstin, television has transformed modern American society to a degree equaled only by the automobile,[3] and, like the automobile, television "has become so inextricably woven into the social fabric that it is extremely difficult to view it as an institution in its own right."[4] Although television's greatest impact probably centers on its non-public affairs programming, its influence on Americans' view of public affairs is greater than any other communications medium. In 1973, a Nielsen survey indicated that the three television network news programs reached 46 million homes in the average week—about 70 per cent of all homes.[5] More significantly, public information polls have demonstrated that television is both the chief source of news and the most believed source of news for most Americans, and that television's position relative to other media is strengthened year by year.[6]

Moreover, television has managed to reverse two of the most important characteristics of the print media's audience. First, greater levels of education tend to produce greater propensities to read, not just books and relatively sophisticated magazines, but also pictorial and general interest magazines. Yet, the least educated in the United States tend to watch more television news than those with higher education levels.[7] Second, television-viewing has reversed the tendency of print media consumers to supplement one medium with another. Generally, the more time readers spend with newspapers, the more time they will spend with magazines and books. Television viewing, by contrast, leads to less contact with competing news media.[8] In other words, public reliance on print media has been influenced by educational level and exposure to other published information, which do not affect television-viewers. The absence of these mediating tendencies in a growing number of Americans, whose information about public affairs is increasingly dominated by television, is a serious challenge to traditional *laissez-faire* notions about the legal status of communications media.

In view of the legal and social environment, it is not surprising that access rights leave the realm of conjecture when it comes to radio and television. From the outset of federal regulation over electronic media, statutes have guaranteed specific rights of access to political candidates. In addition, the Federal Communications Commission has exercised its administrative powers to create further rights of access. Persons or groups attacked on the air during discussion of controversial public issues must be informed of the attack and provided with an opportunity for reply. Editorializing by broadcasters triggers similar access rights for representatives of opposing public positions. In recent years, a lively access controversy has been triggered by the expansive notion that airing advertisements for products creating risks to public health should oblige broadcasters also to present "counter-commercials" informing the audience of the dangers.

Further dispute has centered on presidential addresses aired during prime-time simultaneously by the three networks. Recent presidents have increasingly resorted to this efficient means of building popular support for their policies and, frequently, for their presumed candidacies for re-election. Some suggest that such addresses by presidents should generate a right of reply for their political opposition. Certain observers of this trend have claimed that the absence of a reciprocal opportunity for mass communication may endanger our system's political balance of power.

Many political and minority groups have demanded broader rights of access to radio and television. Some contend that broadcasters should be obligated to accept all editorial advertisements. Others have urged the Commission to guarantee access without cost. To date, broad access obligations have not been imposed on broadcasters. However, existing narrow rights of access indicate that radio and television do not enjoy the First Amendment autonomy of print media. Therefore, the question of whether the electronic media should be subject to further access claims has been viewed as a matter open to legislative and administrative decision, rather than as a constitutional issue.

The question of access has also been at the forefront of recent FCC approaches to cable television. The cable television method of signal transmission by coaxial cable is very different from the radiation of electromagnetic waves from a transmitting antenna used by traditional broadcasting, and it promises great diversity in television programming. A single cable can carry up to 44 different channels within conventional VHF television frequencies and more than one cable can be laid in any given area. As a result, the number of channels available is now limited more by economics than by physical realities. Traditionally, much regulation of electronic media has been justified on the ground that physical outlets were scarce. The potential of cable television is beginning to challenge this theory.

Cable television adds a unique perspective on access. The Commission has required that cable operators set aside three "access channels" for the free use of the public, educational institutions, and local governments. These access channels must be available on a first-come, first-served basis. Thus, cable television has elicited an affirmative access right available to the general public, in contrast to the contingent access rights imposed on traditional broadcasting.

Rights of access to traditional broadcasting and to cable television offer concrete experience with a number of the theoretical and practical questions previously discussed. What are the grounds, in legal theory and public policy, for imposing access obligations on radio and television? Are some of these justifications transferable to print media? Have rights of access to the electronic media caused administrative problems, inhibited certain types of desired expression, or served as a wedge for expanding governmental control over the content of broadcast journalism? Conversely, have rights of access to radio and television increased fairness to individuals, produced a better informed public, or counteracted economic and social tendencies to media concentration? Overall, should a common legal approach to questions of access embrace both print and electronic media? Or does access suggest that the First Amendment and communications policy should diverge when applied to different types of communications media?

Issues of access reach to the foundations of the administrative, statutory, and constitutional law that governs radio and television. Accordingly, this part of the book begins with an overview of radio and television regulation. Subsequent chapters turn specifically to the issue of access, dealing first with the statutory rights of political candidates to airtime, and next with the Fairness Doctrine, which at once supports and inhibits access claims. After that, the discussion will concern the fate of various efforts to impose broad rights of access on radio and television, and will offer suggestions for the future of access to radio and television. This part concludes with a look at the prospects for access to cable television.

An Overview of Broadcast Regulation

*[T]he ether and the use thereof for the transmission of signals,
words, energy, and other purposes . . . is hereby reaffirmed to
be the inalienable possession of the people of the United States
and their Government. . . .*

S. 2930, passed by the United Senate in 1924[1]

*The situation in the American broadcasting industry is not
essentially different in character from that which would be
found if a commission appointed by the federal government had
the task of selecting those who were to be allowed to publish
newspapers and periodicals in each city, town, and village of the
United States.*

Ronald H. Coase[2]

The persistent clinging of First Amendment principles to the
broadcast media, despite fundamental rebuff, shows how adaptable
our tradition of freedom of the press really is. This Anglo-American
tradition began as a reaction against the licensing system that existed
in England virtually from the introduction of the printing press until
the expiration of the Printing Act in 1694. The most assured historical meaning of the First Amendment is that government may
not treat publication as a privilege to be indulged only on condition
of prior license. Yet, this anathematic pattern is the foundation of
the Communications Act of 1934.[3] No one may broadcast without a
license, and the government issues licenses without charge to those it
believes will serve the "public interest." Thus, the Federal Communi-

cations Commission is analagous to the regulatory machinery of the Tudor and Stuart monarchs. Insistence upon freedom of expression in broadcasting, despite the contradiction of licensing, suggests the vigor of our commitment to freedom of expression in general.

But why has our law rejected a free enterprise, market-pricing system as the basis for allocating resources in the electromagnetic spectrum? When one considers the *laissez-faire* thinking that dominated the first third of this century, and our tradition of autonomy for communications media, it seems unlikely that we should have produced a system of broadcast regulation involving such extensive government control. The answer probably lies in early perceptions about the physical characteristics of the spectrum, the nonjournalistic uses to which broadcasting was first devoted, and the rapid, chaotic growth of broadcasting during the 1920s, which seemed to call for sudden and sweeping legislative response.

The Genesis of Regulation

Broadcasting is the transmission of electromagnetic waves over the radio spectrum. When more than one station in a particular geographical area simultaneously attempts to use the same piece of spectrum space, the result is chaos. Thus, for the spectrum to have reliable utility, the right to exclusive use of a portion must be protected. The demand for spectrum space has generally exceeded the usable and available supply, and a system of short-term, cost-free licensing has been the means chosen by Congress to allocate this scarce resource.[4]

From the inception of its use, the spectrum has been regarded as posing a unique regulatory problem. The absence of legal regulation was intolerable even during the early uses of radio in marine communication at the beginning of this century. In 1910, the Department of the Navy called for "placing all wireless stations under the control of the Government." As the Navy complained to the Senate, the independent and uncoordinated use of radio had led to a "state of chaos":

Calls of distress from vessels in peril on the sea go unheeded or are drowned out in the etheric bedlam produced by numerous stations all trying to compete at once. . . . It is not putting the case too strongly to state that the situation is intolerable, and is continually growing worse.[5]

Congress responded with a 1912 enactment that required a license from the Secretary of Commerce for anyone sending radio signals.[6] The licensing power permitted regulation of such matters as location of transmitter, wavelengths to be used, and hours of broadcasting. Although the 1912 law was passed before anyone understood the possibilities of broadcasting, it established a pattern of cost-free administrative licensing as the mechanism for allocating rights to the spectrum.

Six years later, the Navy Department proposed again that the spectrum be allocated exclusively to the Navy, because, as Secretary Josephus Daniels put it, radio is "the only method of communication which must be dominated by one power to prevent interference. . . . The question of interference does not come in at all in the matter of cables or telegraphs."[7] However, the Navy failed to win a monopoly of the spectrum, and the rapid growth of private radio broadcasting in the early 1920s eliminated the feasibility of a government-operated radio monopoly.

The years following World War I were a period of frenetic corporate activity and patent competition in the broadcasting field, but they still gave few hints about the future of the electronic media. As radio became less a hobby and more a business, the commercial purpose of broadcasting was to create an incentive for the purchase of receivers. Westinghouse showed the way with station KDKA in Pittsburgh. David Sarnoff saw the potential, and RCA sales of radio sets, which totaled $11,000,000 in 1922, rose to $50,000,000 two years later.[8] During this period, the Commerce Department was deluged with license applications. Between March 1 and November 1, 1922, the number of broadcasting stations in the United States increased from 60 to 564.[9] However, these stations were assigned to only two frequencies, and interference became a serious problem for broadcasting.

The resulting confusion led Secretary of Commerce Herbert Hoover to convene the Washington Radio Conference early in 1922. All the broadcasters, receivers manufacturers, federal and state officials, inventors, and even a ham operator who assembled for this conference agreed that the Secretary should be given "adequate legal authority" to deal with "the mess" over the air. Hoover enthusiastically declared that "this is one of the few instances where the country is unanimous in its desire for more regulation."[10]

Yet, the unanimity of those who attended the conference was the result of their failure to consider any of the details of the "adequate legal authority" for which they called. Legislative proposals to enhance the Secretary of Commerce's power of licensing met opposition based on congressional concern over the incumbent's political aspirations. Other presidential aspirants in Congress joined together and called for the creation of an independent regulatory commission. A stalemate ensued.[11]

Secretary Hoover, however, faced urgent problems of allocation that could not wait for Congress. Calling the chaos in the air "simply intolerable," Hoover convened a second radio conference early in 1923 and sought industry acquiescence in executive action, under the assumption that new legislation was not close at hand. The conference resolved that Hoover had authority under the 1912 statute "to regulate hours and wavelengths of operation of stations."[12] Armed with this mandate, Hoover imposed regulations not expressly authorized by the 1912 Act, including limits on the number of licenses that would be granted and allocation of portions of the spectrum for different types of broadcasting.

The courts were not persuaded. First, in 1923, a federal court held that Hoover lacked authority to refuse to grant a license or to decline to renew an existing license.[13] Three years later, another court denied him power to restrict the wavelengths at which licensees might broadcast.[14] The Justice Department refused to appeal, conceding the correctness of the two courts' debilitating construction of the 1912 law.[15]

Bedlam was the predictable result. Pressure for comprehensive legislation overcame congressional doubts about regulatory invasion of *laissez-faire* preserves, and the idea of a regulatory commission alleviated concerns about presidential politics. As an interim measure, to preclude any claims of property rights in the spectrum, Congress acted in 1926 and passed a joint resolution declaring that licensees must execute waivers of "any right or of any claim to any right, as against the United States, to any wavelength or to the use of the ether in radio transmission."[16] Permanent arrangements followed the next year.

The Radio Act of 1927 created the Federal Radio Commission. This Commission was given the power to issue broadcast licenses if the "public convenience, interest, or necessity will be served thereby," to control location, power, wavelength, and nature of service, and to make regulations to minimize interference.[17] In accordance with the 1926 Joint Resolution, licensees were required to sign a waiver of property rights in the spectrum. The Radio Commission was also authorized to require applicants for licenses to submit information about their proposed service and about all aspects of their financial, technical, and character qualifications. Moreover, the Radio Act contained four specific regulations pertaining to programming. The most significant regulation for our purposes required that a station which gave or sold airtime to a candidate for public office must also afford equivalent access to other candidates for the same office. This contingent access obligation has remained in the law to this day. The other three programming requirements prohibited obscene, profane, or indecent language, required announcements of the sponsors and producers of paid programming, and prohibited rebroadcasting without the permission of the original broadcaster. Concern for free expression also surfaced in the Radio Act. The Commission was forbidden to censor programs or to interfere "with the right of free speech by means of radio communications."

The Radio Commission existed only from 1927 to 1934, and it did not contribute much of importance to the development of access law regarding the electronic media. One bizarre incident, however, was revealing. John R. Brinkley, who appropriated the title "Dr." after purchasing medical diplomas from Kansas City and St. Louis diploma mills, used medical quackery, snake-oil hucksterism, and electronic charisma to build an illustrious career in the formative days of radio.[18] His "Medical Question Box" was broadcast from a small Kansas town. Combining prescriptions and plugs for his mail-order patent medicines with a mixture of country music, folk wisdom, and fundamentalist religion, Dr. Brinkley's broadcasts became the most listened-to in the country. His diatribes against organized medicine ("a meatcutters' union," "Don't let your doctor two-dollar you to death") eventually attracted the attention of the AMA, which in 1930 opposed renewal of his broadcast license. The Commission declined to renew on the grounds that offering prescriptions to unknown, unseen, and unexamined patients was "inimical to the public health and safety," and that the station operated "only in the personal interest" of Brinkley. "The interest of the listening public is paramount," the Commission concluded, "and may not be subordinated to the interests of the station licensee." Brinkley charged that the Commission's refusal to renew on account of his programming was censorship, in violation of the Radio Act. However, the Court of Appeals rejected his contention:

> It is apparent, we think, that the business is impressed with a public interest and that, because the number of available broadcasting frequencies is limited, the Commission is necessarily called upon to consider the character and quality of the service to be rendered. . . .
>
> When Congress provided that the question whether a license should be issued or renewed should be dependent upon a finding of public interest, convenience, or necessity, it very evidently had in mind that broadcasting should not be a mere adjunct to a particular business but should be of a public character.[19]

Other Court of Appeals' decisions also affirmed the Commission's authority to consider a broadcaster's past programming in deciding whether license renewal was in the public interest.[20] However, the Supreme Court did not accept for decision any cases that would have posed the issue. It was during this formative period that Senator Clarence C. Dill, the primary author of the Radio Act, visited Chief Justice William Howard Taft to express his hope that any radio case would receive careful attention. The genial Chief Justice, Dill later recalled, predicted that the Court would not take jurisdiction of any radio case if it could be avoided, because

> to me, interpreting the law on this subject is something like trying to interpret the law of the occult. It seems like dealing with something supernatural.[21]

The Chief Justice's prediction was correct. No authoritative judicial review of the Radio Commission's powers over the programming of broadcast licensees had occurred when Congress debated a new communications statute during 1933 and 1934. Controversy at that time mainly concerned reforms of the allocation pattern of the 1927 Act proposed by educational institutions and others committed to cultural improvement through radio. The Senate, however, defeated a proposal to reserve one-fourth of the broadcasting spectrum for educational, religious, and other nonprofit institutions.[22]

The Communications Act of 1934 transferred the powers of the Federal Radio Commission to the Federal Communications Commission. Power over telegraph and telephone, formerly held by the Interstate Commerce Commission, was also transferred to the FCC. Yet, the basic allocation pattern of broadcast licenses was not changed. The administrative powers over broadcasting created by the 1927 Act were carried over into the 1934 Act without important revision. Moreover, the 1934 Act has itself remained largely unchanged. Even in these present days of network-dominated commercial television there remains essentially the same statutory basis for broadcast regulation that Congress created back in 1927.

Not until 1943 did the Supreme Court review the basic authority of the Federal Communications Commission. NBC and other networks challenged the 1941 FCC Report on Chain Broadcasting, which prohibited certain types of provisions in contracts between the networks and their affiliated stations. In general, FCC regulations were designed to increase station independence. They ensured that affiliates could broadcast programs of all networks, while granting affiliates the right to reject any network program. At the same time, they prohibited affiliates from having the exclusive right to network programs in a given territory, reduced the length of affiliation contracts from five to two years, and ended network ownership of more than one station in the same listening area.[23] The networks objected to these regulations. They argued that the FCC was limited by the Communications Act to control of the engineering and technical aspects of broadcasting and that it could not regulate the content and source of programming. They also argued that the First Amendment rights of broadcasters were violated when Commission action affected programming.

In the celebrated decision in *National Broadcasting Co.* v. *United States*,[24] the Supreme Court rejected both arguments. It held that the Communications Act authorized more than engineering regulation:

There is a fixed natural limitation upon the number of stations that can operate without interfering with one another. Regulation of radio was therefore as vital to its development as traffic control was to the development of the automobile. . . .

But the Act does not restrict the Commission merely to supervision of the traffic. It puts upon the Commission the burden of determining the composition of that traffic. The facilities of radio are not large enough to accommodate all who wish to use them. Methods must be devised for choosing from among the many who apply. . . .

The Commission was, however, not left at large in performing this duty. The touchstone provided by Congress was the "public interest, convenience, or necessity. . . ."

The "public interest" to be served under the Communications Act is thus the interest of the listening public in "the larger and more effective use of radio. . . ." Since the very inception of federal regulation by radio, comparative considerations as to the services to be rendered have governed the application of the standard of "public interest, convenience, or necessity."[25]

The First Amendment argument also fell before the Court's analysis of the implications of spectrum scarcity:

We come, finally, to an appeal to the First Amendment. The Regulations, even if valid in all other respects, must fall because they abridge, say the appellants, their right of free speech. If that be so, it would follow that every person whose application for a license to operate a station is denied by the Commission is thereby denied his constitutional right of free speech. Freedom of utterance is abridged to many who wish to use the limited facilities of radio. Unlike other modes of expression, radio inherently is not available to all. That is its unique characteristic, and that is why, unlike other modes of expression, it is subject to governmental regulation. Because it cannot be used by all, some who wish to use it must be denied. But Congress did not authorize the Commission to choose among applicants upon the basis of their political, economic or social views, or upon any other capricious basis. If it did, or if the Commission by these Regulations proposed a choice among applicants upon some such basis, the issue before us would be wholly different. The question here is simply whether the Commission, by announcing that it will refuse licenses to persons who engage in specified network practices (a basis for choice which we hold is comprehended within the statutory criterion of "public interest"), is thereby denying such persons the constitutional right of free speech. The right of free speech does not include, however, the right to use the facilities of radio without a license. The licensing system established by Congress in the Communications Act of 1934 was a proper exercise of its power over commerce. The standard it provided for the licensing of stations was the "public interest, convenience, or necessity." Denial of a station license on that ground, if valid under the Act, is not a denial of free speech.[26]

The Supreme Court's first general consideration of the Communications Act thus resulted in a resounding affirmation. The Court's rationale clearly rested on the conception that scarcity of the spectrum in relation to demand for its use justified the Commission's concern with programming for the benefit of the general public.

Not until the *Red Lion* decision in 1969, 26 years later, did the Supreme Court again extensively analyze broadcasting, the Communications Act, and traditional constitutional notions about the autonomy of communications media. As a result broadcast regulation has developed under a single statutory rationale, embodied in the 1927 and 1934 Acts, and under a single Supreme Court precedent, which embraced that statutory scheme without objection.

Useful Perspectives from "an Insight More Fundamental Than We Can Use"[27]

The continuity of legal tradition regarding radio and television tends to generate an assumption that the technological characteristics of broadcasting necessitate the system of administrative spectrum allocation embodied in the Communications Act. This assumption has been forcefully challenged by a number of observers, primarily economists, who maintain that greater social utility would be achieved through operation of a market system in which portions of the spectrum would be sold or leased to the highest bidder. Consideration of this market alternative offers basic insights about the existing law of broadcast regulation and about the role of access in that scheme.

Professor R. H. Coase has contended that, in economic terms, the electromagnetic spectrum is similar to other resources, such as land or printing presses.[28] All valuable resources are scarce, and they are valuable largely because government surrounds them with legal protections against interference. As Coase points out, the fact that governmental protections give value to land and printing presses as property does not cause us to assume that the government should also license these scarce resources to be used in the "public interest." The protections provided by the government in granting exclusive use of portions of the electromagnetic spectrum are more complex than the legal protections needed to give value to land or printing presses. However, they are not different in principle. Coase suggests that the laws of property, trespass, theft, and contracts, among others, which make land or printing presses valuable, are broadly comparable to the licensing and transfer provisions of the Communications Act.

The two main differences between the electromagnetic spectrum and other resources, with respect to allocation and utilization, are the complexity of interference problems and the obviousness of scarcity. Land need only be allocated in terms of length, width, and time.[29] The spectrum involves these same three limits, plus the characteristics of frequency and interference. Even though the same geographical space and time can be occupied by different frequencies of electromagnetic radiation, signal carriage over one part of the spectrum will often cause interference throughout a broader portion. In such a case, the problem of interference is greater than actual beneficial use. Accordingly, allocation of the spectrum is more complicated than allocation of such physical resources as land. Restrictions on the allocation of physical resources ordinarily are limited to preventing incompatible uses of the same resource.[30] Of course, the phenomenon of interference is not altogether unknown in land matters, as the law of nuisance attests. But, despite such problems of interference and the necessity for general restrictions on free use of land, our legal order allocates this resource by a system of ownership, based either on purchase in the open market or on appropriation by first-comers under homestead statutes. And, although certain uses of land are prohibited, our law does not impose general official control over land use to ensure that a given parcel is used "in the public interest." So, why did Congress choose to allocate the electromagnetic spectrum and deal with problems of interference in that resource by a system of short-term licensing under the public interest standard rather than by some form of ownership?

Coase supposes that the answer has to do with the scarcity of the resource. Many people believe that this scarcity differentiates the spectrum from land or printing presses. From the early days of broadcasting, more persons have wished to transmit signals than the spectrum can accommodate without chaos. The finitude of the usable portion of the electromagnetic spectrum is more immediately evident than the finitude of land or of the ingredients of printing presses. The spectrum is just there; we cannot manufacture additional spectrum space in the sense that we can convert a wilderness into usable land, or produce more printing presses and fewer cars.[31] But Coase argues that this difference does not justify departure from the market-pricing system of resource allocation. Scarcity and economic value are common to the electromagnetic spectrum and all other resources as well.

Coase and others have warned that exempting the spectrum from the market system may have unfortunate effects. First, since the FCC must allocate and oversee very valuable resources on the basis of amorphous criteria, the Commission is likely to be subject to political pressures and conflicts of interest. Second, holders of spectrum rights are not encouraged to economize in their spectrum use, because they are not permitted to sell lesser portions of their spectrum rights. Moreover, no transfer is permitted among different types of service (such as land mobile, marine, radio, television, and communications common carriers that use microwave transmission). This is true even if a particular portion of the spectrum is more valuable to some other type of service than to the type of service to which it has been allocated by the Commission. Finally, some suspect that the amount of spectrum allotted to the government for military and other purposes is greater than what the government would be willing to pay for in an open spectrum market.

The Coase thesis has not gone unquestioned. Professor W. K. Jones has pointed out that interference problems are most severe between different types of spectrum users. A market system allowing transfers of spectrum from one use to another would create severe inter- ference problems.[32] Therefore, at least some nonmarket regulation of the spectrum, similar to zoning regulations, is necessary. The Commission might specify what general use would be allowed for designated portions of the spectrum, although market transfers might be allowed within a designated area of use. But, even if circumscribed by such minimal regulation, a market system might be impractical. The phenomenon of intermodulation—interference generated by the combined effects of several signals, which in lesser numbers do not create this interference—requires on-going supervision and adjust- ment of spectrum rights. Adequate supervision and adjustment would be difficult under a system of contract allocations and would challenge both the scientific competence and the remedial capacity of courts. It is doubtful that Coase and other market-enthusiasts have demonstrated, in concrete terms, that the market could cope with the complex problems of interference within the spectrum. More- over, from a practical viewpoint, it is almost inconceivable that Congress would upset the existing system. Professor Kalven acutely characterized the Coase analysis as "an insight more fundamental than we can use."[33]

However, it is not necessary to embrace the Coase critique for it to be useful in a discussion of broadcast regulation and access. Quite apart from its merits as a program for reform, the market critique is a helpful touchstone for analysis of the existing system of regulation. It reveals that resource allocation and utilization of a most unusual sort are the essence of the Communications Act and the entire body of related administrative law developed by the FCC. The basic thesis of this book's analysis of access obligations, in relation to television and radio, is that virtually everything the FCC does in this area must be viewed in light of its problematical responsibility of allocation under the Communications Act.

The actual system of administrative allocation may be viewed best against the background of other methods that have been rejected. As we have seen, a market-pricing system of spectrum allocation was rejected from the beginning. The obvious alternative to market allocation is direct government operation. Such utilization would leave open those allocation questions relating to different official uses—questions of efficiency—but would not encounter the problems of justification that are endemic when benefits in the spectrum are conferred upon private parties at no cost. Yet, despite continuous official rhetoric to the effect that the spectrum is an inalienable part of the public domain, the Navy was not successful in urging direct government control of the spectrum. Private interests in broadcasting had become entrenched before 1927 when Congress, for the first time, focused on basic issues of spectrum allocation and utilization. Direct government operation of the spectrum was neither practical nor politically feasible.

A third possible method of spectrum management would work toward the goal of open access. Anyone might be allowed to buy, lease, or borrow a transmitter and apply for a particular broadcast time and spectrum space, which would be allocated on some neutral basis, such as "first-come, first-served." However, such an "open access" method of allocation would fractionalize broadcasting. There would be little continuity of programming, and broadcasters would have very little incentive to invest in long-term, quality programming.[34]

Any of these three methods of spectrum management would have provided a coherent rationale for government regulation of broadcasting; the Communications Act is a contradictory mix of the three. Section 301 of the Act authorizes "the use of such channels, but not the ownership thereof, by persons for limited periods of time, under licenses granted by Federal authority, and no such license shall be construed to create any right, beyond the terms, conditions, and periods of the license."[35] The FCC is authorized by statute to grant licenses and renewals "in the public interest, convenience, and necessity,"[36] a phrase borrowed from a statute regulating railroads and grain elevators.[37] Moreover, the statutory scheme imposes public interest obligations on broadcast licensees.

Three particular standards are incorporated in the Act to indicate the minimum contours of broadcast service in the public interest. First, the Act requires that the Commission make a fair distribution of licenses among states and communities to ensure diverse local outlets of radio service.[38] Second, the Act generally prescribes that broadcast service shall be "efficient" and "nationwide" and shall afford "a reasonable opportunity for the discussion of conflicting views on issues of public importance."[39] These two aims are mutually exclusive. As the Presidential Task Force on Telecommunications observed in its 1968 Report: "The concept of a nationwide scheme of local stations produced a relatively large number of individual stations but relatively few accessible broadcast signals for the individual listener."[40] The third public interest standard of the Act requires that political candidates be given "equal opportunities" to airtime provided to their rivals.[41]

Just as the Act undercuts any basis in traditional conceptions of private property for broadcaster autonomy, it likewise negates the antithetical notion that broadcasters are purely surrogates for the public at large, or subject to unfettered official control. The Act specifies that licensees are not "common carriers" compelled to accept any message for broadcasting.[42] Moreover, as noted above, the Act expressly withdraws any "power of censorship" from the FCC, and provides that "no regulation or condition shall be promulgated or fixed by the Commission which shall interfere with the right of free speech by means of radio communication."[43] These provisions clearly were intended to give the broadcaster substantial editorial control over programming.

These colliding statutory ground rules governing broadcasters' freedom and obligations have been incorporated into one of the law's most elastic conceptions. The FCC regards a broadcast license as a "trust," with the public as "beneficiary" and the broadcaster as "public trustee."[44] This conception of the broadcaster as a "public trustee" is a natural consequence of the conflicting statutory goals of private use and nonmarket allocation of spectrum space. Since our law has rejected both market allocation and governmental use, the

Commission's dilemma is choosing among various candidates for broadcasting licenses and somehow finding justification for providing a fortunate few with the use of a valuable, scarce resource at no cost. The public trustee concept is designed to dull the horns of the FCC's dilemma. To give away valuable spectrum rights, with no strings attached, would pose stubborn problems of justification.

Since programming is by far the most significant aspect of a broadcaster's operation, it is inevitable that public trusteeship obligations will substantially concern programming. The focus of this concern can be prospective, contemporaneous, or retrospective. That is, the Commission can try to decide whether an applicant for a license will prove to be a satisfactory public trustee by evaluating, in advance, the likely nature of his programming. Or, it can review individual programs more or less contemporaneously, and impose sanctions or require corrective or supplementary programming. Or, the Commission can review the overall programming performance of a broadcaster over an extended period, in retrospect. The FCC's current practice is a rather haphazard mix of these three types of evaluation.

Though we need not sort this mixture out at this time, one general point is worth mentioning. There is a significant possibility that the extent to which one type of evaluation is imposed on a station depends upon the extent to which the other two types of evaluation are imposed. A principle of administrative conservation of energy may operate, so that a reduction in one type of evaluation produces an increase in another. If public trustee obligations with respect to programming cannot be either predicted or mandated in advance, the focus of the Commission's supervision must be contemporaneous or retrospective. Moreover, a retrospective review of public trustee obligations is likely to reveal only gross and consistent deviation. For this reason, there are substantial practical pressures for contemporaneous review. On the other hand, when the FCC reviews specific programs and imposes specific remedies, it runs the serious risk of inhibiting certain types of expression. The values of the First Amendment, therefore, may discourage contemporaneous review. Furthermore, the "no censorship" provision prevents advance prohibitions of specific programs, and the same provision's injunction against interference with "the right of free speech" tends to discourage the imposition of punishments for unsatisfactory programming. The result of all this is that contemporaneous review of whether a license has met public trustee standards tends to focus on corrective and supplementary programming. Rights of access thus become a central issue in the enforcement of public trustee obligations.

The paradox of freedom in a licensed medium centers on access. Should a temporary holder of spectrum space in trust for the benefit of the public be required to permit others to use that means of public expression? Will a medium of expression serve the goals of the First Amendment if there are government-imposed correctives for certain of its editorial decisions? These general themes will be considered after an appraisal of how access guarantees and claims have actually fared in the regulation and operation of television and radio.

Politics and Access:
The "Equal Opportunities" Provision of Section 315

If any licensee shall permit any person who is a legally qualified candidate for any public office to use a broadcasting station, he shall afford equal opportunities to all other such candidates for that office in the use of such broadcasting station.

Section 315(a) of the Communications Act.

From the Radio Act of 1927 to the present, the statutes regulating broadcasting have required that a licensee allowing use of its station by a legally qualified candidate for office must afford equal opportunities to all other legally qualified candidates for that office. This provision, codified in section 315(a) of title 47 of the United States Code, is the most precisely drawn access right in the law governing radio and television. It reflects Congressional concern that politically biased use of a radio or television station could be ruinous to disfavored political candidates. From its inception, the equal opportunities obligation has been at the center of contention as to the freedom and public responsibility of broadcasters, as to guaranteeing equality of access to broadcasting for political candidates as opposed to encouraging serious political expression over the air and allowing flexibility in broadcasters' news judgments, and as to whether access rights for candidates should be affirmative and free of cost as opposed to the type of largely contingent obligations contained in existing law. The equal opportunities provision has also been beset with controversial problems of interpretation and administration. Although this statute is of very considerable political significance in itself, its history and experience also suggest some of the problems and potentialities of access obligations in general.

Of the many proposals to impose more extensive access obligations on radio broadcasters, only the equal opportunities provision survived in both the Radio Act of 1927 and the Communications Act of 1934. It was the residue of wide-ranging debate before passage of the Radio Act of 1927 on the nature of broadcasting in America. Concern centered on what should be the extent of control by broadcasters over material that was aired. Some entrenched radio interests sought autonomy for broadcasters along the lines of that enjoyed by newspapers, as in this testimony by a representative of AT&T:

> . . . we take the same position that is taken by the editor of any publication. He has the right to accept or to reject any material presented to him. You can not walk into a newspaper office to-day and get them to publish anything you care to present. We felt that was a privilege which the owners of the broad-casting stations also possessed.[1]

On the other side were advocates of public utility—common carrier status for radio stations. They urged that material should be accepted for broadcasting just as messages must be accepted for sending by the telegraph company. Somewhere in the middle were the Coolidge Administration and Secretary of Commerce Hoover, who rejected the notion of autonomy in widely quoted words: "We can not allow any single person or group to place themselves in position where they can censor the material which shall be broadcasted to the public."[2]

As originally reported by the House Committee on the Merchant Marine and Fisheries, the bill which became the Radio Act contained no access obligations of any kind.[3] However, broad proposed obligations were added by the Senate Interstate Commerce Committee:

> If any licensee shall permit a broadcasting station to be used as aforesaid, or by a candidate or candidates for any public office, or for the discussion of any question affecting the public, he shall make no discrimination as to the use of such broadcasting station, and with respect to said matters the licensee shall be deemed a common carrier in interstate commerce.[4]

Oddly, it was Senator Clarence C. Dill, chairman of the Committee, who moved on the Senate floor to strike this broad access "common carrier" provision, and to replace it with the specific contingent access obligation for candidates only found in the law today. Dill's reasons for his change of heart are a bit obscure. He stated that "broadcasters were so opposed to having themselves designated as common carriers we thought it unwise at this stage of the development of the art to do it."[5] More important, perhaps, Dill was concerned about the vagueness of common carrier status with respect to "any question affecting the public":

> That is such a general term that there is probably no question of any interest whatsoever that could be discussed but that the other side of it could demand time; and thus a radio station . . . would have to give all their time to that kind of discussion, or no public questions could be discussed.[6]

Dill persuaded the Senate to limit the access obligation to equal opportunities for candidates.[7] The Conference Committee also accepted his proposal,[8] and it was enacted.

The debates in 1934 followed the same pattern. Broad access proposals were originally included in the bills that eventually became the Communications Act of 1934. These proposals would have extended the equal opportunities requirements beyond appearances by political candidates to include supporters of candidates and, more significantly, "the presentation of views on a public question to be voted upon at an election."[9] Both Houses actually passed such a provision in H.R. 7716, but for extraneous reasons the measure was pocket-vetoed by President Roosevelt.[10] The bill that became the Communications Act[11] initially included a similar broad provision and the Senate passed it.[12] However, the equal opportunities provision was later cut back to its present scope by the Conference Committee.[13] Broader access obligations were thus specifically considered and ultimately rejected by Congress in both the 1927 and the 1934 Acts.

From 1934 until the statute was amended in 1959, the equal opportunities language of section 315 of the Communications Act read as follows:

> (a) If any licensee shall permit any person who is a legally qualified candidate for any public office to use a broadcasting

station, he shall afford equal opportunities to all other such candidates for that office in the use of such broadcasting station: Provided, That such licensee shall have no power of censorship over the material broadcast under the provisions of this section. No obligation is hereby imposed upon any licensee to allow the use of its station by any such candidate.[14]

With one exception to be discussed shortly, questions of interpretation have presented no great difficulty for the FCC.

This equal opportunities access right is contingent, not affirmative. That is, the statute provides that "[n]o obligation is imposed under this subsection upon any licensee to allow the use of its station by any such candidate."[15] Moreover, the provision does not require equality of actual use by candidates. If one candidate does not care to make use of free air-time, the opponent may nevertheless appear. Similarly, if one candidate is willing to pay for advertising but opponents are not, the station may sell time to that candidate only.[16] It has also been made clear by repeated rulings that the provision is triggered only by appearances by the candidates themselves and not to air-time given to candidates' supporters.[17] Apart from several essentially minor problems of administration,[18] difficulty for the Commission has centered on what constitutes a "use" of a broadcast station that triggers equal opportunities for competing candidates.

The Commission before 1959 held that even such non-political appearances by candidates as taking a bow on a variety show or selling used cars constituted uses triggering equal opportunities.[19] Such literalism in the service of absolute equality of access among competing candidates also led to rulings that virtually any appearances by candidates in newscasts triggered section 315. The absurd consequences of this approach became apparent in 1959 in the Commission's *Lar Daly* decision. Daly, a futile but perennial candidate in both Republican and Democratic mayoral primaries in Chicago, sought equal access after Mayor Richard Daley (also a candidate) appeared in a newscast greeting a foreign visitor at the airport, and in a televised appeal for the March-of-Dimes. The Commission ruled that these appearances were "uses" entitling Lar Daly to equal opportunities.[20]

The decision set off a furor in Congress and among broadcasters. If every appearance by a candidate resulted in an access right for every other candidate for the same office, the result would be, in the words of the Senate Commerce Committee, "to dry up meaningful radio and television coverage of political campaigns."[21] Thus, Congress set out to prevent the ideal of equality among competing candidates from inhibiting the coverage of public affairs by broadcasters. The result was 315(a)'s amendment in 1959, exempting from the operation of the equal opportunities provision four kinds of news programs that are under the control of the broadcaster rather than the candidate: (1) newscasts, (2) interviews, (3) news documentaries, so long as the appearance of the candidate is incidental to presentation of the subjects covered, and (4) on-the-spot coverage of news events.[22] These exempted programs are governed now by the general Fairness Doctrine, which will be discussed in the next chapter.

Although the 1959 amendment allows considerable freedom to a broadcaster who wishes to feature political candidates in regular news programming without triggering the equal opportunities requirements, controversy continues about section 315's application to coverage of such non-regular occasions as press conferences and specially-arranged debates between candidates. As to the status of candidate debates, the FCC ruled in 1962 that broadcast coverage of a debate between two Michigan gubernatorial candidates was not an exempt "bona fide news event," a ruling which afforded equal time to the candidate of the Socialist Labor Party (which received 1,479 votes out of a total of 3,255,991 cast in the previous state election).[23] Only appearances incidental to news events unrelated to political races should come within the exemption, the Commission concluded. Similarly, the FCC held that coverage of press conferences did not qualify for exemption from the equal opportunities requirements of section 315(a) because such conferences were not regularly scheduled and the formats were not under the broadcaster's exclusive control.[24]

There can be no question that these narrow interpretations of exempt news programming did not suffice to blunt section 315's inhibiting effect on special political programming during elections. A comparison of the 1960 presidential campaign with those of 1964 and 1968 demonstrates the chilling effect of section 315(a). In 1960, the equal opportunities provisions were suspended for the presidential campaign,[25] and the three television networks donated over 39 hours of broadcast time to presidential candidates. The 1960 suspension stimulated the four "Great Debates" between Kennedy and Nixon, who appeared before the largest audience ever to witness two candidates for the presidency. In 1964 and 1968, when section

315 was applicable to the presidential elections, the amount of free time given to candidates was 4 hours and 28 minutes and 3 hours and 1 minute, respectively. Virtually all the 1964 and 1968 appearances were on exempt programs. One major consequence of this small amount of free time in elections after 1960 has been an escalation in the cost of presidential campaigns.

The inhibiting effect of section 315 on broadcast debates stems from the American tradition of fringe party candidates.[26] In the 1960 election fourteen minor party candidates for the presidency surfaced on various state ballots. Had section 315(a) been in effect during 1960, the "Great Debates" either would have had to include the candidates for such parties as the American Beat Consensus and the Prohibition Party, or else stations would have been required to broadcast other special programs giving fringe candidates equal (and therefore free) opportunities for expression. It is not surprising that broadcasters in 1964 and 1968, faced with the economic burden of providing free time to numerous fringe candidates and with airing programs of little interest to a mass audience, declined to afford a significant amount of free time for presidential candidates.

Section 315(a) should be recast in its application to presidential elections. In attempting to guarantee equality for candidates, the Communications Act discourages public debate. In an effort to solve this problem, the Federal Communications Commission has proposed that section 315 be amended to provide equal opportunities only for presidential candidates who meet some minimal test of potential significance, for example, only those who represent a party that polled at least 2 percent of the popular vote in the most recent presidential election, or those whose candidacy is supported by petitions bearing a number of signatures equal to 1 percent of the popular vote in the preceding election. Some reform of this type seems eminently sound.[27] However, the political opportunity for such reform tends to arise only when a president is willing to allow a change in law that will increase materially the time available on the air for the major party candidates in the next presidential election. First-term presidents generally have not been willing to give lesser-known challengers this opportunity for free public exposure.[28]

In contrast with presidential elections, section 315(a) probably does not inhibit free air-time for candidates in most local or statewide elections. Congressional hearings have indicated that, in most of these elections, only two or three candidates are in competition and the equal opportunities problem presented by fringe candidates tends not to be serious.[29] In addition, the alternative to the equal opportunities requirement in local and state campaigns would be general supervision under the Fairness Doctrine, which is a slow administrative process that would moot many problems arising late in a campaign. Furthermore, it is most unlikely that Congress could be persuaded to repeal section 315 as it applies to congressional races. However, an outright repeal of section 315 for presidential races, or a modification along the lines suggested by the FCC, would stimulate greater political expression in the electronic media.

It may be that frustration with political barriers to reform of section 315(a) lies behind a significant reinterpretation by the FCC in September 1975. The Commission reversed its earlier rulings concerning candidate debates and press conferences. Henceforth, the Commission ruled, such political programming will be treated as on-the-spot coverage of bona fide news events, and thus exempted from section 315(a), unless the programming is designed to favor a particular candidate or is clearly not news.[30] The change was justified by reference to a newly discovered Congressional intent to give the 1959 exemption broad scope.

This is a very significant ruling. The effect is to permit coverage of debates and press conferences in which candidates take part, so long as good faith news judgments underlie the broadcasts, without triggering section 315(a)'s unwieldy and inhibiting obligation to grant free reply time to every political hopeful in the field. The Commission's action was challenged in the courts by political and other interests committed to equality of treatment for political candidates. For example, the Democratic National Committee opposed the Commission's ruling because it will allow airing of President Ford's press conferences without a right of reply for other presidential candidates. Moreover, initial Congressional reaction appeared negative.[31] However, the Commission is trying to enhance uninhibited expression on public issues, and its ruling on candidate debates and press conferences contributes to that goal.

The chilling effects of section 315(a) which led the FCC to reverse its position on debates and press conferences would appear not to pose any serious inhibition on acceptance of political advertisements. A broadcaster may refuse to accept all advertising by political candidates. The language and legislative history of section 315 clearly point to a power of absolute refusal. Although other provisions of the Communications Act forbid broadcasters from refusing all noncommercial appearances by candidates,[32] it is doubtful that a licensee would violate the Act by maintaining a policy of refusing short political spot-commercials that attempt to sell politicians as if they were soap.

On the other hand, a station that accepts some candidate advertising does not suffer any economic hardship if it is required to accept other candidates' ads. Candidates given equal opportunities must still pay the same rates as did the candidate whose ad triggered the contingent access right. Admittedly, section 315(a)'s provision that broadcasters "have no power of censorship over the material broadcast under the provisions of this section" may result in political commercials that are highly offensive to a portion of the broadcaster's audience.[33] However, broadcasters are not subject to liability for defamatory material broadcast in a political commercial.[34] Nor does it seem likely that many viewers would avoid a station because of an obnoxious political ad that may well be carried also on competing stations.

Although the FCC appears with its 1975 ruling to be moving away from the notion of equal access for candidates, there is strong sentiment in other quarters that section 315(a)'s contingent access obligations do not go far enough in ensuring both general coverage of political affairs by broadcasters and balanced political exchange. Concern that broadcasters should provide access for political candidates led Congress in 1971 to add the following to section 312(a)'s grounds for revoking broadcast licenses:

> (7) for willful or repeated failure to allow reasonable access
> to or to permit purchase of reasonable amounts of time for the
> use of a broadcasting station by a legally qualified candidate for
> Federal elective office on behalf of his candidacy.[35]

This provision was adopted as part of the Federal Election Campaign Act of 1971, an omnibus reform law which dealt mainly with campaign contributions and expenditures.[36] The provision was largely neglected in the hearings and debates. Its proponents believed that it merely made explicit a duty already embodied in broadcasters' obligations to serve the public interest. However, in view of section 315(a)'s caveat that "no obligation is hereby imposed upon any licensee to allow the use of its station by any such candidate," it appears that the 1971 amendment to section 312(a) does indeed add an important element to broadcasters' statutory duties.

Beyond the generalized aim of ensuring airtime for political candidates that led to the amendment to section 312(a), concern about politics and access has focused on whether section 315(a)'s contingent access obligations go far enough to foster a degree of balanced political exchange between incumbent presidents who are not considered "political candidates" under the statute, because they have not announced their re-election candidacy, and their potential challengers.[37] The use of free, prime-time, and simultaneous broadcasts by presidents has dramatically increased over the last three decades. President Nixon, for example, made more prime-time appearances in his first 18 months in office than the combined total appearances of Presidents Eisenhower, Kennedy, and Johnson in their first 18 months in office.[38] Fred Friendly has suggested that, as presidents increase appearances that are under their control, they become less willing to subject themselves "to the hurly-burly risks of the news conference."[39] President Nixon held only 28 news conferences in his first 4 years in office, as compared with 126 for Johnson in 6 years, 64 for Kennedy in 3 years, 193 for Eisenhower in 8 years, 324 for Truman in 8 years, and 998 for Roosevelt in 12 years.[40]

Not only has it been suggested that these presidential appearances may provide incumbent presidents with an unfair advantage in coming elections, but they may also be a significant ingredient in the trend toward greater presidential power at the expense of Congress.[41] In 1970 Senator Fulbright complained that "television has done as much to expand the powers of the President . . . as would a constitutional amendment formally abolishing the co-equality of the three branches of Government."[42]

The quality, as well as the amount, of air-time afforded to presidents is significant. The fact that the president is able to broadcast simultaneously on the three networks adds greatly to the size of the audience. For example, when President Ford previewed his State of the Union message on the three networks on January 13, 1975, he had an audience estimated at 70 million viewers. Democratic leaders were given reply time by the three networks, but these replies were not broadcast simultaneously. Speaker Albert and Senator Humphrey reached a combined audience of 47 million viewers, and it was assumed that much of this audience was duplicated, because viewers who listened to both Democrats were counted twice.[43] One reason for the president's larger audience is that his office has a greater appeal. But *New York Times* columnist

Les Brown concludes that this larger audience is mostly attributable to simultaneous televising, which is known to advertisers as "road-blocking." Mr. Brown quotes a television adviser for Senator McGovern during the 1972 campaign: "People will watch television no matter what is on, and if you allow them no other choice, they will watch your show."[44]

It is rare that the political opposition or congressional representatives are given an opportunity for extensive and uninterrupted reply to presidential addresses. Commonly, political figures other than the president are given air-time on interview programs, but these are not broadcast in prime-time and do not allow for prepared and uninterrupted statements. Regular newscasts and specials are even more disjointed.

The equal opportunities requirement of section 315(a) is applicable to presidential addresses only when the incumbent happens also to be a nominated candidate for re-election.[45] Most presidential addresses fall outside the reach of the section. Moreover, even some addresses by presidents who were nominated candidates for re-election have been held outside the reach of the equal opportunities provision on the ground that the addresses were "reports to the nation" and not related to the election campaign. Neither President Eisenhower's address on the Suez Crisis in 1956[46] nor President Johnson's address on the Chinese nuclear explosion during the 1964 campaign[47] was covered by section 315(a).

The Fairness Doctrine, not the equal opportunities provision of section 315(a), covers addresses by noncandidate presidents and non-partisan reports by incumbent candidates. As the Fairness Doctrine and its relation to access will be discussed fully in the next chapter, it is enough here to note its treatment for the problem of presidential addresses. The hallmark of the Fairness Doctrine is broadcaster discretion regarding fair coverage of public issues; it involves neither a requirement of equal treatment nor, ordinarily, a right of access for defined persons or groups. Thus, the Fairness Doctrine does not afford an automatic right of reply to presidential addresses. Some have contended that governing the problem of presidential addresses by the Fairness Doctrine results in imbalance in favor of the president. When President Nixon gave five addresses on Vietnam within a period of seven months, the FCC held that fairness required that reply time be given to a suitable representative for contrasting views.[48] The Commission was careful, however, to limit its holding to the peculiar facts: five addresses on one topic within seven months.[49] This instance demonstrates the difficulty of administering an appropriate reply to the president. CBS had voluntarily given time to the Chairman of the Democratic National Committee, Lawrence O'Brien, in response to "the disparity between Presidential appearances and the opportunities available to the principal opposition party."[50]

The Republican National Committee immediately petitioned the Commission for a right of reply to O'Brien's reply. Their complaint was that O'Brien had launched a partisan attack on the Republican Party rather than replied to President Nixon. The FCC agreed, and gave the Republican National Committee reply time.[51] However, this ruling was then reversed by the Court of Appeals for the District of Columbia.[52] The Court severely censured the Commission, holding that the administrative ruling in this case was inconsistent with a ruling in a previous, parallel case in which the FCC had found no right of reply to a reply. Furthermore, the Court declared that no rationale had been spelled out by the Commission to justify the different result. The Court was blunt and uncomplimentary:

> *The Commission's utter failure to come to grips with this problem constitutes an inexcusable departure from the essential requirement of reasoned decision making. . . .*
> *The Commission's handling of this case does not mark its finest hour. Put to the test under pressure it waffled. . . .*
> *[I]ts arbitrary action may not stand.*[53]

This blistering reversal has had a withering effect on the Commission's attitude toward mandatory replies to presidential addresses. In the summer of 1972, the Commission issued a report on political broadcasts. The report advocated a return to the fairness doctrine regime of broadcaster discretion governing presidential addresses and rejected rights of reply beyond those expressly required by the equal opportunities provision of section 315(a). The FCC took the position that the statute should be construed as fixing the outer limits of rights of reply to political broadcasts. Any further extensions of access, the Commission argued, should come from Congress. But the FCC did not invite such statutory reform. It stood firmly against broadened contingent access rights as a matter of principle:

> *. . . increasingly detailed Commission regulation militates against robust, wide-open debate. The genius of the Fairness*

*Doctrine has been precisely the leeway and discretion it affords
the licensee to discharge his obligation to contribute to an
informed electorate.*[54]

Clearly, the Commission is not about to embark on a program of
mandatory access to counter the political and institutional imbalance
generated by increasing numbers of presidential broadcasts. Any
solution to this problem must be legislative.

The imbalance caused by presidential television has two aspects.
One problem is the standing and efficacy of Congress relative to the
power of the Executive. A different problem is the political
advantage that presidential appearances confer as compared to appearances by candidates of opposition parties, or even, occasionally, challengers within the president's own party.

The congressional remedy for the president's dominion over
political broadcasting does not lie in a right of reply to presidential
addresses. Instead, it depends upon more extensive and regular
television coverage of significant legislative activities. The tendency
to view Congress' appropriate remedy in terms of narrowly conceived
rights of reply only emphasizes the president's advantage. The
president is equipped to address a national audience; Congress is not.
The leaders of Congress are not, and should not be, chosen because
they are capable of effectively delivering a fifteen- or thirty-minute
television address. They are leaders because they have a longstanding
grip on their local constituencies, and because they have proven
adroit in the legislative process. If legislative leaders would often
prove ineffective in the format well suited to a typical president, it is
no answer to select some charismatic member, who is not of the
leadership, to deliver the reply. The problem of selection is difficult,
but in any event the lack of a leadership designation would make
such a representative a poor match for the prestige of the president.

If Congress is to try to counter the power the president exercises
through television, it would be far better to encourage the televising
of Congress in action, with its component parts and procedures, than
for the Speaker or Majority Leader to venture onto the unfamiliar
ground of a solo television performance. And we have recent
evidence of the dramatic effect that selected congressional proceedings carried on television can have. Of course, the hearings of the
Ervin Committee and the impeachment proceedings of the House
Judiciary Committee were unusual with regard to the willingness of
both the networks and the public to maintain the patience necessary

to follow those proceedings. But these are only the more recent examples of successful televising of congressional activities. The investigation of Alger Hiss, the Kefauver crime hearings, and the Army-McCarthy hearings were also widely viewed and proved very influential.[55] The success of televising those lengthy affairs suggests the possibility of successfully presenting less sensational, less complex, less unwieldy legislative processes. Congress should demonstrate what it actually does, and what it knows how to do. It should not try to compete with the president in his own peculiarly tailored premises. Scandals in the executive branch, basic questions of foreign policy, the penetration of bureaucratic secrecy and deceit, the investigation of federal programs, ventilation of the unmet or unknown needs of society, and many other issues are staples of congressional activity. In many instances, they would have significant popular appeal. Thus, it is through the televising of such proceedings, rather than through a right of reply, that Congress can best attempt to counter the president's effective use of television.[56]

On the other hand, the problem of partisan imbalance is more amenable to correction through a right of reply. The question here is not so much a matter of how to remedy the imbalance, as it is a matter of whether, or to what extent, the imbalance should be countered. An influential study, authored by former FCC Chairman Newton Minow, has recently recommended that presidential appearances within ten months preceding a presidential election or within 90 days preceding congressional elections should give rise to a specified right of reply. This right of reply would be given to an authorized spokesman of the opposition party whose candidate received the second-highest number of votes in the previous presidential election.[57] Incidental presidential appearances in newscasts or documentaries and appearances by presidents who were formal candidates, and who would therefore be covered by the equal opportunities requirement of section 315(a), would not be covered by this proposal. The Minow proposal is designed to protect the opposition party at election time:

> [T]he opposition party, whether Democratic or Republican, is likely to lack a clear spokesman and a clear position on issues except during a presidential election; and this is why it may not be well qualified to present a rapid, direct, and reasoned response to the president during his term. Reform, therefore, must be directed at protecting the party's primarily electoral function, not at giving it time to present its views between

elections, when neither a party view nor a party spokesman may exist.[58]

There is surely merit in limiting any automatic right of reply for opposition spokesmen to election periods. Our system, which employs the separate fixed-term executive, is far from a parliamentary model. Presumably (except around election-time) it is consistent with our system that the president is, in Woodrow Wilson's phrase, "the only national voice in affairs."[59] The access of presidents to television is a significant unifying force in American society. A president should not be inhibited in his use by the prospect that a presidential appearance not geared to a forthcoming election would automatically trigger a right of reply for a partisan critic. Nor should the networks be encouraged to be ungenerous in considering requests by presidents for time. A right of reply that was operative at all times would require the networks to give up twice as much of their time whenever they acceded to a presidential request.

As for election time, an evaluation of rights of reply to presidential broadcasts by opposition spokesmen requires an assessment of the benefits of required access against its possible costs. One consequence which rights of reply for the opposition party might have is to displace other programming devoted to news and public affairs. If so, the question arises whether appearances by opposition spokesmen would serve the public interest more than the documentaries, public affairs specials, interview shows, and other programming that would be lost. Access rights for opposition party representatives would lead to uniform programming. If displacement of other public affairs programming occurred, the result would be a substitution of uniformity for diversity in this area.[60]

Such a substitution is not necessarily undesirable. Concentrating public affairs programming on opposition party representatives before elections would probably sharpen political issues between the parties, stimulate public interest in elections, and reduce the electoral advantage of incumbent presidents. Certainly, if displacement of other programming did occur, then the agenda for public discussion would be set to a greater degree by party spokesmen. For example, a reply by an opposition party representative might be aired instead of a documentary on a subject that national party representatives had not discussed in detail, such as educational achievement in public schools or consumer issues. However, even if displacement of public affairs programming did result from a right of reply to presidential addresses, audience exposure to public affairs programs might well increase. Political and public affairs programs usually draw a relatively small audience. Even presidents appearing on only one network draw smaller audiences than entertainment programming.[61] However, a large audience will watch politicians if it has no other choice of network programming. Because most presidential addresses are carried simultaneously during prime-time by the three networks, a right of reply for opposition party spokesmen during election periods would also result in simultaneous, prime-time political programming. Accordingly, even if each network reduced its public affairs prime-time programming by the amount of time consumed by the opposition party reply right, the result would be a significant overall increase in public exposure to public affairs broadcasts. Thus, despite certain costs of programming diversity and editorial discretion, such proposals for a right of reply to presidential addresses deserve the support of persons who wish to increase the public's exposure to public affairs and political broadcasts.

The narrow contingent access obligations imposed by section 315(a) deserve mixed evaluation when measured against the values of robust political debate over the electronic media. The inhibiting effects of section 315(a) in presidential elections have been obvious. The tradition of fringe candidates makes it economically infeasible to grant large amounts of free time to serious presidential candidates. On the other hand, in most local and state elections where there are few fringe candidates, the existence of 315(a) prevents favoritism and does not seriously affect the amount of free time stations grant for political debate. However, provisions dealing with the fringe candidate problem at the national level should apply also to local and state elections to take care of the infrequent problems that arise there. Section 315(a) should probably be broadened to create access rights for the opposition party when an incumbent president who is not legally a candidate makes an address in the period preceding elections.

Consideration of a right of reply to presidential addresses is a provocative introduction to the connections and contrasts between specific access rights and the obligations that the general Fairness Doctrine imposes on broadcasters. Section 315(a) outlines a concrete access right that defines precisely the situation which triggers the right (nonexempt appearances by legally qualified candidates), the recipient of the right (other legally qualified candidates for the same office in the same election), and the scope of the right (equivalent treatment). Its precision has led to demands that the Fairness Doctrine also grant a right of reply in situations comparable to those covered by section 315(a) but not actually within its scope.

The Fairness Doctrine, however, has proved to be a rather blunt legal instrument for implementing a right of reply to presidential broadcasts. When the Commission resorted to the Fairness Doctrine to create a right of access in response to presidential appearances, the expansive logic of the Doctrine led the Commission to order a right of reply to the first reply. But because the Doctrine is very general, the Commission could not explain why the Doctrine called for a right of reply to the reply in this particular case, when in other similar circumstances it had not granted a reply right. An embarrassing judicial reversal was the end result. The Commission's unhappy experience in attempting to ground presidential broadcasts in the Fairness Doctrine raises the following question: Can a doctrine that is premised on broad notions of fairness in the discussion of controversial issues of public importance be made the basis for contingent access rights without those rights becoming so vague and so sweeping as to be unmanageable and inhibiting? This question cannot be answered without an overall evaluation of the Fairness Doctrine and access obligations in other related contexts.

11

The Fairness Doctrine
and Access to the Electronic Media

This role of the Government as an "overseer" and ultimate arbiter and guardian of the public interest and the role of the licensee as a journalistic "free agent" calls for a delicate balancing of competing interests. The maintenance of this balance for more than 40 years has called on both the regulators and the licensees to walk a "tightrope" to preserve the First Amendment values written into the Radio Act and its successor, the Communications Act.

Chief Justice Warren Burger[1]

The Fairness Doctrine and access claims exist in a pardoxical relation of support and conflict. The premise of the Fairness Doctrine is that broadcasters are public trustees for the community-at-large. This theory undercuts any constitutional claim of autonomy that would immunize broadcasters from access obligations. Yet the Federal Communication Commission's administrative stance has been that compliance with fairness obligations should be left to the editorial discretion of the broadcaster, with a minimum of official intervention. Thus, the Fairness Doctrine both feeds and frustrates access demands. The public trustee concept invites access claims. But because access obligations displace licensee discretion and, as a practical matter, require extensive administrative oversight for their application, they run counter to what the Commission likes to call "the genius" of the doctrine. Moreover, the existence of the Fairness Doctrine tends to blunt demands for access. It is assumed that, through this doctrine, the goal of informing the public about various positions on important controversies is accomplished. Accordingly, demands for access tend to be viewed more in terms of the interest of those seeking access than in terms of the public interest at large.

Fairness: Beginnings to the *Red Lion* Vindication

The Fairness Doctrine is the most controversial aspect of FCC regulation of broadcast programming. Although general doubts as to the doctrine's constitutionality have been laid to rest by the Supreme Court's holding in *Red Lion*[2], there is still much dispute over the wisdom of the doctrine and the most appropriate method for its implementation.

The Fairness Doctrine is rooted in the basic theory of the Communications Act. If one views the broadcaster as a public trustee who has no indefeasible property interest in his license, then one may also easily conclude that the broadcaster has an obligation to give airtime to views other than his own. As early as 1929, the Federal Radio Commission stated:

> *Broadcasting stations are licensed to serve the public and not for the purpose of furthering the private or selfish interests of individuals or groups of individuals. The standard of public interest, convenience, or necessity means nothing if it does not mean this. It would not be fair, indeed it would not be good service to the public to allow a one-sided presentation of the political issues of a campaign. Insofar as a program consists of discussion of public questions, the public interest requires ample play for the free and fair competition of opposing views, and the Commission believes that the principle applies not only to addresses by political candidates but to all discussions of issues of importance to the public.*[3]

The FCC gave definitive statement to the Fairness Doctrine in its 1949 report on *Editorializing by Broadcast Licensees*.[4] This report concluded that the public interest imposes a two-part duty on broadcasters: (1) to devote reasonable time to the coverage of controversial issues of public importance, and (2) to afford reasonable opportunity for contrasting viewpoints to be heard on these issues. However, the report included a vital administrative doctrine which was premised on the Communications Act's rejection of censorship and common carrier status for licensees, overlaying and moderating fairness obligations. Implementation of the Fairness Doctrine was confided to the editorial discretion of the licensee. The Commission stated that it would overturn the licensee's judgment on a fairness question only when the licensee's *overall* performance constituted an *abuse* of discretion. Under the 1949 statement, no particular program had to be "fair" if overall programming on an issue met the test of fairness. Complaints about lack of fairness would be reviewed at renewal time against the perspective of the broadcaster's entire performance.

Initially, the statutory basis for the Fairness Doctrine was the general provision of section 303, which authorizes the Commission to make regulations in the public interest. Then, in 1959, when Congress exempted several categories of news programming from the equal opportunities requirement, it also added the following language to section 315:

> *Nothing in the foregoing sentence shall be construed as relieving broadcasters, in connection with the presentation of newscasts, news interviews, news documentaries, and on-the-spot coverage of news events, from the obligation imposed upon them under this chapter to operate in the public interest and to afford reasonable opportunity for the discussion of conflicting views on issues of public importance.*[5]

Congress intended this language to be an affirmation of the Commission's Fairness Doctrine.

Interestingly, the evolution of this 1959 statement followed the same pattern as the 1927 and 1934 statutes on equal opportunities: Proposals for broad rights of access, extending beyond the contingent equal opportunities rights for political candidates, were offered, but they failed to pass. Senator William Proxmire's amendment to the Senate Commerce Committee proposal suggested that "all sides of public controversies shall be given as equal an opportunity to be heard as is practically possible."[6] Questioned as to the purpose of his amendment, Proxmire explained: "I am trying to protect all viewpoints in public controversy by providing them an equal opportunity."[7] Later, he added: "What I am trying to accomplish by my amendment is to permit equal opportunity to have candidates or persons speak in the public interest, so that controversial ideas can be heard by the public."[8] Proxmire's amendment passed the Senate, but the Conference Committee replaced it with the words now found in section 315. No reason for the replacement was given; the report stated that the language adopted amounted to a restatement of the "standard of fairness" imposed on broadcasters by the Commission under the 1934 Act.[9] Since the Proxmire proposal failed to make its way into the statute, the FCC seems justified in regarding the 1959 legislation as a ratification of the Fairness Doctrine as set out in its 1949 report.

During the 1960s, the FCC departed from its 1949 standards in several significant ways, which moved the Fairness Doctrine toward an access rationale. In 1962, the Commission initiated the practice of considering fairness complaints promptly, rather than waiting until the broadcaster's license renewal date.[10] Like many shifts in procedure, this one brought substantive changes in its wake. Although prompt consideration of complaints was not intended to diminish the editorial discretion of the licensee, it soon had that effect. Case-by-case review of fairness complaints tended naturally to focus more on particular programs than on the broadcaster's overall performance. This particular focus, in turn, engendered pressures for particular remedies for one-sided broadcasts.

In the following year, the Commission established the *Cullman* principle, which required broadcasters to fulfill fairness obligations at their own expense, if no forthcoming sponsored programming would air other sides of controversial issues.[11] This principle that broadcasters must underwrite the costs of Fairness Doctrine programming is a substantial incentive to those wishing to press access claims.

A third major change resulted from three Commission rulings, made in 1962, that imposed explicit access obligations as the means of carrying out fairness obligations in certain situations. In one case, a station had made a series of personal attacks on local public officials, and the station owner appeared to be active in a rival political faction. The Commission ruled that the Fairness Doctrine required that reply time be offered to the persons attacked, notwithstanding the general rule that satisfying fairness obligations is usually left to the editorial discretion of the broadcaster.[12] A second case involved repeated broadcasts of editorials opposing the creation of public utility districts and criticizing an individual. Here the Commission required the licensee to provide a copy of the editorials to the subject and offer him time to reply.[13] The third case held that a broadcaster who allowed a commentator repeatedly to attack a political candidate must send transcripts of the attacks to the candidate and invite reply from an appropriate representative.[14] In 1964, two years after these 1962 rulings, the personal attack episode that led eventually to the Supreme Court's celebrated *Red Lion* decison came to the Commission. Shortly thereafter, the Commission initiated hearings on new general regulations with the aim of reflecting the new rulings on personal attacks and editorials.

The result was that, in 1967, two specific access regulations were declared, which remain in effect today. According to the first, when a broadcaster takes an explicit position for or against a political candidate in an editorial, he must notify the candidate opposed, or the rivals of the candidate supported, and offer them an opportunity to respond. The second access requirement has broader significance. It specifies that "[W]hen, during the presentation of views on a controversial issue of public importance, an attack is made on the honesty, character, integrity or like personal qualities of an identified person or group," the person or group attacked must be given notice, a transcript of the attack, and an opportunity to respond.[15] In these two administrative rules, contingent rights of access were extended beyond the equal opportunities rights for political candidates provided by section 315(a).

The *Red Lion* episode and the personal attack access rules caused the Supreme Court to consider the constitutional and statutory rationales underlying regulation of radio and television for the first time since the *NBC* decision in 1943.[16] The vehicle for this sweeping review presented the personal attack rules in a sympathetic posture.

The origins of the *Red Lion* case go back to a small Pennsylvania radio station's broadcasts of 15-minute messages by fundamentalist preacher Billy James Hargis as part of a "Christian Crusade" series. Hargis' broadcasts and others of a similar nature had caused much concern in liberal and Democratic Party circles. In fact, author Fred J. Cook had published an article called "Hate Clubs of the Air" in *The Nation*, attacking Hargis and his broadcasts. Hargis was incensed by this article and by a caustic book entitled *Goldwater—Extremist on the Right*, also written by Cook. In 1964, Hargis took to the air to defend Goldwater. He attacked Cook's book as a "smear" and claimed that Cook had been fired by a newspaper for lying about city officials, had written for a Communist-affiliated magazine, had attacked J. Edgar Hoover, the FBI, and the CIA, and had defended Alger Hiss. When Cook heard about the broadcast, he demanded that the station give him an opportunity to reply. The station offered to sell the reply time to Cook for seven dollars. Cook refused to pay and complained to the FCC.

The Commission held that the station had failed to meet its fairness obligations under the three 1962 rulings dealing with personal attacks, and ordered the station to give Cook reply time whether or not he would pay for it. The District of Columbia Circuit Court of Appeals upheld the FCC requirement of reply time.[17] That Court made a fundamental distinction under the First Amendment between suppression of programming and contingent rights of access. "The [Fairness] Doctrine," wrote Judge Edward A. Tamm, "rather than limiting the [broadcaster's] right of free speech, recognizes and enforces the free speech right of the victim of any personal attack made during the broadcast."[18] The fact that Cook had access to other media, such as magazines and books, to disseminate his ideas did not impress the Court.

As the *Red Lion* case moved through the Commission and the Court of Appeals, broadcasters viewed the proceedings with growing anxiety. The case appeared to be a candidate for Supreme Court review. If taken, it would be the first occasion for the high Court to consider the legality of the Fairness Doctrine and only the second time the Court had had an opportunity for broad review of the law of broadcast regulation. Many broadcasters feared that the specific facts of *Red Lion*—a right-wing radio preacher attacking the honesty of an author and a station refusing reply time without payment—would present the Fairness Doctrine and the personal attack reply rules in an inviting light.[19] Accordingly, the Radio-Television News Directors Association sought to challenge the Commission in a case divorced from the *Red Lion* facts and in a forum less sympathetic to the FCC than the District of Columbia Court of Appeals. The RTNDA challenged the legality of the new personal attack rules before the Court of appeals for the Seventh Circuit located in Chicago. More than one year after the *Red Lion* decision of the District of Columbia Court, the Seventh Circuit Court struck down the FCC's new personal attack and editorializing regulations as unconstitutional abridgments of broadcasters' freedom of expression.[20] According to the Seventh Circuit, the rules were unconstitutionally vague for regulations bearing on expression and would inhibit robust political speech because of the substantial economic and practical burdens that they imposed on broadcasters through requirements of notification, provision of a transcript, and arrangement for a reply. Moreover, the Seventh Circuit Court held that these rules were an impermissible

departure from the general Fairness Doctrine, since licensee discretion was replaced by mandatory programming obligations, and
since particular broadcasts, rather than overall performance, were
subject to governmental supervision. Thus, the FCC's move to a right
of reply as the Fairness Doctrine's remedy to personal attacks had
produced two diametrically opposed Court of Appeals rulings.

The *Red Lion* and *RTNDA* decisions were consolidated for review
by the Supreme Court. An enthusiastic vindication of the FCC
followed when the Supreme Court unanimously upheld both the
order of free reply time in *Red Lion*, and the FCC's editorializing
and personal attack rules.[21] As a matter of statutory interpretation,
the Court held these access rules to be consistent with the legislative
intent of the Communications Act. The Court treated the new rules
as merely a specification of the Fairness Doctrine, justified by a
reference to personal attacks in the 1949 report and ratified by
Congress in the 1959 amendment to section 315. "The simple fact
that the attacked men or unendorsed candidates may respond
themselves or through agents is not a critical distinction," asserted
Justice White's opinion for the Court.[22]

The broadcasters' First Amendment claims of autonomy as a
barrier to the personal attack and editorializing rules were swept
aside. Justice White declared:

*Where there are substantially more individuals who want to
broadcast than there are frequencies to allocate, it is idle to
posit an unbridgeable First Amendment right to broadcast
comparable to the right of every individual to speak, write, or
publish. . . .*

*[A]s far as the First Amendment is concerned those who are
licensed stand no better than those to whom licenses are refused. A license permits broadcasting, but the licensee has no
constitutional right to be the one who holds the license or to
monopolize a radio frequency to the exclusion of his fellow
citizens.*

*There is nothing in the First Amendment which prevents the
Government from requiring a licensee to share his frequency
with others and to conduct himself as a proxy or fiduciary with
obligations to present those views and voices which are representative of his community and which would otherwise, by
necessity, be barred from the airwaves.*

*This is not to say that the First Amendment is irrelevant to
public broadcasting. . . . But the people as a whole retain their*

interest in free speech by radio and their collective right to have the medium function consistently with the ends and purposes of the First Amendment. It is the right of the viewers and listeners, not the right of the broadcasters, which is paramount. . . . It is the purpose of the First Amendment to preserve an uninhibited marketplace of ideas in which truth will ultimately prevail, rather than to countenance monopolization of that market, whether it be by the Government itself or a private licensee. [23]

Thus, the Court turned the broadcasters' autonomy arguments back on themselves, and decided that the new access obligations were not only consistent with the First Amendment but were a positive implementation of its values.

First Amendment arguments concerning the vagueness and potential inhibiting effect of the personal attack and editorializing rules were also cast aside, although not conclusively. The broadcasters had convinced the Seventh Circuit that the expense, administrative burdens, and disruption of programming entailed by these rules would inhibit the sort of robust expression that triggers the contingent access obligations. Self-censorship would result, they had argued, causing a net reduction in public debate. The Court called this fear "at best speculative," [24] although it suggested that the argument might be considered at some later time: [I]f experience with the administration of these doctrines indicates that they have the net effect of reducing rather than enhancing the volume and quality of coverage, there will be time enough to reconsider the constitutional implications." [25] The next paragraph, however, suggested a skeptical reception for such an argument:

That this will occur now seems unlikely, however, since if present licensees should suddenly prove timorous, the Commission is not powerless to insist that they give adequate and fair attention to public issues. It does not violate the First Amendment to treat licensees given the privilege of using scarce radio frequencies as proxies for the entire community, obligated to give suitable time and attention to matters of great public concern. To condition the granting or renewal of licenses on a willingness to present representative community views on controversial issues is consistent with the ends and purposes of those constitutional provisions forbidding the abridgment of freedom of speech and freedom of the press. [26]

Arguments that the personal attack rules were impermissibly vague for regulations bearing on expression evoked even less interest from the Court. The Court asserted that FCC adjudications would give precise meaning to the operative concepts in the regulations. It saw nothing vague about the Commission's order to the Red Lion Broadcasting Co. regarding Cook.

The Court's sweeping opinion in Red Lion invited speculation over whether a newly perceived basis for regulation of the electronic media had been developed. Before Red Lion, physical scarcity and the public trusteeship conception of spectrum rights had supported the constitutionality of the Communications Act. The editorial autonomy of licensees, although subject to overall official supervision, had always been a prominent value in Commission and judicial rationales of broadcast regulation. The Red Lion decision ignored this aspect of the traditional understanding, and the editorial autonomy of broadcasters simply disappeared in the Court's opinion. Instead of a public trustee, the broadcaster became a public proxy.

Even more remarkable, the Red Lion opinion suggested an access rationale for regulation of communications media that might reach beyond radio and television. Justice White cited the Associated Press[27] decision, which concerned newspapers, as support for such statements as:

> The right of free speech of a broadcaster, the user of a sound truck, or any other individual does not embrace a right to snuff out the free speech of others.[28]

> It is the purpose of the First Amendment to preserve an uninhibited marketplace of ideas in which truth will ultimately prevail, rather than to countenance monopolization of that market, whether it be by the Government itself or a private licensee.[29]

> It is the right of the public to receive suitable access to social, political, esthetic, moral, and other ideas and experiences which is crucial here.[30]

Moreover, two provocative footnotes also pointed beyond broadcasting. One alluded to "the general problems raised by a technology which supplants atomized, relatively informal communication with mass media as a prime source of national cohesion and news."[31] The other footnote was more explicit, although also tentative:

A related argument, which we also put aside, is that quite apart from scarcity of frequencies, technological or economic, Congress does not abridge freedom of speech or press by legislation directly or indirectly multiplying the voices and views presented to the public through time sharing, fairness doctrines, or other devices which limit or dissipate the power of those who sit astride the channels of communication with the general public.[32]

Thus, the *Red Lion* decision left broadcaster autonomy almost entirely at the mercy of the FCC, and also hinted at what Professor Barron termed "an access-for-ideas" approach to freedom of expression generally.[33] In rejecting constitutional claims of autonomy made by broadcasters,[34] *Red Lion* implicitly challenged the print media's traditional freedom from governmental attempts to guarantee fairness and balance. As a result, the Court provided doctrinal ammunition for the argument that all media, electronic and otherwise, must be opened to those who lack the know-how or resources to gain access otherwise. Barron was quick to stress the broad implication:

My point is that Red Lion *is not just a broadcast case. It is a media case. It represents a look at the First Amendment in the light of new social realities of concentration of ownership and control in a few hands that has been produced by the twin developments of media oligopoly and technological change. It is in the background of these realities that the new First Amendment right of access spoken of by Mr. Justice White should be understood. There is a remarkable sentence in* Red Lion. *It marks the recognition by the Supreme Court of a new constitutional right: "It is the right of the public to receive suitable access to social, political, esthetic, moral, and other ideas and experiences which is crucial here."[35]*

Living with Access: Does Familiarity Breed Retreat?

The FCC's constitutional and statutory authority to require access to broadcast media seemed clear after *Red Lion*. However, it is another question whether access requirements sensibly implement the Communications Act's delicate balance between public trusteeship and private editorial responsibility. Attempts by the Commission to extend access rights beyond specific equal opportunities rights for political candidates have not been encouraging.

The preceding chapter discussed the embarrassment that the Commission suffered as a result of its order to the networks to provide reply time for a spokesman in opposition to President Nixon's telecasts on Vietnam.[36] Because it had viewed Mr. O'Brien's appearance in the narrow perspective of a right to reply, the Commission found itself in the rather ridiculous position of ordering a reply to the reply and received a blistering reprimand from the D.C. Circuit Court of Appeals. One year later, the Commission concluded that only traditional fairness obligations were generated by presidential broadcasts. The creation of new access rights on an administrative level was rejected.[37] Now it seems that if any such right of reply is to be created, outside the context of political campaigns already covered by section 315(a), it must originate in Congress.

Access has also been rejected as a substitute for the traditional Fairness Doctrine approach in the area of commercial advertising because it resembled Pandora's box. In a 1967 ruling that now appears aberrational, the Commission held that broadcasters who carry ordinary cigarette commercials must also air counter-commercials indicating the health hazards of smoking.[38] The ruling was a departure from past practice, and effectively constituted a right of access for the Heart Association and the American Cancer Society. In connection with liquor commercials, the FCC consistently had ruled that, although product commercials might raise questions of public policy and health, the obligations of the Fairness Doctrine were satisfied if other views about advertised products were covered in regular programming.[39]

The Commission sought to justify and to make an exception of its cigarette ruling. It pointed to what it thought was a unique combination of the official health hazard status of cigarettes considering the Surgeon General's Report of 1964, the popularity of smoking, and the dangers of normal use. However, having ordered counter-commercials as a fairness obligation, the FCC faced some hard questions. First, the FCC had to decide how many counter-commercials were required. It rejected the idea of parity with regular advertising, out of concern that cigarette advertising would be driven off the air. But once the Commission had rejected parity, it realized that governing the counter-commercial obligation by manageable standards required obviously arbitrary line-drawing. Although the Commission declined to specify a required proportion of counter-commercials to regular cigarette ads, it found ratios of one-to-five during prime time and one-to-three overall "not unreasonable."[40] Furthermore, broadcasters who concentrated anti-smoking spots outside prime time were required to air some counter-commercials during prime time.[41] The Commission did not hold the stopwatch for long, however. In 1969 it opened for consideration a proposed ban on cigarette commercials,[42] and Congress reacted in that same year with a statutory ban on all advertising of cigarettes over radio and television.[43]

The cigarette counter-commercial ruling also raised a second problem: How might this principle affect commercials for other products posing potential personal or social dangers? The FCC apparently did not enjoy its exercise in stopwatching cigarette ads and counter-ads for it resolutely refused to order counter-commercials again as a balance for other products' commercials. A series of complaints demanded counter-commercials to ads for cars, gasoline, the military draft, phosphate-based detergents, and the Alaska pipeline.[44] However, even when the Commission agreed that regular commercials constituted commentary on one side of a controversial public issue, as in the case of Alaska pipeline advertisements, it decided that fairness obligations were being satisfied by presentation of other views in regular programming.

In July 1974, the FCC made a major policy statement on the Fairness Doctrine. This statement demonstrated that its refusal to administer a counter-commercial requirement again reflected its considered view:

> If in the future the Commission is confronted with a case sim-ilar to that presented by the cigarette controversy, it may be more appropriate to refer the matter to Congress for resolution. It is questionable whether the Commission has a mandate so broad as to permit it to scan the airwaves for offensive material with no more discriminating a basis than the "public interest" or even the "public health." The Commission does not believe that the usual product commercial can realistically be said to inform the public on any side of a controversial issue of public importance. In the future, the Commission will apply the Fair-ness Doctrine only to those "commercials" which are devoted in an obvious and meaningful way to the discussion of public issues. . . .

> *The Commission will not adopt a proposal of the Federal Trade Commission to create a right of access to respond, in effect, to all product commercials. The decision to cover consumer issues appropriately lies with individual licensees in fulfillment of their public trustee responsibilities. The fairness Doctrine does not provide an appropriate vehicle for the correction of false and misleading advertising. If an advertisement is found by the FTC to be false and misleading, the proper course is to ban it altogether.*[45]

The Commission further announced that commercials consisting of "direct and substantial commentary on important public issues" would not give rise to a right of access for counter-commercials. Instead these commercials would be treated under the traditional Fairness Doctrine.[46] Thus, as with the question of reply to political broadcasts outside the specific campaign context of section 315(a), the Commission has yielded to Congress any further consideration of access as a means of countering commercials.

Commission antipathy toward counter-commercials suggests problems for access obligations grounded on the broad concern that the public should hear different points of view on matters of vital interest to it. The counter-commercial rationale quickly showed expansionist tendencies that threatened to swamp the commercial foundation of broadcasting. Once the Commission perceived this, it retreated to traditional Fairness Doctrine precepts as it had with the issue of replies to political addresses.

How does this tendency to retreat from access obligations apply to the personal attack and editorializing rules already sanctioned by *Red Lion?* There are indications here also that access requirements have shortcomings as a mechanism for carrying out the public trustee obligations of broadcasters. The major difficulty has been vagueness and the fact that the contingent obligations of both the personal attack and the editorializing rules have a chilling effect on certain types of expression.

Not all personal attacks trigger the access obligation. The only attacks covered are those that "occur within the context of a discussion of a controversial issue of public importance."[47] The aim of these rules is not to vindicate the victim of a personal attack; the law of defamation is left with that task. Rather, the personal attack rules simply specify fairness doctrine requirements in a particular situation. The aim is to inform the public about issues of general importance. The theory of the rules is that, when an attack occurs during discussion of such an issue, the target of that attack is the best person to give the public another point of view. As an extrapolation from the Fairness Doctrine, the requirement that a personal attack be related to a public issue is critical to justifying the rules. However, determining whether discussion of a controversial issue of public importance is involved, and whether an attack is connected to such a discussion presents great difficulties for predictable administration.

Another troublesome question concerns the kind of comments that should be judged as personal attacks. The rules apply to "an attack . . . upon the honesty, character, integrity or like personal qualities of an identified person or group."[48] Commission decisions indicate that the language of the regulation encompasses attacks relating to moral turpitude, but not to derogatory comments about an individual's ability or intelligence,[49] nor even to offensive hyperbole reflecting strong disagreement.[50]

In view of the amorphous nature of the distinctions which the Commission must make under the personal attack rules, it is not surprising that the sixty or so reported Commission decisions made since 1967 reveal confusion over the central questions of: (1) What is an attack? (2) What is a controversial issue of public importance? And (3) when are the two considered to be connected? For example, in attempting to define what constitutes a personal attack, the Commission has held:

1. A statement that a particular legislator's private interests appeared to create a conflict of interest was not a personal attack; however, the statement that a particular professor was trying to promote the Soviet form of government and destroy the American form of government was considered by the Commission to be a personal attack.[51]

2. An assertion that a person was likely to engage in physical abuse, disruption, and violence was a personal attack; an assertion that a school was a breeding ground for revolutionaries, terrorists, and guerrillas was not a personal attack.[52]

3. An assertion that a person had lied and was mentally unstable was a personal attack; an assertion that a public official hoodwinked a government agency, wasted public money, and illegally gave away public land was not a personal attack.[53]

4. An assertion that a person was a Communist or, in another case, that a person was subversive and Communist was a

personal attack; an assertion that a person was a patriotic extremist was not a personal attack.[54]

5. An assertion that a teacher's union was engaging in blackmail, was seeking to extract blood money, and was using children as pawns was not a personal attack; an unelaborated reference to a Congressman as a coward for failure to appear on the air was a personal attack.[55]

The Commission's conclusions concerning what constitutes a controversial issue of public importance are even more difficult to reconcile:

1. An assertion that a person is Communist may or may not be held to raise a controversial issue of public importance.[56]

2. An assertion that union leaders were gangsters and connected with the Mafia did not relate to a controversial issue of public importance because a union representation election affected only 1,230 employees. On the other hand, one doctor's conduct was covered by the rules.[57]

3. No personal attack was found in a derogatory reference to the mental stability of a segregationist who, in connection with a discussion of the need for brotherly love, momentarily touched on integration. However, had the discussion been focused on integration, that same reference would have fallen within the purview of the rules.[58]

Viewed individually, most of the Commission's decisions under the personal attack rules do not seem unreasonable. But when the rulings are read together, the decisions seem haphazard, and they hopelessly confuse any effort to figure out what general principles delineate the scope of the personal attack rules.

The Commission itself is becoming aware of how difficult the personal attack rules are to administer in a coherent and principled fashion. Thus, when the Commission recently decided that no personal attack was involved when Mayor Frank Rizzo of Philadelphia stated that leaders of a teachers' union were engaging in "blackmail," had "placed a gun to the heads of the taxpayers," and were seeking "to extract blood-money ... with the educational welfare of our children as pawns," while the aforementioned reference to a Congressman as a "coward" was held to constitute a personal attack, two Commissioners complained that the two rulings could not be squared. The dissenter added:

It may be, of course, that these are among the species of cases for which principles do not really suffice, and that must consequently be decided according to the length of the Chancellor's foot. If a certain amount of arbitrariness is necessary to finish important business in realms where mere language will not carry us, so be it. But in such cases, it is the Chancellor's duty at least to try to keep his foot from changing size like Alice in Wonderland.[59]

Nor is vagueness the only problem in the administration of the personal attack rules. An additional problem is what Henry Geller, the knowledgeable former General Counsel of the FCC, has called the "crazy quilt pattern of exceptions."[60] Originally, the personal attack rules did not cover attacks on foreign groups and foreign public figures, or attacks made by candidates on other candidates. Reply rights for foreign groups or figures were exempted on practical grounds, and the latter type of attack was thought to be taken care of by the equal opportunities requirement of section 315(a). Shortly after adoption, the Commission also made the rules inapplicable to both newscasts and on-the-spot coverage of news events, two of the four categories of news programming exempted by Congress in 1959 from the equal opportunities requirement of section 315(a).[61] A few months later, the Commission added two more exemptions to the rules: news interviews and news commentary or analysis contained in newscasts. News documentaries, the other exemption from the equal opportunities requirement, continue to be covered by the personal attack rules. The Commission's stated reason for exempting most news programming from the personal attack rules was that such requirements would be "impractical and might impede the effective execution of the important news functions of licensees or networks," causing news broadcasts to be replaced by responses to personal attacks.[62] Apprehensive about the disruptive and potentially inhibiting impact of the personal attack rules, the Commission has instead relied on the general Fairness Doctrine and broadcaster-originated programming to provide countervailing opinion on public issues.

These exceptions, and the inherently intractable nature of questions that arise under the personal attack rules, tend to make the rules a trap for the unwary broadcaster who cannot be certain when the Commission will decide that the rules' vague standards have been transgressed. Henry Geller's conclusion is amply warranted:

We suggest that the FCC end this detailed and tortured categor-

izing and return to the basic principle of fairness; namely, determining whether the licensee has afforded reasonable opportunity for the contrasting viewpoint. This would afford the responsible broadcaster greater discretion—a factor conducive to more wide-open debate and, we believe, would not result in any significant lessening of such debate by a failure to present the side of the person attacked fairly and robustly.

To an irresponsible broadcaster who ignores his fairness duties, the revision will lead to the same result—denial of renewal for failure to comply with the requirements of the rule and the doctrine.[63]

Access rules respecting political editorializing are less troublesome than the personal attack rules because vagueness and unpredictability of administration are not a problem. Nevertheless, these rules too almost certainly have the effect of seriously inhibiting broadcast editorials, and they constitute a departure from the usual pattern of fairness obligations. Geller has noted that the editorializing rules, with their requirements of notification and an invitation to respond, apply only to editorials endorsing or opposing a candidate. They do not apply to editorials taking positions on ballot issues. He attributes the difference in treatment to Congress' attitude toward political editorializing by broadcasters.[64] Congressional committees have indicated displeasure with political editorializing. In fact, Congress has flatly prohibited editorializing by noncommercial stations.[65] Geller suggests that the FCC may have declared a right of access for candidates in reply to political editorials as a means of disarming Congressional critics. In any event, Geller sees no principled basis on which to distinguish editorializing about candidates from editorializing on ballot issues. In his considered view, the editorializing rules represent an unjustifiable burdening of one type of political editorializing with contingent access obligations, while another type of political editorializing is handled under the Fairness Doctrine. Geller points out that the number of political editorials has significantly decreased since the editorializing access rules went into effect.[66] When a number of candidates are in competition, the rules restrain political editorializing in favor of one candidate in the same way that section 315(a)'s equal opportunities requirement inhibits broadcasters from giving free air time to presidential candidates.

The FCC's personal attack and editorializing rules depart from the traditional pattern of the Fairness Doctrine, which weeks to implement the public trustee obligations of broadcasters without intrusive official second-guessing of day-to-day editorial decisions and without officially mandated programming. There is no sound justification for carving out these exceptions from the general policy of licensee discretion subject to official supervision. As a result, it is no surprise that the rules are replete with exemptions and differential treatments. Moreover, the administration of the personal attack rules has been unpredictable, vague, and controversial. Subjecting broadcasters to burdensome complaint procedures under these amorphous rules is a tempting weapon for persons offended by particular broadcasts. The Commission should reconsider its attempt to fit access obligations within Fairness Doctrine theory. Possible results of such a rethinking are suggested in the next chapter. Those suggestions, however, must be viewed within the context of the Supreme Court's most recent consideration of access to radio and television.

Access to Electronic Media and the First Amendment: The Supreme Court's Latest Statement

After the *Red Lion* decision in 1969, the Supreme Court maintained a prudent silence about broadcast regulation and the First Amendment for four years. *Red Lion* constituted a major statement, and both the Commission and the lower courts needed time to digest and explore the implications of the new rationale. During the period following *Red Lion*, a number of developments made the Supreme Court's next confrontation with broadcasting especially interesting. Problems surfaced over the Commission's resort to access in dealing with product commercials and presidential addresses. Also, the appointment of Warren Burger as Chief Justice portended a new activism and sophistication by the Supreme Court in dealing with broadcast regulation. Burger had long been a member of the Circuit Court of Appeals in the District of Columbia. A major proportion of that Court's work consists of reviewing FCC actions, and Burger had achieved a well-deserved reputation for vigorous and imaginative action in broadcast cases. Moreover, public-interest law firms and citizens groups, dedicated to significant changes in broadcast regulation, were focusing more attention on the FCC than ever before. Finally, the Nixon administration's attitude toward the press heightened concern about relations between government and communications media. All these factors created great interest in the Supreme Court's next action in the broadcast field.

In 1973, the Supreme Court provided its latest statement on access to radio and television. Two cases joined for decision under the name *Columbia Broadcasting System, Inc.* v. *Democratic National Committee* tested the legality of broadcasters' refusals to accept non-candidate-oriented political advertisements on an equal basis with commercial ads.[67] One case arose from the efforts of the Democratic National Committee (DNC) to place television ads for the Democratic Party. The second case concerned whether a radio station could rightfully refuse to air an anti-Vietnam ad from a group called Business Executives' Move for Vietnam Peace (B.E.M.). Both the DNC ad B.E.M. had been prepared to pay for the ads at regular commercial rates.

The broadcasters' refusal to air the ads was upheld by the FCC on the ground that the licensees were obligated by the Fairness Doctrine only to cover controversial issues as they deemed appropriate within their editorial discretion. The Fairness Doctrine was interpreted as granting access rights to particular parties only in matters falling within section 315(a) or the personal attack and editorializing rules.[68] The District of Columbia Court of Appeals reversed the Commission in an opinion of great potential sweep by Judge J. Skelly Wright.[69] Judge Wright viewed broadcasters as analogous to "state action,"[70] and applied a somewhat diluted version of the equality principle developed in the public forum cases. Because the broadcasters had accepted product commercials, Judge Wright held that they could not flatly refuse to air all non-candidate-oriented political ads. The First Amendment, as Judge Wright read it, did not require that all political ads must be broadcast. However, a "flat ban" by licensees on any particular type of ad was unconstitutional. The Court of Appeals made the Commission responsible for implementing the constitutional obligation to broadcast some, though not all, political ads.[71] The court was careful to limit the scope of its ruling to time voluntarily relinquished by broadcasters to advertising:

In normal programming time, closely controlled and edited by broadcasters, the constellation of constitutional interests would be substantially different. In news and documentary presentations, for example, the broadcasters' own interests in free speech are very, very strong. The Commission's Fairness Doctrine properly leaves licensees broad leeway for professional judg-

ment in that area. But in the allocation of advertising time, the broadcasters have no such strong First Amendment interests. Their speech is not at issue; rather, all that is at issue is their decision as to which other parties will be given an opportunity to speak.[72]

Although the focus was on advertising, Judge Wright's opinion emphasized the broad changes in the theory of broadcast regulation signified by the *Red Lion* decision. Judge Wright spoke of the state action doctrine as a traditional barrier to invoking First Amendment rights against private entities, including broadcasters, but declared that "the path is now clear of such doctrinal impedimenta." Turning specifically to *Red Lion*, he endorsed a broad interpretation:

> . . . *[T]he Court's opinion went well beyond the scarcity rationale of the* National Broadcasting Co. *case. It justified the Commission's interference with broadcasters' free speech by invoking specifically constitutional rights of the general public which, it said, underlie and support the Fairness Doctrine rules at issue. . . .*
>
> *Of course, the* Red Lion *Court had to invoke the public's First Amendment interests for a narrow purpose only—to uphold legislative and administrative action already taken. It did not have to reach the issue, presented in these cases, of invoking those interests for a direct attack on broadcasters' policies approved by the Commission. However, the language used by the Court is significantly expansive. It spoke of a First Amendment "right" held by "the people as a whole." A constitutional "right" is hardly deserving of the name if it can function only to permit legislative and administrative action and if its content depends entirely upon the current policies of the legislative and executive branches.*[73]

The Court of Appeals' opinion in *B.E.M.—DNC* suggested that *Red Lion* would be read to the outer limits of its implications for access rights. Broad rights of access grounded in the First Amendment seemed likely for radio and television, with expansive potential for other types of communications media as well. Great anticipation awaited Supreme Court review.

The Supreme Court emphatically reversed the Court of Appeals. It offered a new perspective on broadcast regulation, one which constituted a significant departure from the theory of *Red Lion*.

The Supreme Court decided that the First Amendment did not obligate broadcasters to air the message of any particular sponsor. This decision sustained the FCC's position, as did the decision in *Red Lion*. Yet the opinions of the Justices contributed substantially to a new understanding of state action principles, of the nature of the Fairness Doctrine and its relation to the First Amendment, and of access obligations in general. Chief Justice Burger, joined by Justices Stewart and Rehnquist, rejected the argument that broadcasters constitute "state action" because of the licensing system. Justice Douglas essentially agreed with this position. These four Justices also rejected the analogy between broadcasters and the public forum cases. Justices White, Powell, and Blackmun found the state action question unnecessary to decide. They believed that the traditional Fairness Doctrine, which did not require access in these circumstances, was sufficient to meet First Amendment demands even if licensees were considered to be state action. (Chief Justice Burger and Justice Rehnquist also subscribed to this view.) Only Justices Brennan and Marshall maintained the view that broadcast licensees should be considered state action.

Although the Court in *B.E.M.—DNC* is fragmented, important themes about the First Amendment and electronic media emerge from the majority coalition. Chief Justice Burger and Justices Rehnquist, White, Powell, and Blackmun all viewed broadcasting as "a special situation to which traditional constitutional doctrines should not be mechanically applied."[74] One major theme of these five Justices was deference to the legislative and administrative branches in broadcast regulation. The result is that they approved the Fairness Doctrine as applied. But Chief Justice Burger also strongly supported broadcaster editorial autonomy and was sharply critical of access requirements. He viewed the Communications Act as a careful balance between maximum broadcaster autonomy and public trustee responsibilities. He believed that access obligations upset this balance:

> [S]o sweeping a concept of governmental action would go far in practical effect to undermine nearly a half century of unmistakable congressional purpose to maintain—no matter how difficult the task—essentially private broadcast journalism held only broadly accountable to public interest standards. . . .
> [I]t would be anomalous for us to hold, in the name of promoting the constitutional guarantees of free expression, that the day-to-day editorial decisions of broadcast licensees are

*subject to the kind of restraints urged by respondents. To do so
in the name of the First Amendment would be a contradiction.
Journalistic discretion would in many ways be lost to the rigid
limitations that the First Amendment imposes on government.*[75]

Moreover, he criticized access obligations for the administrative
supervision their application would require:

> *By minimizing the difficult problems involved in implementing
> such a right of access, the Court of Appeals failed to come to
> grips with another problem of critical importance to broadcast
> regulation and the First Amendment—the risk of an enlarge-
> ment of government control over the content of broadcast
> discussion of public issues. . . .*
>
> *Under a constitutionally commanded and government super-
> vised right-of-access system urged by respondents and mandated
> by the Court of Appeals, the Commission would be required to
> oversee far more of the day-to-day operations of broadcasters'
> conduct, deciding such questions as whether a particular
> individual or group has had sufficient opportunity to present its
> viewpoint and whether a particular viewpoint has already been
> sufficiently aired. Regimenting broadcasters is too radical a
> therapy for the ailment respondents complain of.*[76]

However, the Chief Justice was careful not to exalt broadcaster
autonomy beyond the reach of regulation: "The use of a public
resource by the broadcast media permits a limited degree of
Government surveillance." Nor did he shut the door to access
requirements: "Conceivably at some future date Congress or the
Commission—or the broadcasters—may devise some kind of limited
right of access that is both practicable and desirable."[77] Moreover,
he carefully distinguished between the constitutional status of
electronic media and that of newspapers:

> *The tensions inherent in such a regulatory structure emerge
> more clearly when we compare a private newspaper with a
> broadcast licensee. The power of a privately owned newspaper
> to advance its own political, social, and economic views is
> bounded by only two factors: first, the acceptance of a suffi-
> cient number of readers—and hence advertisers—to assure
> financial success; and, second, the journalistic integrity of its
> editors and publishers. A broadcast licensee has a large measure*

of journalistic freedom but not as large as that exercised by a newspaper. A licensee must balance what it might prefer to do as a private entrepreneur with what it is required to do as a "public trustee."[78]

Although he did not grant broadcaster autonomy the status of a constitutional guarantee, Chief Justice Burger clearly viewed autonomy as an essential value in the existing statutory scheme of broadcast regulation.

Justices Stewart and Douglas went beyond the other Justices in the majority. They saw First Amendment principles as barring access requirements to all branches of the communications media. Justice Stewart, in his heated but rather opaque concurrence, stated that he joined *Red Lion* "with considerable doubt" regarding the personal attack and editorializing rules as "within the outer limit of First Amendment tolerability."[79] As for the access arguments in the present case, he declared:

If we must choose whether editorial decisions are to be made in the free judgment of individual broadcasters, or imposed by bureaucratic fiat, the choice must be for freedom.[80]

Justice Stewart also stated that imposing access obligations on newspapers

would be . . . grossly violative of the First Amendment's guarantee of a free press. For that guarantee gives every newspaper the liberty to print what it chooses and reject what it chooses, free from the intrusive editorial thumb of Government.[81]

Meanwhile, Justice Douglas viewed the case as very simple. In his opinion, the First Amendment absolutely prohibited the imposition of access obligations on any medium of expression:

TV and radio stand in the same protected position under the First Amendment as do newspapers and magazines. . . .
I did not participate in [Red Lion] and, with all respect, would not support it. The Fairness Doctrine has no place in our First Amendment regime. It puts the head of the camel inside the tent and enables administration after administration to toy with TV or radio in order to serve its sordid or its benevolent ends. . . .

> *What kind of First Amendment would best serve our needs as*
> *we approach the 21st century may be an open question. But the*
> *old-fashioned First Amendment that we have is the Court's only*
> *guideline; and one hard and fast principle which it announces is*
> *that Government shall keep its hands off the press.*[82]

Only Justices Brennan and Marshall maintained that the broadcasters' ban on political advertisements violated the First Amendment. They insisted that broadcasters constitute state action in the
constitutional sense. To support this view, they pointed to the public
"ownership" of the electromagnetic spectrum, to the fact that
licensees owed to the government their "right" to operate, to the
pervasive government control of the broadcast industry, and, most
important, to "the *specific* governmental involvement in the broadcaster policy presently under consideration,"[83] referring to the
broadcasters' claim that the Fairness Doctrine authorized the ban on
editorial advertisements. Accordingly, the two dissenters contended
that the First Amendment did control broadcasters' policies and, in
this context, required a balancing of "the competing interests of
broadcasters, the listening and viewing public, and individuals seeking
to express their views over the electronic media."

Justice Brennan insisted that the First Amendment supported
rights of access in these cases:

> *But freedom of speech does not exist in the abstract. On the*
> *contrary, the right to speak can flourish only if it is allowed to*
> *operate in an effective forum—whether it be a public park, a*
> *schoolroom, a town meeting hall, a soapbox, or a radio and*
> *television frequency. For in the absence of an effective means*
> *of communication, the right to speak would ring hollow indeed.*[84]

He recognized the broadcasters' First Amendment interest "in
exercising journalistic supervision over the use of their facilities."[85]
But since *B.E.M.–DNC* involved only the allocation of advertising
time, which broadcasters relinquished in any event to the expressions
of others, Justice Brennan found the broadcasters' "supervision"
interest to be insubstantial.

Thus, the attitude toward access rights of a substantial majority of
the Supreme Court in the *B.E.M.–DNC* decision ranged from
skepticism to downright hostility. It is a remarkable contrast to the
enthusiasm with which a unanimous Court had embraced access only

four years earlier in *Red Lion*. Admittedly, the holdings of the two decisions are consistent. In each, the Constitution was disclaimed as the wellspring of decision, and the position of the FCC was sustained. However, in the *B.E.M.–DNC* decision, the Court criticized access obligations for the electronic media as contrary to both the premises of the Communications Act and the spirit of the First Amendment.

The majority opinion in *B.E.M.–DNC* likewise marked a shift in the Court's articulation of the theory of broadcast regulation. In *Red Lion*, the Court intimated a rationale for regulation that viewed broadcasters as proxies for the public, with no rights of autonomy over their temporarily licensed frequencies. Access obligations were judged as consistent with this proxy theory. In fact, the Court even hinted that access to radio and television might be required by the First Amendment ideal of a free and open marketplace of ideas. These hints ripened into constitutional doctrine, briefly, in the *B.E.M.–DNC* decision of the District of Columbia Court of Appeals.

But when the *B.E.M.–DNC* decision reached the Supreme Court, that Court rejected the notion of broad access rights required by the First Amendment. Instead, it reverted to a theory of broadcast regulation which was grounded in the legislative history of the Communications Act and which stressed the editorial autonomy of broadcasters. Thus, the current approach of the Supreme Court rests on the view that broadcasters are public trustees rather than proxies designed to serve as a conduit for public expression. Under this trustee theory, broadcasters are obliged to operate in the public interest and are subject to periodic evaluation. However, they are still allowed a considerable degree of trustee discretion and editorial autonomy in day-to-day operations. According to the Court, the Fairness Doctrine serves both as a means of enforcing the public obligations of broadcasters and as a way of preserving a core of editorial autonomy.

After considering the *B.E.M.–DNC* decision, one may wonder how FCC-mandated access obligations will fare under this current view of the Fairness Doctrine. *B.E.M.-DNC* did not involve such an administrative obligation, but rather the notion of a constitutionally mandated right of access to electronic media for political advertising. It is understandable that any court might be reluctant to apply sweeping First Amendment principles to a legal context that it views as a delicate balance of competing values. In such a situation, First Amendment principles may be too categorical to use as a practical source of legal rules. However, the fact that the First Amendment has been discounted as the basis for imposing access obligations does not necessarily mean that statutory or administrative rules of access would likewise be rejected.

12

Access, Autonomy, and the Public Interest in Broadcasting: Concluding Observations

. . . I have attempted a reconciliation of the existing system of telecommunication regulation and the developing schema of the First Amendment. I don't want to leave the impression that this attempt leaves me entirely satisfied; far from that, the more I study the relation of these two areas the more uncertain and troubled I become. Particularly intractable to my mind is the relation of modern notions of "chilling effect" or "breathing space" for First Amendment freedoms and a comprehensive system of governmental licensing of speakers.

Chief Judge David Bazelon[1]

The system of broadcast regulation established under the Communications Act of 1934 is a rough accommodation of competing policies. As a result, virtually any specific regulation in the field is an inviting target for criticism because it may be held up against whichever of the statutory policies it happens to contradict. So it is with access. A balanced appraisal of access questions must take into account the tensions within our system of broadcast regulation. The difficulty of this task cautions against confidently asserting that a particular administrative policy of the FCC does or does not accord with the Communications Act and the First Amendment. Thus, the following conclusions and suggestions are offered provisionally. Nevertheless, consideration of both the basic principles of the Communications Act and of recent experience with various access requirements offers some useful lessons.

On the whole, the experience of radio and television does not support contingent access obligations for communications media. Section 315(a)'s requirement of "equal opportunities" for political candidates has made broadcasters less willing to provide free time for debate between candidates in presidential and other elections in which there are a number of fringe candidates. Such obvious inhibiting effects led to the creation of exemptions. Yet, though these exemptions were necessary to prevent the section from disrupting news programming, they are difficult to administer and they implicitly undermine the logic of applying the section to any programming other than political advertisements. Moreover, section 315(a) indicates a serious danger for access rules. The issue of reforming this section has become a notorious political football; public interest in robust debate is a sorry loser to the political anxieties of presidents and their parties, who are understandably reluctant to encourage access for their serious competitors. Many types of access requirements would be so embroiled with the political fortunes of the lawmakers responsible for promulgating these requirements that the public interest and First Amendment values would likely receive short shrift. According to Henry Geller, similar political pressures have produced the special access rule for broadcast editorials about political candidates but not for other editorials.

Nor have access obligations derived from the general Fairness Doctrine had a happy experience. When the FCC attempted to rectify imbalances caused by presidential addresses under the right-of-reply rationale, it found itself trapped because those replies only generated further rights of reply. And, as a result of the counter-commercial ruling in the cigarette advertising case, the Commission and the courts had to embark on a futile search for limiting principles. In both areas, the Commission soon repudiated access obligations and returned to reliance on the more flexible Fairness Doctrine. This pattern is likely to be repeated whenever contingent access rights are premised on broad notions of fairness to the listening public.

Even when access rights have evolved through general rulemaking, rather than *ad hoc* rulings, the results have not been fruitful. The personal attack access rules have had to be severely qualified to prevent them from overwhelming the public with trivia or becoming unmanageable for the broadcaster. Where the rules apply, they require the Commission to make close judgments on such imponderables as whether a given issue is "controversial" and of "public importance" in the broadcaster's community, and whether derogatory words constitute a covered personal attack or an uncovered criticism of competence. Punitive measures for failure to comply with the personal attack rules should not turn on decisions having such a tendency to vagueness and inconsistency.

After so many difficulties and unhappy experiences, the Commission has lately become wary of access. And, no doubt, it has also been affected by the Supreme Court's unsympathetic response to access claims in the *B.E.M.–DNC* decision. There is reason to question, however, whether the Commission has gone far enough in rejecting access rights as an aspect of broadcast regulation. The Commission's 1974 report on the Fairness Doctrine, as discussed previously, rejected access rights in the contexts of political addresses and product commercials. Moreover, the Commission phrased its rejection in terms that were broadly critical of access obligations in general. Thus, the Commission was uncomplimentary in speaking of its own cigarette counter-commercial ruling: "we believe that this mechanical approach to the Fairness Doctrine represented a serious departure from the doctrine's central purpose."[2] A similar outlook had permeated the Commission's 1972 report on the question of responses to political broadcasts:

> [I]ncreasingly detailed Commission regulation militates against robust wide-open debate. The genius of the Fairness Doctrine has been precisely the leeway and discretion it affords the licensee. . . .[3]

> [T]raditional fairness works better by setting out broad principles and permitting the licensee to exercise good faith and reasonable discretion in applying those broad principles.[4]

Along the same lines, the Commission's 1974 report rejected access for the discussion of public issues:

> Our studies during the course of this inquiry have not disclosed any scheme of government-dictated access which we consider "both practicable and desirable." We believe, to the contrary, that the public's interest in free expression through broadcasting will best be served and promoted through continued reliance on the Fairness Doctrine which leaves questions of access and the specific handling of public issues to the licensee's journalistic discretion. This system is far from perfect. However, in our judgment, it does represent the most appropriate accommodation of the various First Amendment interests involved, and

provides for maximum public enlightenment on issues of signif-
icance with a minimum of governmental intrusion into the
journalistic process.[5]

In view of these general rejections of access, one may wonder why the Commission did not discuss the personal attack and political editorializing access rules in its 1974 report. Although the Commission often expounded the themes of licensee discretion, nonintrusion in specific programming judgments, and skepticism about the feasibility of access requirements, it made no effort to justify the personal attack and editorializing rules. Yet these rules undoubtedly involve the most significant displacement of licensee discretion, the most economically and administratively burdensome programming obligations, and the vaguest access requirements that have been imposed on radio and television. The Commission's failure to consider the personal attack and editorializing rules in a report that claimed to reflect thorough reconsideration of the Fairness Doctrine is an incredible oversight. Without apparent justification, the Commission has maintained a mechanistic survivor from an earlier day of untested enthusiasm for broad access guarantees.

The personal attack rules are ripe for reconsideration. Fred W. Friendly's recent investigations into the political background of the *Red Lion* case seem certain to add an important perspective to the controversy about the constitutionality and wisdom of the personal attack rules. Friendly has uncovered evidence that in 1963, as the Commission moved toward recognition of a right of reply to personal attacks, the Democratic National Committee used the evolving reply right for partisan political purposes.[6] Democrats saw that the Fairness Doctrine could be used to force broadcasters to present the Democratic point of view. They also saw that it could be used to inhibit broadcasts favoring positions associated with Senator Goldwater. According to Friendly, the DNC set up a dummy "non-partisan" committee that, with contributions channeled from the DNC, monitored right-wing broadcasts. By demanding free reply time to broadcasts that attacked individuals or groups, the DNC sought to harass stations that carried right-wing broadcasts. If their aim had simply been to force broadcasters to give airtime to Democratic viewpoints, the result would have been quite consistent with the premises of the Fairness Doctrine. But the fact that the DNC also intended to inhibit anti-Democratic broadcasts, a result at odds with the goals of the doctrine and the First Amendment, is indicated by this statement from a report by Wayne Phillips, the executive at the DNC who set up the monitoring effort:

> [E]ven more important than free radio time, however, was the effectiveness of this operation in inhibiting the political activity of these right-wing broadcasts.[7]

And Friendly quotes another DNC memorandum, which was even more blatant:

> [T]he right-wingers operate on a strictly cash basis and it is for this reason that they are carried by so many small stations. Were our efforts to be continued on a year-round basis, we would find that many of these stations would consider the broadcast of these programs bothersome and burdensome (especially if they are ultimately required to give us free time) and would start dropping the programs from their broadcast schedule.[8]

The technique of the DNC was apparently manifest in the *Red Lion* case itself. Fred Cook had been hired by a public relations firm associated with the DNC effort to write articles and broadcast copy that attacked right-wing broadcasting. Ironically, it was such an article that piqued Hargis' anger and led to the radio attack on Cook that generated the litigation. The DNC monitoring effort picked up Hargis' broadcast and, according to Friendly, the DNC staff helped Cook prepare and send demands for free reply time to all the stations that had carried the Hargis broadcast.

The critical point in Friendly's disclosure is that seasoned politicians in the Democratic National Committee invested a significant amount of personnel and money in the belief that monitoring right-wing broadcasts and demanding a right of reply to all personal attacks would inhibit political expression unfavorable to the Democratic party. It is hard to imagine more compelling evidence that the personal attack rules do, indeed, have the "chilling effect" that the Supreme Court in *Red Lion*, with none of this evidence known to it, called "speculative."

Evidence that professional politicians have acted on the assumption that the personal attack rules have a significant chilling effect is particularly damaging to the tenability of these rules. It is true that rules of law may inhibit freedom of expression and still be sustained because they serve overriding legitimate social policies. However, the personal attack rules are intended to implement the Fairness Doctrine, which is supposed to afford the public more, rather than less, speech on controversial public issues. In short, the purpose of the personal attack rules is to increase expression. A finding of chilling effect, therefore, not only runs counter to the values of the First Amendment, but also undercuts the basic justification for the rules.

Experience has verified the fears of vagueness and inhibiting effect that the Supreme Court dismissed in *Red Lion*. The personal attack rules stand virtually alone as an unjustified exception to the Commission's current commitment to licensee discretion in carrying out fairness obligations, nonintrusion in individual programming judgments, and encouragement of robust, uninhibited debate on public issues.

However, as stated before, it is easy to criticize official policy in the area of broadcast regulation, and the FCC's access rules are an especially easy mark. It is far more constructive, and far more difficult, to formulate a system of regulation that does not include problematic access obligations and still gives due weight to the public responsibilities of a licensee. Critics do well to remember that access obligations have evolved as one means of justifying and implementing the Communications Act's nonmarket, nonownership method of allocating rights in the electromagnetic spectrum. Some broadcaster responsibility for programming in the public interest is virtually inevitable in a system that grants free temporary use of a coveted resource to only a few applicants. The question is not whether public trustee responsibilities should be implemented, but how they should be implemented.

In the past two years, the FCC, the federal courts, individual jurists, and influential commentators have all exhibited a fundamental change in attitude toward broadcast regulation. The Supreme Court's change in mood toward access between *Red Lion* and *B.E.M.—DNC* is symptomatic of basic rethinking by the front-line institutions—the Commission and the Court of Appeals for the District of Columbia—that oversee broadcast regulation in the United States.

As the Federal Communications Commission has moved away from access obligations, it has found other less intrusive means of implementing broadcasters' public responsibilities. The Fairness Doctrine is no longer tied so strictly to access and the notion of reviewing specific programs. The move now is toward evaluation of overall performance. The potential force of the Fairness Doctrine in

license renewal proceedings had been demonstrated in the 1960s in a
formidable pair of opinions by Judge Warren Burger, then serving on
the District of Columbia Court of Appeals. His opinions effectively
removed the license of station WLBT in Jackson, Mississippi, for
routinely refusing to air the viewpoints of a substantial local black
community.[9] And a second more recent case also suggests the
current potency of the Fairness Doctrine in the license renewal
process. In 1970, for the first time, an AM radio station owned by
fundamentalist preacher Carl McIntire was denied renewal of its
license by the FCC for failure to comply with fairness obligations.
The Court of Appeals for the District of Columbia upheld the refusal
in *Brandywine—Main Line Radio, Inc.* v. *FCC,* although only one of
the three judges based his opinion squarely on fairness violations, and
Judge Bazelon, in dissent, argued that the Fairness Doctrine should
not be the basis for refusal to renew.[10] This decision suggests that
licensees can expect a forceful review of their overall performance
under the Fairness Doctrine at renewal time.

In 1975, two additional refusals to renew rested on violations of
fairness or related public interest standards in programming. One
very significant ruling denied renewal applications made by the
Alabama Educational Television Commission (AETC) for its eight
educational television stations in Alabama.[11] The Commission found
that AETC followed "a racially discriminatory policy in its overall
programming practices during the license period."[12] Moreover,
AETC was found to have excluded blacks from policy-making staff
positions, and to have failed to consult with the black community
about programming policies. A general lack of programs suited to the
special educational needs of the state's black population was also a
factor in the Commission's decision to deny renewal. Several other
aspects of the AETC decision merit notice. The Commission refused
renewal even though substantial improvements had taken place
toward the end of the license term.[13] Also, renewal was denied even
though AETC was a noncommercial broadcaster and an agency of
the state. Two dissenters protested the Commission's decision as
vindictive, and spoke of it as "a new chapter . . . in the history of the
Federal Communications Commission."[14]

The second refusal to renew early in 1975 involved not direct
fairness violations but slanted newscasts designed to further certain
political candidacies. The decision rests on a finding of intentional
slanting, which has traditionally been considered a separate and
serious dereliction. However, this refusal does show the willingness of

the Commission to resort to denials of renewal as a means of enforcing trusteeship standards in programming.[15]

The Fairness Doctrine appears to be assuming real importance in the renewal process. The Commission evidently meant what it emphasized in the 1974 Fairness Doctrine report: " 'we regard strict adherence to the Fairness Doctrine . . . as the single most important requirement of operation in the public interest—the "sine qua non" for grant of a renewal of license.' "[16]

As renewal proceedings have developed recently into serious tests of compliance with public trustee obligations, they have become an important source of leverage for minority groups wishing to make their voices heard over the air. The primary tool on this front has been settlement agreements, in which challenges to renewal are withdrawn in return for licensee promises concerning employment and programming. The Court of Appeals has stated that statistical evidence of a very low rate of minority employment may, if unrebutted, constitute evidence that the licensee is not operating in the public interest and should not have its license renewed.[17] On the other hand, the court has also held that a broadcaster's policy of actively recruiting minority group members for placement in responsible jobs can overcome the negative implication of contrary statistical evidence. The situation is made to order for challenges and settlements. The threat of expensive and lengthy hearings on renewal challenges, and the possibility of nonrenewal if an overall pattern of fairness violations or employment discrimination can be established, are substantial inducements for broadcasters to seek constructive settlements with minority and other citizen groups.[18] Furthermore, the Court of Appeals has bolstered efforts of this sort by ruling that citizen groups may be reimbursed for legal expenses by a licensee with whom a settlement is negotiated.[19]

It is shortsighted to view the Fairness Doctrine, without broad access rights, as a pious bromide that will have no effect on the actual operation of broadcasting in the United States. Application of the doctrine in renewal proceedings has been far more effective than specific access rights in opening broadcasting to the views and participation of minority groups.

The rapid shift by the Commission and courts from enthusiasm to disfavor concerning access rights to electronic media cautions against predictions about the future place of access guarantees in broadcast regulation. Moreover, two recent and important proposals for reform of broadcast regulation have taken an even dimmer view of access rights than the FCC has. In December 1973, Henry Geller, the Commission's respected former general counsel, proposed a comprehensive reform in the administration of the Fairness Doctrine. In broad outline, Geller called for an end to Commission review of specific programs and imposition of specific remedies, such as access rights, for particular fairness violations. Instead, he advocated a return to the pre-1962 practice of not ruling on fairness complaints on an *ad hoc* basis, but rather withholding review until renewal proceedings. Then, Geller suggested, the overall performance of the licensee should be evaluated and renewal granted unless flagrant disregard of fairness obligations can be shown.[20] However, Geller would require a prompt resolution of fairness complaints concerning political broadcasts during campaigns not covered by section 315(a)'s equal opportunities requirement.[21] He would also dispense with prompt complaint review for personal attacks, and would eliminate the current right-of-reply remedy. Instead, Geller would simply require that a broadcaster who had presented a personal attack comply with the general Fairness Doctrine for the public issue in question through programming under the broadcaster's control.[22] He also advocated that the Commission adopt percentage guidelines as a means of indicating to broadcasters how much programming in particular subject areas would constitute performance in the public interest and justify renewal.[23]

The second important proposal for reform of broadcast regulation surfaced in two brilliant, excursive opinions by Chief Judge David Bazelon of the Court of Appeals for the District of Columbia. Bazelon has reconsidered the problems of broadcast regulation and the First Amendment, after more than twenty years of experience in reviewing actions of the FCC, and has moved to a fundamentally different approach.

The opinion in which Bazelon first departed from traditional assumptions about broadcasting and the First Amendment was evoked by the Court of Appeals' affirmation of the Commission's refusal to renew Reverend McIntire's broadcast license in the *Brandywine* decision. Bazelon wondered how the First Amendment could condone the silencing of WXUR, which broadcast controversial religious and political views, and he complained that "ancient assumptions and crystallized rules have blinded all of us to the depth of the First Amendment issues involved here."[24] He therefore embarked on an ambitious attempt to "come to grips with the conceptual underpinnings which have led the Commission to such ironic consequences."[25] Beginning with the assumption that the "marketplace of ideas" is the goal of the First Amendment, he argued that no broadcasting regulation that abridged a station's right of free expression could be justified unless that regulation also enhanced public access to the marketplace of ideas. Thus, he concluded that public trustee obligations "cannot be extended beyond what is required to preserve the marketplace of ideas from the dangers which scarcity may threaten."[26]

Bazelon expressed two fears about the Commission's action. First, he contended that, in removing the station from the air, the Commission had eliminated a unique and controversial viewpoint from public debate. Second, if the station had been allowed to remain on the air, but required to comply with the personal attack rules, Bazelon feared that the result would have been "strangulation."[27] Monitoring obligations and the high ratio of reply time required for each issue discussed "would have forced WXUR to censor its views."[28] The scarcity of broadcast frequencies, in Bazelon's view, was a doubtful basis on which to enforce balanced expression, if enforcement meant silencing a controversial point of view. He stressed that the number of broadcast outlets exceeded the number of newspapers, both nationally and in virtually every locality. And furthermore, Bazelon pointed out that, with the development of cable television technology, only economic constraints limited the number of broadcasters. All these factors, he argued in dissent, called for a remand to allow the Commission to reconsider its refusal to renew Brandywine's license in the light of First Amendment values.

Judge Bazelon refined his views in a 1974 case which reviewed the Commission's approval for transfer of a radio station's license to a new licensee who planned to change the station's format from classical to rock music. In recent years, with the prodding of the Court of Appeals, the Commission has attempted to preserve a diversity of formats in its rulings on license transfers and proposed format changes. For example, in a 1970 ruling, the Court of Appeals held that format changes could properly be left to market forces unless the format to be discontinued was unique to the area served. In such a case, the court ruled, the Commission must hold a hearing to determine whether the proposed format change would serve the public interest in diversity.[29] Late in 1974, the court affirmed this holding in *Citizens Committee to Save WEFM* v. *FCC* and Judge Bazelon concurred in a lengthy opinion.[30]

This opinion invites careful attention because Judge Bazelon raised basic questions about access obligations in relation to First Amendment theory. He challenged the assumption that diversified ownership of broadcasting outlets means diversity of ideas. Although free competition for advertising dollars is the goal of antitrust law as applied to broadcasting, the paradoxical result of this competition is not diversity of expression, but the opposite. Mass audience programming, essentially devoid of direct commentary on public affairs, has proven most efficient in the business of selling advertising time. Having posed this paradox of a competitively free marketplace that does not generate diversity of ideas, Bazelon raised the critical question: Does the First Amendment permit the government to go beyond efforts to ensure "a multiplicity of tongues unrestricted in speech," and undertake direct efforts to increase diversity of ideas?[31] Bazelon saw potential dangers in direct concern with diversity of expression, since it might involve "picking and choosing among speakers on the basis of the content of their speech. This process of choice, once begun, may well be difficult to halt short of the disaster."[32] The question then becomes: What failures in outlet diversity would justify direct regulation designed to achieve diversity of expression? Bazelon responded that direct concern with diversity of expression can be justified only when the government must, of necessity, choose which speaker will have access to a communications outlet. In the broadcasting field, therefore, the FCC may be concerned with the content of programming only in comparative licensing proceedings—where there are competing applications for the same license. In Bazelon's view, an application to transfer a license to a licensee planning a format change would be an appropriate occasion for FCC choice as to preferred format only if the old licensee would remain in operation and retain the old format if transfer were not approved.

Overall assessment of Judge Bazelon's ideas for broadcast regulation will not be made here.[33] In passing, however, one obvious question about his theory should be raised. If the Commission may properly choose between competing licensees on the basis of their planned programming, why may the Commission not require the licensee to program in accordance with its representations at the comparative hearing? For example, if the Commission, in a comparative hearing, decides to award a license to an applicant who promises to give all persons criticized an automatic right of reply, then why should the Commission not insist that this promise be carried out? In general terms, the question is whether Judge Bazelon's notion that direct concern with diversity should only surface in comparative hearings would logically limit FCC intervention in programming decisions. It is not easy to create airtight compartments of broadcaster autonomy under our system of broadcast regulation. But we need not pursue a critique. For present purposes, it is notable that Judge Bazelon's creative efforts to find a new approach to broadcasting and the First Amendment make no room for access obligations.

A second highly respected member of the Court of Appeals for the District of Columbia has also expressed disquiet about Fairness Doctrine review of specific editorial decisions. In December 1974, Judge Harold Leventhal wrote an opinion which reversed an FCC ruling that NBC had presented a critical and one-sided view in a documentary and so was obligated under the Fairness Doctrine to present other points of view.[34] This was the first time a broadcaster had been held to violate the Fairness Doctrine for airing a news documentary. Judge Leventhal's opinion for the court is a notable effort to accommodate the Fairness Doctrine to statutory and First Amendment principles mandating wide journalistic discretion for broadcasters.

The NBC documentary, "Pensions: The Broken Promise," portrayed a number of older workers who were left after retirement without pension benefits because of failures in their pension plans. All persons interviewed suggested that serious defects existed in many private pension plans, and the narrator of the program stated at the end: "The situation, as we've seen it, is deplorable." A complaint was filed with the FCC charging that NBC had distorted and presented only the bad side of the overall operation of private pensions. NBC responded that the program did not address the issue of the overall performance of pensions; rather it claimed that the program dealt with the noncontroversial issue of some problems in some pension plans. The Commission rejected the charge of distortion, but agreed that the documentary had presented only one side of the issue. It ruled that the issue was controversial and of public importance, and that the Fairness Doctrine therefore obligated NBC to program views on the other side. NBC appealed this ruling.

The Court of Appeals for the District of Columbia initially reversed the Commission. Judge Leventhal, writing for a majority of the three-judge panel, pointed to "the circumspection" with which the *Red Lion* decision had approved the personal attack and editorializing rules. According to that Supreme Court opinion, "if experience with the administration of those doctrines indicates that they have the net effect of reducing rather than enhancing the volume and quality of coverage there will be time enough to reconsider the constitutional implications."[35] And Judge Leventhal also pointed to the Supreme Court's approach in *B.E.M.–DNC* regarding broadcasters as "free agents" with "initial and primary responsibility for fairness, balance, and objectivity."[36] From these and similar Supreme Court statements, he fashioned the principle that in Fairness Doctrine cases

> *[T]he editorial judgments of the licensee must not be disturbed if reasonable and in good faith. . . . It has wide discretion and latitude that must be respected even though, under the same facts, the agency would reach a contrary conclusion.*[37]

Thus the FCC's function is limited to correcting the licensee for *abuse* of discretion.[38] But, Judge Leventhal reasoned, the court's function in reviewing cases in which the FCC has upset a broadcaster's editorial discretion is not the usual judicial role of according deference to the agency's judgment. Rather, the court must take a "hard look" at the agency's action to ensure that it has not interfered with the primary journalistic responsibility of broadcasters unless the broadcaster has abused its discretion.[39]

The court, unlike the FCC, found NBC's judgment to be reasonable: that only some problems in some private pension plans were covered, that this issue was therefore not a controversial one, and that the Fairness Doctrine did not require further programming presenting other points of view. An important element in the court's holding was its view of "Pensions" as an example of "investigative journalism," which necessarily concentrates on evils and abuses. According to Judge Leventhal, to convert descriptions of abuses in a system into broadsides against the overall system would result in the Fairness Doctrine inhibiting investigative reporting on radio and television.

Judge Leventhal's approach to the Fairness Doctrine is designed to minimize official interference with editorial judgments by broadcasters. What is notable about his approach is his forthright acknowledgment of the inhibiting effects of fairness review by the FCC and the courts. In a supplemental statement, speaking of fairness obligations, Judge Leventhal pointed to

. . . the stultifying burden on journalism. Even the monetary burden is not inconsequential. . . . [T]he problem is that the incremental burden will lead a licensee to acquiesce in the Government's instruction as to what he should broadcast. . . .

[T]he risks of government interference are so oppressive as to require a plain showing of journalistic abuse before a government official can issue a direction that the journalist's report must be supplemented with a codicil.[40]

After the initial panel decision concerning "Pensions," the case had a tortuous procedural history. The entire Court of Appeals first ordered rehearing *en banc* (a full ten-judge court review of the three-judge panel's decision), but later vacated that ruling in light of the Commission's suggestion that the case had become moot. The case was then sent back to the original panel for consideration of this mootness problem. Mootness is a concept whereby federal courts limit their exercise of judicial power to real controversies that have not been resolved. The Commission argued that the passage of comprehensive federal pension reform legislation in 1974[41] made the issue of private pension reform non-controversial, and so ended any obligation upon NBC to air further programming on the subject. In its first encounter with the case, the panel had decided that the passage of legislation did not end the case. However, on second thought, the panel was persuaded to dismiss the entire controversy. It treated the FCC's mootness suggestion as, in effect, a request that the Commission be allowed to vacate its order that NBC put on further programming. The upshot was that the initial reversal of the Commission and the Court's opinion were erased as actual judgments, although, as Judge Fahy commented, the opinions of Judge Leventhal and dissenting Judge Tamm "remain for their influence in the development of the law."[42] As a final complication in the case, Judge Bazelon submitted a lengthy dissent which argued that, if the Fairness Doctrine was not to be challenged frontally, the Commission's judgment in this particular case ought to be respected.

The "Pensions" decision is a fascinating study in the current attitudes of broadcasters, leading judges, and the FCC toward the Fairness Doctrine. Although the case did not involve a question of access specifically, it did raise questions concerning the propriety of Commission review of a particular programming decision by a broadcaster, a central issue in the controversy over contingent access obligations under the Fairness Doctrine.

Another recent decision by the Court of Appeals, this one dealing directly with questions of access under the personal attack rules, has also limited the Commission to a narrow scope of review in reviewing broadcasters' judgments. The case involved a radio station devoted to telephone call-in programming. A moderator called a local congressman a "coward" after the congressman had refused to be interviewed over the air about his role in a consumer meat boycott. The station contended that the "coward" remark had nothing to do with the meat boycott (the remark was separated by about two hours from discussion of the boycott, and the moderator had stated his agreement with the congressman on the boycott), and thus was not made "during the presentation of views on a controversial issue of public importance" within the terms of the personal attack rules. However, the FCC concluded that the remark "was part of a continuing discussion of the nation-wide meat boycott" and held that the station had violated the personal attack rules.

In *Straus Communications, Inc.* v. *FCC*, the Court of Appeals reversed the Commission.[43] Judge J. Skelly Wright reasoned in his opinion for a unanimous court, that "abiding First Amendment difficulties" and Congress' intent in the Communications Act required that in Fairness Doctrine controversies, including personal attack cases, the FCC reverse a broadcaster only when the broadcaster's judgments "have been unreasonable or in bad faith."[44] The court found that the Commission had improperly substituted its "own *de novo* judgment" for that of the broadcaster on the crucial question of whether the coward remark was connected to discussion of a controversial public issue. Thus, it vacated the Commission's ruling and remanded the case for further administrative proceedings under the proper, limited scope of agency review. The *Straus* decision constitutes a square holding that the FCC must defer to reasonable broadcaster judgments in dealing with "all components" of the Fairness Doctrine.

The Federal Communications Commission, the Court of Appeals for the District of Columbia, the Supreme Court, and two influential and imaginative proponents of reform in broadcast regulation, Geller and Bazelon, all appear to be moving away from access rights and other types of official supervision of specific programming decisions. Experience reveals that such interventions in day-to-day editorial decisions upset the dialectical tension in the Communications Act between the autonomy and the public responsibilities of radio and television licensees. The question is whether and how broadcasters' public trustee responsibilities under the Communications Act can be enforced without resorting to access obligations under the Fairness Doctrine. It is too soon for a final consideration of this ultimate question. We must await a review of the FCC's approach to access issues in the regulation of cable television, and an analysis of the Supreme Court's statement on the constitutionality of access obligations for the print media.

13

Access to Cable Television

We are in great haste to construct a magnetic telegraph from Maine to Texas; but Maine and Texas, it may be, have nothing important to communicate.

Henry Thoreau[1]

Watching public access programming is much like spending an evening in Times Square. It is exhilarating, frustrating, shocking and boring—above all, it is simply amazing.[2]

Broadcasting developed in the United States by radiation of electromagnetic waves from a transmitting antenna, and interception and decoding of such waves by radio and television receivers. However, as was discussed in Chapter 9, the tendency of these waves to interference physically limits the number of separate broadcast signals that feasibly can be received on ordinary television receivers at any particular place and time. A different method of signal transmission is by coaxial cable, which can carry, under present technology, up to 44 different channels within conventional VHF television frequencies.[3] This method of transmission has, in recent years, opened up the possibility of a communication revolution.

Since 1972, cable television has been the vehicle for the most ambitious and far-reaching access obligations yet attempted in the United States. Cable television thus offers the general public concrete experience with access rights of the kind that have been hotly debated for traditional broadcasting. However, the distinguishing features of cable television and the special characteristics of the access guarantees developed in this novel medium tend to set the cable access experience apart from that of traditional broadcasting. Indeed, the contrast between cable and traditional broadcasting, in physical, economic, and legal terms, is so striking that cable seems more akin to newspapers when one is considering access.

Because cable is a form of "television" that bears a strong resemblance to print communication, it challenges our law's traditional preoccupation with the differences between broadcast and print media. The development of cable invites a comprehensive approach to the law of mass communications. However, it is not clear in which direction this coalescing pressure ought to push. Cable television bridges some of the major differences between television and newspapers. But the question remains whether this development means that broadcasting should be given the same constitutional freedom that has been given to print publications, or whether some of the patterns of official supervision developed for radio and television should be extended to include the print mass media as well.

Although cable provides a fascinating perspective for a study of access to the media, there are several grounds for caution in assessing the general importance of cable's experience with access obligations. For one thing, the access rules imposed on cable systems by the FCC date only from 1972. Consequently, all potential problems involved in these access obligations have not as yet been uncovered. Moreover, the FCC's approach to cable regulation so far has been erratic and convoluted. The fundamental premises of the current pattern of regulation could be revised in the near future. After only three years, the FCC already seems to be retreating from some of the broad goals of the 1972 rules, and this trend may portend the end of the novel public access obligations. Furthermore, even if the current rules remain in effect, it is hard to measure their practical impact because of complicated "grandfathering" exemptions[4] and widespread waivers of the rules' applicability. The brief and volatile life of federal cable regulation provides a shaky basis for assessment.

A second reason for caution in assessing access and cable television is that the access obligations developed for cable are quite different from those developed and proposed for traditional broadcasters. They differ both in the nature of access rights conferred on the public and various other designated beneficiaries, and in the type of obligation imposed on the medium. Thus, the existence of broad access rights in the medium of cable television may offer little basis for extending such access rights to other media, and the experience of access in this setting may not provide general lessons. Even so, cable television does offer an important new approach to rights of access to communications media.

Cable television is in a state of uncertain adolescence. The first modest cable systems were established in the 1940s to bring regular television into isolated mountain communities. A tall antenna, receiving distant signals, was connected to customers' homes by coaxial cable. By 1952, there were some 70 systems of this sort serving about 14,000 customers; by 1962 the number of systems had grown to 800 with 850,000 customers.[5] During the 1960s, cable grew even more rapidly and was extended into urban areas. Cable's capacity for improving reception gave it a useful function in cities with special reception problems, such as New York, San Francisco, and Los Angeles. Meanwhile, signal importation was attractive in cities such as San Diego, which had been allocated few broadcast licenses because of special geographical interference problems and so presented a natural opportunity for importing signals from Los Angeles. Moreover, cable began to offer locally originated programming not available over broadcast channels. By 1973, there were over 3000 cable systems serving 8 million households, and, in 1974, the Cabinet Committee on Cable Communications estimated that the cable industry would continue to grow at a rate of more than 10 percent per year.[6] Other projections have been less restrained. The Sloan Commission predicted that by 1980, 40 to 60 percent of all television households would be served by cable systems.[7] Although most observers no longer take this figure seriously, it suggests the potential sweep of cable operations. As of 1975, cable had some 10 million subscribers, representing about 15 percent of all television households.[8]

The past, present, and likely future of cable television disclose three rather different communications functions:

Cable can mean the true "community antenna," a four- to six-channel operation simply enhancing the clarity of existing television signals; the typically twelve-channel "CATV," augmenting local transmissions with broadcast programming imported from other markets; or the modern "Cable-TV," whose twenty-four to forty-eight channels and two-way circuitry provide a communications network for a broad

spectrum of private information as well as general enter-
tainment services.[9]

At the present time, Professor Don Le Duc points out, cable television is just beginning to move out of its community antenna and program importing stages. It remains "predominantly an auxiliary broadcast service rather than a distinct medium in its own right."[10] How far and how soon cable can realize its potential to provide a vast range of television programming, to serve as a conduit for a wide variety of specialized communications services, and to offer an opportunity for individualized feedback by its viewers, are questions that have revolutionary implications for the future of our society.[11]

A brief sketch of the background of cable regulation is helpful in assessing the 1972 rulemaking that produced the current set of cable regulations, including broad guarantees of access. The FCC paid little attention to cable television in the early years when it simply provided extended reception of local stations into isolated rural places. This service aided local stations by increasing the size of their audiences. However, in the mid-1950s when a few cable systems began to import, by means of microwave relays,[12] distant signals into localities already served by local stations, local broadcasters responded to this threat of audience fragmentation by pressing the FCC for protection. The FCC demurred for several years, assuming that cable was a passing phenomenon that would disappear as over-the-air broadcasting expanded and hoping that Congress would legislate a system of cable regulation.[13]

But Congress did not act, and, in 1962, the FCC began a case-by-case restriction of microwave relays of distant signals by cable systems in order to protect local broadcasters.[14] During this period, the FCC still continued to avoid extensive regulation of cable in the hope that judicial enforcement of broadcaster program rights would protect broadcasters without the need for administrative action. However, the federal courts dispelled this hope in 1964 by rejecting all protections for programming other than those based on federal copyright laws.[15] A year later, cable's increasing penetration of urban markets caused the Commission to react with the first of a series of orders designed to protect broadcasters from cable competition. The FCC issued an across-the-board order: Carriers that served cable systems were required to condition relay service on the cable systems' agreement to carry the signals of local stations, and to refrain from duplicating the programs of local stations, both simultaneously and within 15 days before or after the local broadcast.[16] The Commission justified its protection of broadcasters on the ground that cable systems would not serve rural areas where homes were scattered or viewers were unwilling to pay directly for their television. Furthermore, the Commission reasoned that cable could not act as an outlet for local self-expression since its only function was to relay signals from other areas. In 1966, carriage and nonduplication rules were extended from microwave relays to the cable systems, as the FCC asserted jurisdiction over cable systems for the first time.[17] The nonduplication period was reduced from 15 days to one day. A major additional regulation was imposed in that same year on any new cable systems: The major market distant signal rule provided that distant signals could not be brought by cable into the top 100 markets (which serve almost 90 percent of the viewing public[18]) except on a showing in an evidentiary hearing that such importation would not damage local UHF stations.[19] These rules had the effect of freezing cable systems in the top markets, but did not produce an expansion of UHF broadcasting as the Commission hoped.[20] Indeed, the distant signal rule may have hurt UHF stations because such restrictions deprived UHF of the better reception that cable could provide.[21]

At roughly the same time as the Commission was restricting cable from the major markets, a lower federal court ruled that cable transmission of a program without the program owner's consent was an infringement of the owner's copyright protection. This decision appeared to give broadcasters control of cable systems' use of most available programming. However, the Supreme Court ruled in 1968 that cable systems did not "perform" (within the meaning of the copyright laws) programs they received and transmitted to their subscribers.[22] One week earlier, the Supreme Court had ruled that the FCC had statutory power under the Communications Act to regulate cable systems in upholding the 1966 signal carriage and nonduplication rules.[23] These decisions both ended the hope of a judicial copyright solution to cable broadcaster competition and affirmed the FCC's power over cable television. The Court thus invited an active administrative role in the evolution of cable television.

The Commission's reaction to the 1968 Court decisions followed what Professor Le Duc has termed "its decade-long objective of delegating cable control to the broadcast industry."[24] Because the

Commission concluded that cable's nonpayment for programs had an unfair competitive effect on broadcasting, it excluded cable carriage of distant signals into the top 100 markets.[25] This action, together with the nonduplication rules declared in 1966, reduced the threat of cable systems to broadcasters in the large markets.[26]

After 1968, a different approach to cable gathered momentum in political, business, and academic communities, and the Commission moved away from its attitude of stopgap hostility. One stimulus for this change was the arrival of Dean Burch as FCC Chairman in October 1969. Decisive and suspicious of restrictive government controls on technological development, he pushed for reconsideration of the Commission's attitude toward cable. Moreover, when Burch came to the FCC, criticism of mass media was reaching a crescendo and cable television was being viewed as a panacea for the ills of the media and even of society. Professor Monroe Price has recalled the extraordinary melange of supporters for cable during this period.[27] The bland uniformity of broadcast television was blamed for much of the homogenization of American life, and cable became a symbol of pluralism powerfully attractive to media critics from both left and right. Proponents of equality and participatory democracy saw that the abundance of cable channels might provide an opportunity of access to the media for political, ethnic, and cultural groups excluded from the mass merchandising of broadcast television. Others looked to cable as a means of decentralizing television programming and regenerating local communities. Supporters of cable's promises of diversity, localism, and public access found allies among critics of press concentration and bias. Policy planners decried the FCC's protectionist attitudes in behalf of traditional broadcasting. Thus, the Nixon Administration (whose feud with the networks made support of cable an appealing political weapon), communications egalitarians, futurists fascinated with new hardware and technology, critics of government intervention in economic development, and video radicals all combined to form an unusual constituency for change in official attitudes toward cable.[28]

In December 1971, representatives of broadcasters, program producers, and cable interests met with FCC Chairman Burch and Clay Whitehead, the head of the Office of Telecommunications Policy. They produced, under pressure, an extraordinary "consensus agreement" that provided the basis for the comprehensive 1972 cable rulemaking.[29] According to the industry bargain, as codified in the 1972 rules, cable systems were obliged to carry local broadcasters' signals without simultaneous duplication, but were also allowed to import a number of distant signals measured by reference to the size of the market in which they operated.[30] Cable systems in the top 100 markets were allowed to import at least two distant signals. Complex rules were also adopted to protect network and syndicated programming.[31] These rules dealing with distant signals, program exclusivity, and pay television were the result of bargaining between competing industry interests.

However, the 1972 rulemaking proceeding was more than a forum for bargaining between different segments of the television industry. Foundations presented detailed proposals for public access. Educational groups sought a pedagogical role for cable. Minority groups fought for effective means of access to cable systems. Even the "alternate culture" was attracted to the proceeding by cable's promise of access and program variety. Reflecting the concern of these diverse representatives of the "public interest," the 1972 regulations also included rules that concerned matters not subject to competition within the television industry and not covered by the consensus agreement. These rules dealt with various types of access to cable television, with locally originated programming, with multiple channel capacity, and with two-way communications potential.[32]

The Commission had found the goal of locally originated programming through cable appealing even before it abandoned its vacillating hostility toward cable. In 1969, the Commission ordered cable systems with 3,500 or more subscribers to originate programming and make facilities available for local production and presentation of programs.[33] This rule was to go into effect in 1971, but the Commission never enforced that requirement, and a federal court of appeals decided that the Commission lacked statutory authority for the rule. As a result, the Commission stayed the requirement, and did not reinstate it even after the Supreme Court had reversed the lower court's decision and upheld the Commission's authority.[34] Finally, in 1974, the requirement was lifted by the Commission.[35]

Even so, the Commission did not abandon its goal of enhanced local programming over cable. Rather, the 1972 rules revealed that the Commission's hopes for local programming had shifted to access channels available for nonoperator cablecasts. Cable systems were required to have a minimum 20-channel capacity; for each broadcast signal transmitted, a second channel had to be available for cablecasts (nonbroadcast programming).[36] Moreover, the Commission required that one access channel each be kept available for cablecasting by the general public, by educational institutions, and by local government. The remaining channels reserved for cablecasting were set aside for lease to any program producers, with the cable system acting essentially as a common carrier.[37] As the use of these cablecasting channels became significant, the Commission required that new access channels be activated. The Commission also required cable systems to build in the capacity for two-way circuitry, allowing for feedback from a subscriber to the system. The 1972 access and minimum capacity rules were imposed only on new cable systems in the top 100 markets. All systems already in existence when the rules were declared initially were given until 1977 to comply. Moreover, in July 1975, the Commission postponed these obligations indefinitely in response to objections from existing cable operators that upgrading the system to meet requirements, particularly the 20-channel minimum, would be inordinately expensive. However, the Commission maintained that it was not thereby abandoning "our commitment to foster the community access services cable is so uniquely capable of providing."[38]

The public access channel was designed by the Commission to "offer a practical opportunity to participate in community dialogue through a mass medium."[39] This channel must be available without charge at all times on a first-come, first-served, nondiscriminatory basis. Live studio presentations not exceeding five minutes must be subsidized by the cable system, but other production costs are borne by the access user.[40] The Commission has held that the public access channel must be set aside specifically for that use; a proposal by a cable system to use distant signal channels to fulfill the public access obligation when those channels were blacked out by the exclusivity or duplication rules was held unacceptable.[41] However, the Commission did allow a cable system serving a number of small separate communities to provide only one set of access channels, subject to a requirement for expansion if sufficient demand should develop.[42]

Although the Commission embraced the hope of free and easy public access to the most influential medium of mass communications, access issues still faced formidable difficulties. Access guarantees were established in law, but effective implementation of these guarantees was left largely to chance. As Professor Le Duc has noted:

The fact that this new function of "narrow"—rather than "broad"—casting runs counter to a half-century of industry

experience and audience conditioning and therefore demands an
extremely high level of support and guidance during this
formative era seems to trouble neither the cable leaders nor the
Commission.[43]

The history of public access channels in New York City reveals some of the problems. As of July 1, 1971, the two cable companies operating in Manhattan were required by New York City franchising regulations to set aside two public access channels, one for sporadic or one-time users, the other for users who wish to reserve given time periods. New York enjoyed several unique advantages for its experiment with public access. New York is the home of several major foundations committed to supporting cable access as a worthwhile innovation in television. And the city also had, in Manhattan, a large number of cable subscribers, two healthy cable operators, and a cable audience with varied tastes who might support unorthodox programming. New York's other advantages included a unique range of cultural and artistic activities, and an unmatched presence of performers, program producers, and avant-garde video enthusiasts.

Yet, despite all these promising conditions for the development of viable access cablecasting, the first few years of experience in New York call into question the worth of the entire cable access venture. Special publicity efforts by a private foundation were not successful in making the general public aware of the availability of the access channels.[44] Moreover, those who did use the channels were confronted by formidable organizational problems and expense. A 1972 analysis concluded that the access channels were not useful in reaching a general audience:

> *If a large, distributed audience is desired, public access channels*
> *are ineffective. Informing the potential audience of a program*
> *can be as expensive as the production itself. Because public*
> *access channels will not reach broad audiences in the near*
> *future, they are not adequate substitutes for conventional*
> *television; they are not yet adequate as a forum for the*
> *presentation of competing views on controversial issues.*[45]

Instead, public access channels developed " as a kind of closed-circuit medium for internal communication within already established organizations."[46] Even regarding such narrow intra-group communication, the study found that costs and organizational requirements limited the usefulness of the access channels to groups with resources or foundation backing. "Disenfranchised groups," the 1972 study emphasized, "will find that production barriers and difficulties in developing a viewer constituency are often as great as difficulties in obtaining access."[47]

A useful follow-up study published in 1973 by the Fund for the City of New York provides an overview of the first two years of open access by cable in Manhattan.[48] In the first year, some 650 hours of original programming were shown over Manhattan's public access channels. By June 1973, use had grown to about 500 hours per month, an average of over 16 hours per day.[49] Most of these programs were narrowly directed to geographical communities, providing information about community events and services, or perhaps the need for a traffic light at a specific intersection. Or else, they were designed to appeal to special interest groups, such as homosexuals or practitioners of transcendental meditation. A bewildering variety of other types of shows were also aired. These access programs tended to be produced either by use of one of the free studios supplied by the cable operators or by special suppliers of public access programming funded largely by foundations, such as the Ford or Markle Foundations, which have special interests in communications matters. A number of organizations found production of access programs to be a useful adjunct to their more general activities. Unions, religious groups, organizations for the deaf, neighborhood councils, and others used public access to communicate with their members or to proselytize other cable viewers.

The two most significant problems with public access in Manhattan proved to be attracting audiences and financing. How many persons actually watch public access programming in Manhattan remains a mystery. Audience measuring has been neglected and even resisted by access users because they feel that public access should not be concerned with audience size in the manner of commercial broadcasting. Shows seeking audience feedback have had little or no response. However, a random survey of 250 cable subscribers undertaken by the 1973 study revealed that 30 percent knew what public access is, 20 percent reported that they watched access programming occasionally, and about 5 percent claimed to watch it regularly. The survey found that public viewing of access programming was spontaneous and haphazard; most subscribers did not know what programs were scheduled for the access channels.

Financing programs for public access is an unresolved problem in Manhattan. The study estimated that over $1 million was spent on access programming in the first two years, and that 60 percent of the money was supplied by foundations.[50] Much of this foundation support will not be forthcoming in the future. Cable operators in general are hard-pressed financially, and cannot be expected to support public access programming, beyond the rather spare studio facilities that they are required to make available.

Nor are the problems of financing and audience apathy limited to the Manhattan area. The same two general problems are the greatest obstacles to cable access programming everywhere.[51] In Seattle, an advocate of access actually accused the city council of engaging in a subterfuge by authorizing a no-charge public access channel without subsidizing the costs of access programming:

> In its infant stages, then, public access demands legislative prodding and public funding if it is to be more than an empty promise to Seattle's citizens.[52]

And in Canada, where cable television developed earlier and has far greater penetration, two studies have found no measurable audience for public access programs.[53] By contrast, several Canadian cable systems have had considerable success in drawing viewers to the systems' own originated programs.

The FCC recognizes the problem of financing for public access channels, but, in 1974, it clearly stated that it would not impose the financial burdens of supporting public access on operators:

> We envision this access program as an opportunity for a multiplicity of persons and groups to become active in the use of the communications media for the first time. For access channels to work the individuals and groups being offered access must design their own programs, develop their own resources, and foster the use and value of the channels. This is not accomplished by demanding that the cable operator, having provided the free channels, should now also pay to program the channels. An unfortunate misconception seems to have developed because of some over-expectations at the prospect of free access channels. Demands are being made not only for excessive amounts of free equipment but also free programming and engineering personnel to man the equipment. Cable subscribers are being asked to subsidize the local school system, govern-

ment, and access groups. This was not our intent and may, in fact, hamper our efforts at fostering cable technology on a nationwide scale. Too often these extra equipment and person- nel demands become franchise bargaining chips rather than serious community access efforts. We are very hopeful that our access experiment will work. We recognize the difficulties inherent in developing access programming and will have more to say on the subject later. We do not think, however, that simply putting more demands on the cable operator will make public access a success. Access will only work, we suspect, when the rest of the community assumes its responsibility to use the opportunity it has been provided.[54]

Such financing uncertainties are likely to have two major effects on the nature of public access programming. Ambitious and imaginative access programming probably will become the preserve of organized interest groups that can use access to further their general aims. Unaffiliated persons and groups without cohesion or resources may not be able to produce imaginative programming. Both lack of predictable audiences and current failure to publicize access programs make financing even more difficult.

The remaining access channels, those set aside for educational institutions, local government, and leased programming, have also failed to live up to hopes of significant use. As of 1974, the Commission found that the educational channel was used only infrequently. One cable operator described the situation: "Cable is tremendously intriguing at the university when it starts. But it's work, takes time and effort to put together a meaningful program; and there's not much audience, and they lose enthusiasm."[55]

The 1973 study of Manhattan's access channels found that the two channels set aside for use by municipal government remained virtually unused. Critics blame limited cable penetration throughout Manhattan for the city's failure to initiate training programming for the police and fire departments. But, in addition to the difficulties caused by cable's selective penetration, the study indicates that an absence of both money and imaginative leadership has affected use of the municipal access channels.[56] Thus, even local government, an organized beneficiary of special access rights having great interest in communicating with special constituencies and with the general public, has failed to take advantage of an access opportunity specially designated for its use.

Nor are neglect, lack of adequate financing, and failure to draw audiences the only problems that have surfaced. One additional problem area is restrictive regulation of access programming by the cable operator. Although the Fairness Doctrine, the personal attack and political editorializing rules, and the equal opportunities requirements apply generally to cablecasts in the same manner as to broadcasts,[57] the access channels are relieved of these regulations because open access is thought to make these requirements redundant.[58] However, other restrictions do apply to access programming. Cable systems may not transmit access programs (except on the local government channel) that present advertising material for products or political candidates, lottery information, or obscene or indecent matter.[59] Persons or groups presenting access programming must be identified. Moreover, the liability of cable operators for libel has been a source of concern. The Commission has tried to dispel this concern by pointing to the *Rosenbloom* rule and arguing that malice could not be imputed to cable operators for programming over which they lack content control. The Commission has also suggested that any state law holding a cable system liable civilly or criminally for access programming "may unconstitutionally frustrate Federal purposes,"[60] and it has invited Congress to pass legislation protecting system operators. But the Commission's efforts to relieve fears of defamation liability have not been successful. The *Gertz* holding substitutes a standard of some degree of fault in the place of malice as the requisite for "private defamations" and this will undoubtedly add to cable operators' concerns. Moreover, cable operators show as much concern over the expense of defending lawsuits as they do over the fear of losing them. These uncertainties and fears, along with responsibilities for some control over access programming imposed by the Commission, have led cable operators to impose prescreening requirements, indemnification agreements, and other potentially restrictive controls. It has been suggested that it is in the cable operator's economic interest to discourage access programming because such programming reduces the system's audience for channels that provide advertising income, involves administrative and studio expenses, and may offend the system's subscribers.[61] A series of shows on a New York City access channel, for example, emphasized nudity and sexual aberrations, but it is hard to know whether this stimulated or discouraged additional subscriptions. To date, no legal challenges to the cable system have been undertaken. What conclusions can be drawn from this combination of neglect, lack of financing, failure to draw audiences, and operator suspicion that appears to have characterized the first few years of access to cable television? A basic lesson is the inadequacy of focusing only on the legal definition of access rights. The rights of access applied to cable television are the broadest rights of access found in the law of mass communications. Yet, even these broad legal rights have not solved the related problems of drawing audiences and financing attractive programming. With respect to broader evaluation, the Manhattan study cautions against judging the effectiveness of the cable access channels at this point: "The temptation to try to develop a cost-benefit analysis must be resisted at this point. One can scarcely evaluate the effectiveness of a half-built bridge over a river."[62] And a more comprehensive study of cable access concludes: "The overriding conclusion . . . has to be that the only major block to the vitality [of public access cable television] is ignorance of that idea's existence."[63] Yet, some observers have ventured strong negative opinions. Martin Mayer, reflecting on the cable experience in his popular study *About Television*, has written:

> [A]ccess to media *means nothing at all. . . . Access to* audience *might have some value. . . . [B]ut access to audience must be earned, with talent. There is something bittersweet funny about the sight of all these groups of ardent young lawyers and graduate students and junior executives at foundations, none of whom can write a song anyone would sing or a book anyone would read or a play anyone would act, none of whom holds a position which gives his thought significance in the lives of others or could gather twenty-five people to hear him speak at a meeting—"demanding" access to the great audience of an entertainment medium.*[64]

This rather savage appraisal points to a basic distinction between access to cable television and access to traditional broadcasting. A cable system offers a *spectrum* of communications services, whereas a broadcaster has only a single *channel* of communications. As Professor Le Duc has pointed out, access means something altogether different in these different settings. In the context of traditional broadcasting, an access obligation consumes an unreclaimable portion of the finite time available for generating revenues, tends to reduce the audience for subsequent programming (further reducing revenues), and, in effect, piggybacks on the mass audience drawing power of the broadcaster's regular programming. Thus, the chilling effects of contingent access obligations are severe for broadcasters. In traditional broadcasting, the access user seeks an audience who is not drawn to his or her message and not even aware in advance that the access message is coming. Moreover, an access demand upon a broadcaster interferes with a medium in which the broadcaster has general responsibility for content and some justifiable interest in editorial autonomy.

The special access rules developed for cable television are different. Because they are not contingent, cable access obligations do not inhibit other programming. Of course, public access is expensive. However, since the cable operator sells a spectrum of communications, an obligation to light up a channel for public access may increase the operator's revenues from subscribers. This is especially true when lewd programming is presented, and large audiences are drawn for which the the operator would rather not be responsible. Aside from the cost of lighting up the access channel, the operator loses revenue if public access reduces the audience for other channels in which the operator has a special interest, either through advertising revenues or pay-television. Moreover, the cable access user is not piggybacking on the mass audience created through other programming to the same extent as someone who demands access to traditional broadcasting.[65] Finally, no issue of the operator's editorial autonomy is involved.

These differences do not necessarily mean that the public access rules developed for cable are sensible as a matter of policy. Access channels cost something to transmit, as do the limited obligations imposed on cable operators to maintain studios for the public and to underwrite certain costs of producing access programs. It is an open question, at this point, whether the values of access cablecasting are worth even these relatively modest costs. However, the First Amendment "costs" of access in the context of traditional broadcasting—chilling effects, invasion of editorial responsibility, imposition on a mass audience "earned" by the broadcaster—are negligible for special access channels in a cable television system.

Cable television raises additional questions that pertain to this general study of media access and that go beyond the special access channels. For one thing, because of its nonaccess channels, cable is also subject to traditional acess rules under the Fairness Doctrine and the equal opportunities requirement of section 315(a). Whether this is sensible is a provocative question. More broadly, the physical and economic aspects of cable call into question the theoretical basis of our entire system of radio and television regulation, including the public trustee concept, which has been the foundation of the Fairness Doctrine.

The FCC has treated programming originated by cable operators as it has treated conventional broadcasts with respect to equal opportunities and fairness requirements.[66] The Commission's theory was that, unlike programs on the access channels, original programming is under the operator's control and, therefore, public trustee obligations should apply. However, the Commission has made a fascinating exception for cable transmission of printed material:

> The American Newspaper Publishers Association has urged that we add a new section to make clear that our requirements as to equal time for political candidates, the Fairness Doctrine, political editorials and personal attacks, advertising, and sponsorship identification are not applicable to the dissemination of newspapers. We agree with the thrust of this petition that we did not intend to apply these requirements to the distribution of printed newspapers to their subscribers by way of cable.[67]

This exception surely is sound. If a newspaper is delivered via facsimile reproduction over a cable system, rather than by a newsboy, the difference in delivery mechanism hardly seems an appropriate basis for a fundamental change in legal status. But the lifting of Fairness Doctrine constraints on cable delivery of newspapers, like many exceptions, casts doubt on the general rule. Cable operators have used originating channels to disseminate teleprinter type from the wire-services or even from best-selling books. Should this presentation of printed matter be exempted from the Fairness Doctrine? If so, are we in the position of the child who can spell "banana" but doesn't know where to stop? Where does the electronic dissemination of printed matter, which is not subject to the Fairness Doctrine, end, and where do the normal types of television programming, which are covered by the Fairness Doctrine, begin? To make the answer dependent on whether something other than words appears on the viewer's screen seems formalistic. Why should reading a newspaper or book over the air justify an imposition of Fairness Doctrine constraints any more than teletyping the words on the screen? Almost all television programming emanates from printed scripts. The distinction between print media and cable television is hard to identify once it is conceded that, in disseminating newspapers or books in facsimile or teletype form, cable television is to be treated as a print medium not subject to the traditional regime of broadcast regulation.

The same coalescing of electronic and print media suggested by the above example can be seen deductively, by testing the premises of broadcast regulation against the physical nature of cable. Certainly the most widely accepted justification for imposing public trustee responsibilities on broadcasters, and the one embraced by the Supreme Court in *Red Lion*, is the scarcity of frequencies. This includes the notion of physical limits on available broadcast channels, scarcity in relation to demand, and a consequent need for government allocation in accordance with the public interest.[68] But whatever the dubious underpinnings of this scarcity as a rationale for distinguishing the broadcast spectrum from other scarce economic resources in terms of regulatory consequences, the emergence of cable has put an end to the notion that television frequencies are scarce by nature in any special physical or economic sense.[69] With cable, it is physically feasible to transmit a virtually infinite number of channels to any location through the proliferation of coaxial cables and receivers. With available cable technology, the number of television channels that any home can receive is limited only by economics—the costs of capital investment in cable systems and receivers in relation to the return from subscribers and advertisers. The reasons for the scarcity of television channels thus coincide with the reasons for the scarcity of newspapers. If scarcity in the newspaper industry and in television have similar roots, then the question is: Should the two media be brought under the same First Amendment regime with respect to the Fairness Doctrine, equal opportunities requirements, and related access obligations?

The conclusion of two influential commissions, one public and one private, that have studied the legal and policy implications of cable television is that the advent of cable requires a rethinking of our law's basic approach to electronic media and a challenge to the tradition of disparate First Amendment regimes for print and electronic media. The Sloan Commission on Cable Communications concluded:

> *Cable television, by freeing television from the limitations of radiated electro-magnetic waves, creates for television as a whole a situation more nearly analogous to that of the press. . . .*

> [T]he copiousness of cable television makes it possible to
> conceive of far broader access to its channels by competing
> entrepreneurs and hence opens up the possibilities of a far
> broader expression of opinion.[70]

The Cabinet Committee on Cable Communications also believed that

> [C]able development has the potential of creating an electronic
> medium of communications more diverse, more pluralistic, and
> more open, more like the print and film media, than our present
> broadcast system. . . . Cable would offer unfettered access for
> those who wish to use its channels to promote their ideas, state
> their views, or sell their goods and services; and the cable custo-
> mer would have the freedom to pick and choose from among a
> diverse range of entertainment, information, and services.[71]

The future of access to cable television depends upon the future
development of this novel medium. In attempting to assess the
significance of cable to the law of broadcast regulation, we are
doomed, in the words of the old Chinese curse, to live in a time of
transition.[72] Even this tentative review of access to cable television,
however, has led us full circle. These chapters devoted to radio and
television began with some rather academic questions about the
long-accepted notion that the electronic media's special features
justify a legal status different from the print media, a difference that
centers on access questions but permeates the constitutional status of
these two branches of the mass communications media. The
emergence of cable television makes these questions stark and
compelling. Our review of the place of access in radio and television
law thus leads irresistibly back to the problem of access and public
trustee obligations for newspapers and other forms of the print
media.

PART IV

THE *MIAMI HERALD*
DECISION AND
THE FUTURE OF ACCESS

During June 1974, the case of *Miami Herald Publishing Co.* v. *Tornillo*[1] gave the Supreme Court an opportunity to consider the constitutionality of a statute providing a right of access to newspapers. The issue was unprecedented. However, other access questions had previously been before the Court in defamation cases, in radio and television Fairness Doctrine decisions, in several antitrust cases, and in cases testing rights to expression in public forums. The public forum cases, in particular, had produced an impressive body of lower federal and state court precedents, including several decisions dealing directly with the question of access to print media. Thus, the stage was set for consideration of access in the perspective of recent controversial developments in First Amendment law. Would expansion of the press' freedom from defamation liability justify access rights because such expansion had diminished legal protection of the individual? Would the *Miami Herald* decision make clear whether the First Amendment should apply to print and electronic media in a unitary or differential fashion? Would trends toward media concentration and doubts about the objectivity and diversity of modern journalism undermine the First Amendment's premise of an active and open marketplace of ideas? And, overall, how would the Court review legislative efforts to guarantee access to the print media with virtually no historical experience or direct precedent?

Those who hoped that the *Miami Herald* decision would explicate these and other important issues must have been disappointed by the Supreme Court's rudimentary treatment of the case. The Court announced a seemingly unqualified position on enforced access to newspapers: enforced access violates the First Amendment because it penalizes newspapers, inhibits criticism of public officials, and intrudes on the editorial function. However, on analysis, the Court's treatment leaves almost as many constitutional questions unresolved as answered.

The concluding part of this book will discuss the Supreme Court's decision in *Miami Herald,* examine the justifications that the Court offered, and explore how this decision relates to First Amendment law generally. Then, discussion will turn to the implications of *Miami Herald* for other access issues not directly dealt with in the case, such as access for advertising or access obligations for radio and television under the Fairness Doctrine. The book concludes by considering the extent of mass media's freedom from legal access obligations and by offering some thoughts about the responsible exercise of this freedom by the press.

Miami Herald Publishing Co. v. Tornillo

*Those freedoms which are neither challenged nor defined are
the most secure. . . . The conflict and contention by which we
extend freedom seem to mark, or at least to threaten, a con-
traction; and in truth they do, for they endanger an assumed
freedom, which appeared limitless because its limits were untried.
Appearance and reality are nearly one. We extend the legal
reality of freedom at some cost in its limitless appearance. And
the cost is real.*

Alexander M. Bickel[1]

Few cases involving freedom of the press have generated more
interest in advance of Supreme Court review than did the *Miami
Herald* case. The Florida Supreme Court's decision that a statute
granting access to newspapers was constitutional made the case seem
almost like an academic invention designed to pose basic questions of
First Amendment theory. The case did not call simply for reviewing
the comparative constitutional status of broadcast and print media.
Another issue was whether the Supreme Court would view the First
Amendment's guarantee of freedom of the press as an instrumental
policy favoring maximum diversity of expression or as a general
guarantee of autonomy from government regulation. It was fascinating to speculate how traditional First Amendment approaches might
apply to this novel setting. A common element in many established
doctrines was that challenged official action had the design or effect
of suppressing speech. Some of these doctrines were the doctrine

that expression may be prohibited if it creates a clear and present danger, the doctrine that interests in expression should be balanced against and should sometimes give way to countervailing social interests calling for suppression, the doctrine that certain categories of speech (obscenity, for example, or "fighting words") should be deemed outside First Amendment protection, and the doctrine that prior restraints on expression are especially obnoxious. Yet, the purpose of the Florida statute was to increase expression. Thus, established First Amendment doctrines did not seem to provide an adequate framework for analysis of the *Miami Herald* case. New theory, it appeared, would be forthcoming, no matter how the Court resolved the case.

The theoretical character of *Miami Herald* was reinforced by other circumstances as well. The Florida courts had totally ignored the facts of the case and had considered only the constitutionality of the statute in the most abstract and sweeping terms. As a result the statute came before the Supreme Court without the type of state court appraisal of concrete facts that tends to produce discriminating weighing of constitutional issues and offer possibilities for judgment on narrow grounds. Moreover, although the statute was a criminal prohibition, the validity of which would normally be asserted by the state Attorney General, state law enforcement authorities in this case had refused to enforce the statute or to argue its constitutionality. Instead, in a final push toward a broad theoretical posture, the argument for the statute's validity was advanced by a defeated political candidate, who was represented by the leading academic proponent of imposing broad access obligations on the mass media, Professor Jerome Barron. The case thus took on the dimensions of a wholesale test of Barron's access theories.

The Florida Proceedings

The Florida statute involved in *Miami Herald* granted a right of reply to political candidates attacked by newspapers:

Newspaper assailing candidate in an election; space for reply—*If any newspaper in its columns assails the personal character of any candidate for nomination or for election in any election, or charges said candidate with malfeasance or misfeasance in*

office, or otherwise attacks his official record, or gives to
another free space for such purpose, such newspaper shall upon
request of such candidate immediately publish free of cost any
reply he may make thereto in as conspicuous a place and in the
same kind of type as the matter that calls for such reply, pro-
vided the reply does not take up more space than the matter
replied to. Any person or firm failing to comply with the pro-
visions of this section shall be guilty of a misdemeanor of the
first degree, punishable as provided in § 775.082 or § 775.083.[2]

Curiously enough, although this statute had been in existence
since 1913, it had never been applied to any newspaper before the
Miami Herald case. In one previous case, brought in 1972, a trial
court judge had held the statute unconstitutional, and the state
Attorney General had refused to appeal because he also doubted the
statute's constitutionality.[3] So, as far as reported cases indicate,
Florida's right-to-reply statute existed only on the books.

This unenforced Florida misdemeanor provision became the basis
for a leading Supreme Court precedent as a result of a continuing
quarrel between the *Miami Herald* newspaper and Pat L. Tornillo, Jr.,
head of the Dade County Classroom Teachers' Association. During
1968, this association, a group of some 8,000 local public school
teachers, had participated in a statewide strike of public school
teachers. These events had involved Tornillo in civil and criminal
litigation under "no-strike" and other laws. In the fall of 1972,
Tornillo ran for the Democratic party nomination for the Florida
House of Representatives. The primary election was scheduled to
take place on October 3, 1972. On September 20, 1972, the *Miami
Herald* ran its first editorial concerning Tornillo's candidacy:

The State's Laws and Pat Tornillo

LOOK who's upholding the law!
Pat Tornillo, boss of the Classroom Teachers Association and
candidate for the State Legislature in the Oct. 3 runoff election,
has denounced his opponent as lacking "the knowledge to be a
legislator, as evidenced by his failure to file a list of contribu-
tions and expenditures of his campaign as required by law."
Czar Tornillo calls "violation of this law inexcusable."
This is the same Pat Tornillo who led the CTA strike from
February 19 to March 11, 1968, against the school children and
taxpayers of Dade County. Call it whatever you will, it was an

illegal act against the public interest and clearly prohibited by the statutes.

We cannot say it would be illegal but certainly it would be inexcusable of the voters if they sent Pat Tornillo to Tallahassee to occupy the seat for District 103 in the House of Representatives.

Tornillo responded on September 27 with the following letter to the *Herald**:

Pat Tornillo and the CTA Record

Five years ago, the teachers participated in a statewide walkout to protest deteriorating educational conditions.

Financing was inadequate then and we now face a financial crisis.

The Herald *told us what we did was illegal and that we should use legal processes instead. We are doing just that through legal and political action.*

My candidacy is an integral part of this process.

During the past four years:

—CTA brought suit to give Dade County its share of state money to relieve local taxpayers.

—CTA won a suit which gave public employees the right to collectively bargain.

—CTA won a suit which allowed the School Board to raise $7.8 million to air-condition schools and is helping to keep this money.

Unfortunately, the Herald *dwells on past history and ignores CTA's totally legal efforts of the past four years.*

We are proud of our record.

However, the reply was not published, and the *Herald* went after Tornillo with a second editorial blast on September 29, just four days before the primary election:

See Pat Run
[Picture of empty classroom]

FROM the people who brought you this—the teacher strike of '68—come now instructions on how to vote for responsible

---

*The Supreme Court's rendition of the facts, ironically enough, set out the newspaper's editorials but not Tornillo's replies.

government, i.e., against Crutcher Harrison and Ethel Beckham, for Pat Tornillo. The tracts and blurbs and bumper stickers pile up daily in teachers' school mailboxes amidst continuing pouts that the School Board should be delivering all this at your expense. The screeds say the strike is not an issue. We say maybe it wouldn't be were it not a part of a continuation of disregard of any and all laws the CTA might find aggravating.

Whether in defiance of zoning laws at CTA Towers, contracts and laws during the strike, and more recently state prohibitions against soliciting campaign funds amongst teachers, CTA says fie and try and sue us—what's good for CTA is good for CTA and that is natural law. Tornillo's law, maybe. For years now he has been kicking the public shin to call attention to his shake-down statesmanship. He and whichever acerbic prexy is in alleged office have always felt their private ventures so chock-full of public weal that we leap at the chance to nab the tab, be it half the Glorious Leader's salary or the dues checkoff or anything else except perhaps mileage on the staff hydrofoil. Give him public office, says Pat, and he will no doubt live by the Golden Rule. Our translation reads that as more gold and more rule.

The next day, Tornillo formally sought his statutory right of reply:

Editorial Reply

Since the Herald *has chosen to publicly attack my record, accomplishments, and positions on various issues, and those of the CTA, I again request that under Florida Statute 104.38, the* Herald *print the following record of affirmative and legal action.*

In 1968, CTA signed a no-strike affidavit.

In 1969, CTA filed and won a suit in the Supreme Court of Florida, which gives all public employees the right to bargain collectively without the right to strike.

In 1971, CTA filed the Tornillo suit, which enabled the School Board to receive $7.6 million and is presently cooperating with the Board in their effort to retain this money and avoid further financial chaos.

Since 1968, CTA has reimbursed the taxpayers of Dade County for the full salary and all fringe benefits of its President.

Since 1970, CTA has not used the school mail service to communicate with its members.

Since 1970, CTA has paid all costs of payroll deduction of dues for its members.

We have attempted to obey all the laws of the state, not intentionally violating any, while continuing our efforts to alert the public to the impending financial crisis facing the schools.

We have, however, also retained our belief in the right of public employees to engage in political activity and to support the candidate of our choice, as is the right of any citizen in this great country of ours.

Aye, there's the rub.

The *Herald* also refused to publish this reply and on October 1, Tornillo sued the *Herald*, seeking both damages and an injunction ordering the *Herald* to print this reply. On October 2, a county court judge entered an oral ruling that the reply statute was, on its face, an unconstitutional restraint on freedom of the press and, furthermore, the statute was unconstitutionally vague. The judge explained his ruling in a written opinion filed October 20.[4] He amalgamated statutes directing publication with those prohibiting publication, and, accordingly, struck down the reply statute because it did not protect "a substantial public interest threatened by a clear and present danger." He also declared why he felt that section 104.38 was unconstitutionally vague: "[n]o editor could know from the statute exactly what words would offend the statute or the scope of the reply intended to be mandated." Tornillo appealed. In the meantime, on October 3, he lost the primary election.

The Florida Supreme Court reversed the lower court ruling on July 10, 1973.[5] Because the trial court had held the reply statute unconstitutional on its face, the Florida Supreme Court made no mention of the specific facts of the case. Instead, it considered the reply statute at large and concluded that the statute served the essential governmental purpose of "maintaining conditions conducive to free and fair election."[6] This purpose, in the court's view, did not conflict with First Amendment principles: "[t]he entire concept of freedom of expression as seen by our founding fathers rests upon the necessity for a fully informed electorate."[7] Rather than inhibiting freedom of the press, the court asserted that the reply statute

is designed to add to the flow of information and ideas and does not constitute an incursion upon First Amendment rights or a prior restraint, since no specified newspaper content is ex-

cluded. There is nothing prohibited but rather it requires, in the interest of full and fair discussion, additional information.[8]

The court also justified the reply statute as a counterbalance to concentration of the mass media: "The First Amendment did not create a privileged class which through a monopoly of instruments of the newspaper industry would be able to deny to the people the freedom of expression."[9] Finally, the state court noted that the right of reply statute imposed the same obligation on newspapers that was already imposed on broadcasters under the personal attack rules, which *Red Lion* had held to be consistent with the First Amendment.

Having thus disposed of the basic First Amendment issues, the Florida Supreme Court also quickly dispensed with vagueness objections. The court emphasized that its duty was to interpret the reply statute so that all constitutional doubts would be resolved. However, the only portion it explicated was the term "any reply":

> [T]he mandate of the statute refers to "any reply" which is wholly responsive to the charge made in the editorial or other article in a newspaper being replied to and further that such reply will be neither libelous nor slanderous of the publication nor anyone else, nor vulgar nor profane.[10]

The Florida Supreme Court thus reversed the lower court's constitutional objections to the reply statute. However, because the *Herald* had reserved the right to enter nonconstitutional objections to the statute's application to the newspaper under the particular circumstance of the case, the Florida Supreme Court remanded the case back to the trial court for further proceedings.

The Supreme Court's Response

Assessment of the U.S. Supreme Court's action in *Miami Herald* can begin with the Court's election to decide the case. At best, the litigation reached the Court in a state of semi-ripeness: no state court had applied the Florida statute to the facts of the case. Both the trial court and the Florida Supreme Court had considered the reply statute on its face. Neither the *Herald* nor Tornillo had submitted anything in writing concerning possible nonconstitutional defenses. And, accordingly, the state courts had not really focused on whether a newspaper could trigger the statute by editorials, as opposed to straight news items, even though the statute was limited to attacks "in its columns." Moreover, no definition had been given to such phrases as "assails the personal character," "charges . . . with malfeasance or misfeasance in office," or "otherwise attacks his official record."

Counsel for Tornillo initially argued that Supreme Court review was inappropriate: The case was not a final judgment by the state courts because the *Herald* had refused to concede its nonconstitutional defenses. Affirmance by the Supreme Court, therefore, would have to result in a remand to the state courts for resolution of these claims. In short, state litigation had not run its course. In the end, the *Herald* might not have been obliged by the statute to print Tornillo's reply or pay him damages. An adequate state ground for decision having no constitutional overtones might have surfaced if all aspects of the dispute had been adjudicated, rather than just the constitutionality of the statute on its face.

Under the circumstances, the Supreme Court had several acceptable grounds for deferring constitutional review: the potentiality that the appellant might not be bound by state law in the end, the chance that vague terms in the statute might be given meaning during additional state litigation (and aid the consideration of federal constitutionality), and the possibility that an adequate and independent state ground for decision might emerge.

The rules of finality and ripeness-for-review, like other jurisdictional requisites, have been watered down during recent years until they have become little more than optional grounds on which the Supreme Court can decline to review a case. They gave the Court, in effect, a choice of either deciding the constitutionality of the Florida statute or remanding the case to the Florida courts and waiting for it, or another case, to present a concrete application of the statute on a full record. The Court's election to decide on the merits in *Miami Herald* suggests that it considered the constitutional issues to be too important for deferral and sufficiently clear that factual concreteness was not needed to aid analysis and decision. Thus, *Miami Herald* plays a counterpoint with the *DeFunis* v. *Odegaard*[11] decision of the same year, in which the Court, on questionable mootness grounds, declined to rule on whether the Fourteenth Amendment allowed preferential admission of racial minorities to a state law school.

After reaching out to embrace the access question, the Supreme Court was surprisingly apologetic in its decision in *Miami Herald.* Most constitutional decisions try to justify their result in terms of social utility, historical commitment to freedom, or both. But Chief Justice Burger, in his opinion for the Court, made a greater effort to describe the arguments favoring access guarantees than he did to refute them. The Chief Justice spoke sympathetically about the trend toward media concentration and the economic barriers to entering the communications industry that have fueled demands for access:

> *The result of these vast changes has been to place in a few hands the power to inform the American people and shape public opinion. Much of the editorial opinion and commentary that is printed is that of syndicated columnists distributed nationwide and, as a result, we are told, on national and world issues there tends to be a homogeneity of editorial opinion, commentary, and interpretative analysis. The abuses of bias and manipulative reportage are, likewise, said to be the result of the vast accumulations of unreviewable power in the modern media empires. In effect, it is claimed, the public has lost any ability to respond or to contribute in a meaningful way to the debate on issues. . . .*
>
> *The obvious solution, which was available to dissidents at an earlier time when entry into publishing was relatively inexpensive, today would be to have additional newspapers. But the same economic factors which have caused the disappearance of vast numbers of metropolitan newspapers, have made entry into the marketplace of ideas served by the print media almost impossible.*[12]

The opinion also pointed to statements in the *Asssociated Press* opinion that were congenial to access rights: "Freedom to publish means freedom for all and not for some. . . . Freedom of the press from governmental interference under the First Amendment does not sanction repression of that freedom by private interests." And, Burger also referred to the *Sullivan* decision and its recognition of a "profound national commitment to the principle that debate on public issues should be uninhibited, robust, and wide open."

Burger's response to these arguments favoring access was rather lame:

> *However much validity may be found in thesc arguments, at*

each point the implementation of a remedy such as an enforceable right of access necessarily calls for some mechanism, either governmental or consensual. If it is governmental coercion, this at once brings about a confrontation with the express provisions of the First Amendment and the judicial gloss on that amendment developed over the years. . . .

A responsible press is an undoubtedly desirable goal, but press responsibility is not mandated by the Constitution and like many other virtues it cannot be legislated.[13]

The Chief Justice's opinion for the Court enlisted two arguments to strike down the Florida statute. First, the opinion ruled that contingent access obligations of the sort contained in the Florida statute would impose a penalty on newspapers that published criticisms of political candidates, and thus cause a net reduction in public debate:

The Florida statute exacts a penalty on the basis of the content of a newspaper. The first phase of the penalty resulting from the compelled printing of a reply is exacted in terms of the cost in printing and composing time and materials and in taking up space that could be devoted to other material the newspaper may have preferred to print. It is correct, as appellee contends, that a newspaper is not subject to the finite technological limitations of time that confront a broadcaster but it is not correct to say that, as an economic reality, a newspaper can proceed to infinite expansion of its column space to accommodate the replies that a government agency determines or a statute commands the readers should have available.

Faced with the penalties that would accrue to any newspaper that published news or commentary arguably within the reach of the right-of-access statute, editors might well conclude that the safe course is to avoid controversy. Therefore, under the operation of the Florida statute, political and electoral coverage would be blunted or reduced. Government-enforced right of access inescapably "dampens the vigor and limits the variety of public debate.". . .[14]

This is a striking contrast to the Court's conclusion five years before in *Red Lion* that a right of reply to personal attack would enhance public debate, and that the claim of broadcasters that such reply rights would have a chilling effect was "at best speculative." Yet, the *Miami Herald* decision does not even cite *Red Lion,* much less explain the contradiction between the two Supreme Court views as to the chilling potential of contingent access rules.

Perhaps because the Court was aware of the inconsistency with *Red Lion*, it was careful not to rest its decision in *Miami Herald* on the chilling effect point alone:

> *Even if a newspaper would face no additional costs to comply with a compulsory access law and would not be forced to fore-go publication of news or opinion by the inclusion of a reply, the Florida statute fails to clear the barriers of the First Amendment because of its intrusion into the function of editors.*[15]

An opinion which brusquely rejects arguments that are obviously deemed to have merit normally relies on well-considered precedents that have already resolved the matter in question. So the *Miami Herald* opinion treated the issue of enforced access, but the precedents did not substantiate the claims made for them. The Chief Justice stated that "[t]he Court foresaw the problems relating to government enforced access as early as its decision in *Associated Press*." That decision, in a footnote to the statements quoted above, had stated:

> *It is argued that the decree interferes with freedom "to print as and how one's reason or one's interest dictates." The decree does not compel AP or its members to permit publication of anything which their "reason" tells them should not be published. It only provides that after their "reason" has permitted publication of news, they shall not, for their own financial advantage, unlawfully combine to limit its publication. The only compulsion to print which appears in the record is found in the By-Laws, previously set out, which compel members of the Association to print some AP news or subject themselves to fine or expulsion from membership in the Association.*[16]

However, a matter not presented for decision in *Associated Press*, and mentioned only in passing in a footnote, does not give much support to a claim of prior Supreme Court consideration of enforced access. Neither the *Lorain Journal* decision nor any other antitrust cases that have produced orders to publish ads, were mentioned in *Miami Herald*. The *Associated Press* footnote seems an unlikely foundation on which to erect a general constitutional principle governing access. Yet, the Chief Justice writes:

> *The clear implication has been that any such compulsion to publish that which " 'reason' tells them should not be published" is unconstitutional.*[17]

Other precedents that the Court relied on in the *Miami Herald* case also consist of passing references to matters not presented for decision. *Branzburg* v. *Hayes,* concerning whether journalists may maintain the confidentiality of sources in the face of grand jury subpoenas, is cited for the statement that the issues there "involve . . . no express or implied command that the press publish what it prefers to withhold."[18] In the same vein, *Pittsburgh Press,* which upheld an administrative order that a newspaper not segregate help-wanted ads by sex, is cited for a statement on a matter not at issue in the case:

> *Nor,* a fortiori, *does our decision authorize any restriction whatever, whether of content or layout, on stories or commentary originated by* Pittsburgh Press, *its columnists, or its contributors. On the contrary, we reaffirm unequivocally the protection offered to editorial judgment and to the free expression of views on these and other issues, however controversial.*[19]

Finally, *B.E.M.-DNC*, which concerned access to electronic media for advertising, is cited for this statement:

> *The power of a privately owned newspaper to advance its own political, social, and economic views is bounded by only two factors: first, the acceptance of a sufficient number of readers—and hence advertisers—to assure financial success; and, second, the journalistic integrity of its editors and publishers.*[20]

The *Miami Herald* opinion's inflated treatment of these decisions, none of which gave careful consideration to the question of enforced access to newspapers, is especially surprising since other relevant cases were either not discussed or were mentioned only in passing. As mentioned before, the Court failed even to cite *Red Lion*, which is the one Supreme Court decision sustaining guarantees of access to the electronic media. No discussion at all was offered of the divergent constitutional treatment of print and electronic media with respect to enforced access. Although the Court did cite the language of the *Rosenbloom* plurality opinion, which virtually invited creation of access rights, the significance of the defamation cases to access was not discussed, and the significance of the *Rosenbloom* statement was not elaborated. Moreover, no mention was made of any of the public forum cases, of the state action problem in the context of access to the media, or of the potential power of Congress to override the state-private distinction in imposing access guarantees (as it has sometimes done in cases of race discrimination). The *Miami Herald* opinion is as casual in its selection of cases discussed as in its analysis of those on which it relied.

In view of the small number of precedents offered in support, and the Court's sympathetic recitation of conditions that have created demands for guarantees of access, the Court's skimpy justification is certain to create doubts about the constitutional rule announced in *Miami Herald*. What is this "function of editors" that the First Amendment protects from "intrusion"? The Court considered it in two ways. One definition, drawn from the *Associated Press* footnote, considered access as "compelling editors or publishers to publish that which 'reason' tells them should not be published." The fact that 'reason' is set off in quotes within quotes calls attention to what is, in any event, a rather odd statement. Editors are not said simply to have a right to decide what goes in or out of a publication; they are said to have the right to do what their "reason" tells them to do. Are these prospective words of limitation? It is easy to think of cases in which an editor's decision not to publish might be regarded by a reviewing court or be categorized by statute as not based on "reason." For example, it is easy to distinguish between a refusal to accept an ad for anti-competitive reasons and an instance in which "reason" counsels against publication. Is the Court suggesting that access obligations might properly overcome "unreasonable" refusals to publish? Perhaps an editor's refusal to publish a correction of an established error of fact might also be judged as not based on "reason."

The Court's second description of the protected "function of editors," at the close of the opinion, is much broader:

The choice of material to go into a newspaper, and the decisions made as to limitations on the size and content of the paper, and treatment of public issues and public officials—whether fair or unfair—constitute the exercise of editorial control and judgment. It has yet to be demonstrated how governmental regulation of this crucial process can be exercised consistent

*with First Amendment guarantees of a free press as they have
evolved to this time.*[21]

This definition protects any choice to publish or not publish,
"whether fair or unfair." There is no hint here that only
"reasonable" editorial decisions are insulated from regulation. Thus,
the opinion of the Court offers two descriptions of the protected
editorial function that differ considerably in their implications for
future cases posing constitutional questions about enforced access.

The statements of three concurring Justices suggest that the future
may lie with the narrower of the two descriptions—that description
which limits editorial discretion to decisions based on "reason."
Justices Brennan and Rehnquist stated that they understood the
Court's opinion

> *addresses only "right of reply" statutes and implies no view
> upon the constitutionality of "retraction" statutes affording
> plaintiffs able to prove defamatory falsehoods a statutory action
> to require publication of a retraction.*[22]

These two justices obviously did not view *Miami Herald* as having
rejected all forms of enforced access to the print media.

Justice White also suggested a less-than-absolute view of the First
Amendment's protection of editorial autonomy:

> *Whatever power may reside in government to influence the
> publishing of certain narrowly circumscribed categories of
> material . . . we have never thought that the First Amendment
> permitted public officials to dictate to the press the contents of
> its news columns or the slant of its editorials.*[23]

That *Miami Herald* probably does not stand for absolute protection of the print media from all access obligations seems likely
when one reflects on the nature of the First Amendment principles
in other contexts. An absolutist view of the First Amendment,
championed by Justice Black in many vigorous opinions, has never
won a majority on the Court.[24] Even in the area of "the central
meaning of the First Amendment," which is criticism of the
governmental acts of public officials, there is no absolute protection
for expression. Inaccurate statements may be penalized under
defamation law, if the court finds that they have been published with

knowledge of falsity or reckless disregard for the truth. Perhaps the most stringent First Amendment guarantee applies to prior restraints. Yet, the Court's pronouncements on that subject state only that a prior restraint "carries a heavy burden of showing justification."[25] In other First Amendment contexts, such as use of public forums or subversive advocacy, the scope of constitutional protection varies. However, absolute First Amendment protection is never afforded.

From the perspective of First Amendment law generally, *Miami Herald* would be a stark and unexplained deviation if one were to read the decision as creating absolute prohibitions on access obligations. One would expect some rationalization in support of such a course if it were actually intended. The fact that the Court offers no discussion as to why First Amendment rules respecting access should be absolute, while all other rules emanating from that Amendment are relative, suggests that the principle of *Miami Herald* probably is destined for uncharted qualifications and exceptions.

If *Miami Herald* does not announce an absolute rule against enforced access, for what does it stand? How can one account for the absence of qualifications in the Court's opinion? One explanation might be that the Court was satisfied, in this first case involving access to a newspaper, to establish a general principle that the First Amendment contains a guarantee of publisher autonomy that is infringed upon by access obligations. Under this view, later cases would be left the task of defining the scope of the protection and when it could be surmounted by particular social objectives, or the goal of diversity of expression. This limited understanding of the decision seems reasonable, especially when one considers the character of most writing about access and certain earlier stages in the evolution of First Amendment theory.

Before the decade of the 1960s, First Amendment doctrine embodied the so-called "two-level theory" for categorizing protected and unprotected speech. Characteristic of this view is a statement by Justice Murphy writing for the Court in *Chaplinsky* v. *New Hampshire*:

> *There are certain well-defined and narrowly limited classes of speech, the prevention and punishment of which have never been thought to raise any Constitutional problem. These include the lewd and obscene, the profane, the libelous, and the insulting or "fighting" words.*[26]

The two-level theory defined certain categories of speech as outside

First Amendment protection. Libel was treated in this fashion before *Sullivan*,[27] as were obscenity,[28] and "fighting words."[29] The result of the two-level theory was to leave expression within certain defined categories subject to full legislative authority.

Although the two-level theory has largely been eradicated by decisions during the past two decades,[30] devotees of enforced access to the press advanced a roughly analogous claim in their writings. They argued vigorously that access guarantees, far from conflicting with the First Amendment, actually served First Amendment values. Professor Barron, the most enthusiastic proponent of access, even asserted that the First Amendment *required* courts to guarantee rights of access.[31] If his theory were generally accepted, then legislative power to declare and enforce access guarantees would not be hampered by the First Amendment.

The *Miami Herald* decision constitutes a firm rejection of the Barron thesis. This decision establishes that the First Amendment is not simply a barrier to preventing or punishing expression. The autonomy of the press—at least that part of it which the Court refers to as "the function of editors"—is also a guarantee of constitutional dimension.

Because the dominant theme of access literature differs so radically in its perspective, the Court may have been moved to convey unreservedly its message of publisher autonomy as a constitutional freedom. On this speculation, *Miami Herald* stands in relation to access guarantees roughly as the first part of *Sullivan* stands in relation to the traditional law of defamation. *Sullivan*, it will be recalled, contained two main doctrinal advances. First, it reversed the "two-level" doctrine that defamation was outside the protection of the First Amendment. Second, it formulated the scope of First Amendment protection for defamation of public officials. If the parallel with the first part of *Sullivan* is accurate, then *Miami Herald* has established that editorial autonomy is protected by the First Amendment. Later decisions will formulate the scope of the protection.

It seems plausible that the Supreme Court had its eye on the recent wave of writing about access. Professor Barron was counsel for Tornillo in the case, and his brief contained many references to his own writings. Moreover, the opinion of the Florida Supreme Court under review was a judicial endorsement of the most sweeping themes of Barron's writing. The curious procedural history of the case, in which both state courts dealt with the reply statute on its face and on wholesale grounds, may have led the Court to view the appeal as a vehicle for the treatment of access in its broadest ramifications. Finally, end-of-term pressures have become an increasingly serious problem for the Court in the management of its growing docket.[32] *Miami Herald* was handed down toward the end of June on what ordinarily would have been the final day of the term. In addition to the usual end-of-season rush, the Court was pressured by the upcoming appeal of the President in the Watergate tapes case, *Nixon v. United States*.[33] In view of all these circumstances, it is not surprising that the Supreme Court treated the problem of access in a general and truncated fashion.[34]

If this speculation about the meaning of *Miami Herald* is valid, access guarantees now hold roughly the same relation to the First Amendment as other types of regulation of expression. Sweeping access rights will not be approved. Narrow, specific access guarantees, designed to implement particular and weighty social objectives with the least possible jeopardy to editorial autonomy, may be upheld.

15

Conclusion:
Access, Autonomy, and the First Amendment

No lawyer worthy of the name can ever be truly a conservative or truly a radical: at one and the same time we must somehow devote ourselves to the preservation of tradition, which we don't greatly respect, and to the promotion of change, in which we do not greatly believe.

Grant Gilmore[1]

Despite the unprepossessing character of its analysis, the *Miami Herald* decision will probably be viewed as a landmark in First Amendment theory. *Miami Herald* is the first occasion the Court has had to suggest a guarantee of autonomy under the freedom of the press clause of the First Amendment. Although one holding is not a reliable indication of directions in constitutional doctrine—especially when that holding is so skimpy in its rationale—*Miami Herald* still may signify several important turns in First Amendment theory.

The Court's failure to accord any weight to the interest in diversity of expression, presumably protected by Florida statute, indicates the inadequacy of efforts to cast the First Amendment solely in instrumental terms. The Court sees a core of principle in the First Amendment from which it will not exact instrumental justification. In fact, the Court appears to share Justice Stewart's appraisal, in his concurring opinion in *B.E.M.–DNC,* of "the dangers that beset us when we lose sight of the First Amendment itself, and march forth in blind pursuit of its values." If this view of *Miami Herald* is warranted, the decision represents a judicial preference for

237

the principle of publisher autonomy over the competing policies of diversity of expression. Without fanfare and almost without an acknowledgment of what it was doing, the Court broke new ground when it declared that its decision was not necessarily based on assumptions of the "chilling effects" of Florida's reply statute.

Because the Court's opinion is so sparse, it is hard to predict whether other doctrinal innovations may result from its holding. However, one important possibility is that *Miami Herald* may mark the beginning of an interpretation of the "freedom of the press" clause that departs from the First Amendment's guarantee of freedom of speech. Such a reading was suggested by Justice Potter Stewart in a notable speech a few months after the *Miami Herald* decision:

> *It seems to me that the Court's approach to all these [the defamation, journalists' privilege,* Pentagon Papers, *and access decisions] has uniformly reflected its understanding that the Free Press guarantee is, in essence, a* structural *provision of the Constitution. Most of the other provisions in the Bill of Rights protect specific liberties or specific rights of individuals: freedom of speech, freedom of worship, the right to counsel, the privilege against compulsory self-incrimination, to name a few. In contrast, the Free Press Clause extends protection to an* institution. *The publishing business is, in short, the only organized private business that is given explicit constitutional protection.*
>
> *This basic understanding is essential, I think, to avoid an elementary error of constitutional law. It is tempting to suggest that freedom of the press means only that newspaper publishers are guaranteed freedom of expression. They* are *guaranteed that freedom, to be sure, but so are we all, because of the Free Speech Clause. If the Free Press guarantee meant no more than freedom of expression, it would be a constitutional redundancy. . . .*
>
> *It is also a mistake to suppose that the only purpose of the constitutional guarantee of a free press is to insure that a newspaper will serve as a neutral forum for debate, a "marketplace for ideas," a kind of Hyde Park corner for the community. A related theory sees the press as a neutral conduit of information between the people and their elected leaders. These theories, in my view, again give insufficient weight to the institutional autonomy of the press that it was the purpose of the Constitution to guarantee. . . .*

The primary purpose of the constitutional guarantee of a free press was . . . to create a fourth institution outside the Government as an additional check on the three official branches.[2]

Whether one considers Justice Stewart's thesis to be a sound rendition of First Amendment theory, it is clear that *Miami Herald* may point in that direction.[3] If so, doctrines of freedom of the press may increasingly center on the concept of publisher autonomy, becoming more like guarantees of religious liberty in theoretical content, while policies of diversity of expression and equality may have to find their primary outlet in the guarantee of freedom of speech.

Another basic question of First Amendment law raised by the *Miami Herald* decision is whether the constitutional status of radio and television is ripe for reconsideration. After *Red Lion,* many observers felt that the policies of enhancing diversity of expression, which provided one basis for the Court's approval of the personal attack rules, would also support an application of similar rules to newspapers. To recall the words of Professor Barron: "My point is that *Red Lion* is not just a broadcast case. It is a media case."[4] *Miami Herald* appears inconsistent with *Red Lion,* but it is not clear whether this inconsistency will be tolerated as a reflection of basic differences in the constitutional status of the print and electronic media, or whether the *Red Lion* rationale will be revised.

Other important questions for the future concern whether the guarantee of editorial autonomy established by *Miami Herald* leaves room for certain narrow types of access obligations. If so, what kinds of access obligations might conceivably be sustained? Rules of access might come from two sources. One source is legislation by Congress or state legislatures, including any rules of access declared by such administrative bodies as the FCC, which operate under legislative mandates. The other source is the First Amendment, through the implementing agency of the courts.

Access as a Constitutional Right

Even before the *Miami Herald* decision, it was difficult to conceive that a right to access to privately owned media could be premised solely on the First and Fourteeenth Amendments. There is no evidence that First Amendment tradition has ever reflected the idea of access as a constitutional right. Under established theory, a constitutional right of access would have to be premised on a finding of state action. With respect to government-owned or -operated media, access guarantees derived from the Constitution may be invoked if the government has no legitimate interest in exclusion. But the *Avins* decision indicated the readiness of courts to deny access and uphold the editorial autonomy of publications that are part of state institutions.[5] Even where access has been ordered, as in the school newspaper cases[6] or the state bar journal case,[7] this right has been given only to a member of the particular school community or professional group served by the publication. Moreover, these cases involved only a right to have advertisements accepted. The First Amendment has not required state media to subsidize the costs of an individual's public expression.

When constitutionally based access has been sought to media that are not governmental instrumentalities, the courts' responses have been predictable and sound. The courts uniformly have rejected claims that the privately owned print media should be treated as state action. Even the broadcast media, licensed by the government and subjected to rather pervasive administrative supervision, were found not to constitute state action. Clearly, the Supreme Court did not wish to impose on radio and television the inflexible rules of equal access that the First Amendment properly fastens on public places that have been opened to public expression. The *Miami Herald* decision reinforced the private status of the communications media. The notion of access as a constitutional right has called attention to the principles of liberty implicit in the state action limitation on the reach of constitutional obligations.[8]

An access right to private communications media guaranteed by the Constitution would argue for a version of the First Amendment having no support in historical understanding, in the constitutional text itself, or in the uniform holdings of courts that have considered the question. Even if a court could be persuaded to turn its back on these sources of principle, it would still face the problem of evaluating the desirability of access as a matter of public policy. This is not a task for the courts; enforced access raises not only questions of constitutional values, but also complex questions of fact that are ill-suited to judicial determination. If rights of access are to exist, they will do so through the legislative or administrative process.

Miami Herald and the Electronic Media

Perhaps the most important question raised, though not answered, by *Miami Herald* is whether that decision calls for a change in the legal status of radio and television with respect to access. In granting newspapers freedom from access obligations, the *Miami Herald* opinion made no effort to accommodate *Red Lion*'s denial of any such guarantee for broadcasters. Several reasons might account for the Court's failure even to mention *Red Lion*. Perhaps individual justices had developed different views of the problem of access to radio and television and elected not to surround their agreement about print media with individual statements about broadcast regulation. Also, the decision was handed down at the end of the Court's term during a time of immense pressure, and this too may have discouraged individual opinions. Or, some justices may have wished to postpone reconsideration of *Red Lion* in light of *Miami Herald*, especially those not on the Court when *Red Lion* was decided, to take account of lower courts' reflections on the problem, the possibility of new FCC approaches to the Fairness Doctrine, the reactions of commentators, and other sources of insight that ripen over time. Whatever the reasons, the Supreme Court's reticence in *Miami Herald* has left room for a wide range of speculation about the continuing validity of *Red Lion*.

At one extreme are those who argue that *Miami Herald* is simply irrelevant to broadcasting because constitutional decisions pertaining to the print media have no application to radio and television. Judge Tamm of the U.S. Court of Appeals for the District of Columbia Circuit asserted in the *Pensions* case:

> I cannot conclude that Tornillo *has any effect on the constitu-*
> *tionality of the Fairness Doctrine; I find the decisions "flatly*
> *consistent." Arguments advanced to the contrary are only*
> *reflective of broadcasters' desires to become indistinguishable*
> *from the print media and to be freed of their obligations as*
> *public trustees. While the relevancy of* Red Lion *was fully briefed*
> *in* Tornillo, *that decision contained no reference to* Red Lion *or*
> *to implications for the broadcast media. I read the Court's*
> *striking down a reply rule for newspapers in* Tornillo *after*
> *upholding a similar rule for broadcasters in* Red Lion *as demon-*
> *strating the Court's continuing recognition of the distinction*
> *between the two media, which is primarily manifested in the*

unique responsibilities of broadcasters as public trustees.[9]

The Commission has also put a similar argument to the D.C. Circuit Court of Appeals in responding to a challenge to the personal attack rules that relies in part on *Miami Herald*.[10] And, such a view was implicit in the Commission's failure to discuss the *Miami Herald* decision in its 1974 comprehensive report on the Fairness Doctrine, issued shortly after the Supreme Court's decision.[11]

At the other extreme, one may point to Justice Douglas' statement in *B.E.M.-DNC* that "TV and radio stand in the same protected position under the First Amendment as do newspapers and magazines."[12] Although Douglas took that position before *Miami Herald* was decided, he would no doubt have contended that the decision applied equally to both electronic and print media. A more sophisticated argument to the same effect has been advanced by Chief Judge Bazelon of the D.C. Circuit.[13]

Between these extremes are a variety of efforts to apply the lessons of *Miami Herald* to the law of broadcast regulation, without making print and electronic media constitutionally indistinguishable on critical issues of access and related fairness obligations. Judge Leventhal's opinion in *Pensions* represents such an effort.[14] Although he evidently felt that the Supreme Court in *Miami Herald* gave less than clear guidance, Leventhal tries to accommodate the Fairness Doctrine to *Miami Herald*'s teaching that contingent access obligations inhibit expression and invade editorial autonomy. He appears to read *Red Lion* essentially as upholding the notion of some administrative power to require programming in the interest of fairness, but little more. *Miami Herald*'s disapproval of the chilling effects of contingent access obligations and its concern to protect editorial discretion are injected into the Fairness Doctrine, in Leventhal's approach, by means of standards of review of broadcaster judgments which minimize FCC involvement in specific programming decisions. The FCC may not set aside broadcaster conclusions unless they are an abuse of reasonable judgment, while courts will give deference not to the administrative agency but to broadcasters. The recent *Straus* decision, dealing with the personal attack rules, suggests that this approach of strictly limiting the FCC's scope of review will govern future Fairness Doctrine cases, although two members of the D.C. Circuit, Judges Bazelon and Tamm, have already expressed disagreement.

Henry Geller has offered a different approach for applying the lessons of *Miami Herald* to broadcasting without rejecting *Red Lion* altogether. He would maintain the legal concept that broadcasters are public trustees with obligations to program in the public interest:

> [U]ntil we are ready to substitute a system which is not based upon the public trust concept, I believe we are stuck with the Fairness Doctrine and that we must learn how to live with it. That means we have to somehow minimize the problem of governmental intervention in broadcast journalism.[15]

Geller suggests that the FCC abandon both review of particular broadcasts and the notion of specific programming remedies for "unfair" broadcasts. Instead, he urges that the FCC review, at the time of license renewal, whether a broadcaster has operated in flagrant or reckless disregard of fairness obligations. If access obligations are to be imposed on broadcasters, then Geller argues for an "open time" approach, under which a particular period would be open on a nondiscriminatory basis "to all those who wish to put on a contrasting viewpoint to the broadcaster's other programming." This type of access, he contends, would minimize official interference with specific editorial judgments.

How *Miami Herald* will affect the law of broadcast regulation in general, and *Red Lion* in particular, is an august question for the future. The answer will probably come from the Supreme Court, unless Congress steps in with a basic reform of the Communications Act, a most unlikely prospect.

If the general pattern of First Amendment law is followed, we can neither expect the two branches of the communications media to be joined in a unitary body of constitutional principles, nor can we expect the constitutional status of one branch to be cleanly divorced from that of the other branch. The differences in the legal and economic situations of the two types of mass media are too great for undifferentiated constitutional treatment, yet the similarities in function will not allow total separation. Instead, First Amendment law concerning the print and broadcast media is likely to maintain a tension between symmetry and divergence, a reflection in this area of the balance between the general and the particular that gives the First Amendment its power and resiliency.

Thus, *Miami Herald* probably will not apply to the electronic media in any mechanical, total way. But its underlying principles will have force in the law of broadcasting to the extent that they are consistent with the precepts of the Communications Act and the nature of broadcasting. The two grounds for decision in *Miami Herald* were the chilling effects of contingent access rights and the editorial autonomy of newspapers. How those different bases for judgment are applied to broadcasting will have implications that transcend the problem of access obligations.

In terms of both Congress' clear intent in the Communications Act and the leading judicial precedents concerning broadcasting and the First Amendment, the chilling effect rationale of *Miami Herald* should apply similarly to radio and television as to newspapers. The Act expressly withdraws "any power of censorship" from the FCC and prohibits interference "with the right of free speech by means of radio communication."[16] Many Commission and judicial decisions have pointed to the preeminent value of diversity of expression over the air. Along with *Red Lion,* the decision most often cited in the Commission's Fairness Doctrine pronouncements is *New York Times* v. *Sullivan,* with its commitment to "robust, uninhibited, and wide-open" public debate. And *Red Lion* itself upheld the personal attack reply rules by reference to the paramount First Amendment rights of the viewers and listeners. The assumption was that such rights of reply encouraged rather than discouraged expression. Arguments in *Red Lion* that such reply rights might actually chill expression got lost among the sweeping contentions of some broadcasters that their programming was immune from regulation in the public interest. Meanwhile, the Court dismissed the chilling effect potential as speculative.

But it is hard to see how the chilling effect challenge to the personal attack rules can be dismissed after *Miami Herald.* The assumption of the Commission and of the Court in *Red Lion,* that such reply rights enhance diversity of expression, has been reversed. If the personal attack rules are viewed as inhibiting expression, then they run counter to the instrumental policy of encouraging diversity of expression that *Red Lion* held to be the essence of the First Amendment as applied to broadcasting.

If such contingent access rights continue to be sustained for broadcasting, despite the chilling effect assumption of *Miami Herald,* it can only be on the theory that inhibitions of expression of the kind that the First Amendment bars for print media are permissible for radio and television. Such a theory would invite a new First Amendment approach to the electronic media. Diversity of expression for listeners and viewers (the First Amendment's dominant goal in broadcasting according to *Red Lion*) could not be the basis for continued approval. Rather, rights of reply in broadcasting would have to rest on the notion that regulation of the content of expression, including inhibition of certain types of expression, is permitted for broadcasting though it is not for print media. This would be a significant departure. In place of a First Amendment that allows government to enhance the quantity and variety of expression in broadcasting, we would have a First Amendment that allows restriction of the type and quality of expression over the air. Such a development in First Amendment theory would have large significance across the entire range of problems of free expression in broadcasting, from obscenity and indecency to libel, as well as a central impact on fairness questions.

The second pronouncement of the *Miami Herald* decision, that newspapers enjoy a guarantee of editorial autonomy under the First Amendment, will probably not have much effect on the constitutional status of radio and television, although it will reinforce existing trends in the interpretation of the Communications Act. In *B.E.M.-DNC*, the Supreme Court had already found the editorial freedom of broadcasters to be a prime concern of the Communications Act. *Miami Herald* simply supports this reading. The courts routinely read constitutional values into such broadly worded statutes as the Communications Act. It is quite possible that future holdings may eventually establish, under the "public interest" standard of the Communications Act, a degree of autonomy for broadcasters from FCC program-by-program review that will resemble the constitutional autonomy guaranteed to print publications in *Miami Herald*.

However, *B.E.M.-DNC* did not undercut the public trustee concept that is the foundation of the Communications Act's licensing system. Moreover, nothing in *Miami Herald* suggests that the Supreme Court will grant broadcasters the constitutional autonomy enjoyed by publishers. The public trustee concept is virtually inevitable in a system of non-market allocation of valuable temporary rights in the spectrum. If electronic mass media are ever to enjoy the constitutional autonomy of the print media, it will be because new communications technologies make obsolete the system of spectrum allocation we have had since the Radio Act of 1927.

Access to Print Media

With respect to enforced access to the print media, the major constitutional question for the future is whether *Miami Herald* establishes a First Amendment prohibition on all rights of access, no matter what is required to be published or why. As indicated in the preceding chapter, the Supreme Court will probably adopt a skeptical, but not wholly resistant, attitude to access statutes. *Miami Herald* indicates that sweeping access obligations, designed to foster notions of equality or fairness to the public through completeness of public discussion, will definitely be rejected. Such access obligations would have destructive implications for the preservation of press autonomy. Moreover, because *Miami Herald* recognized First Amendment protection of editorial autonomy, any access guarantee requiring official editorial supervision will not be upheld. For example, the Fairness Doctrine as it has developed in broadcast regulation could not be imposed on print media. However, if the pattern of First Amendment adjudication in other areas is followed, one can expect that narrowly drawn access requirements, designed to achieve specific legislative policies, will have a good chance of surviving judicial review. Narrowly drawn access statutes might be upheld as remedies for victims of defamation or antitrust violations, or as an incident of the broad legislative power to regulate advertising.

The idea that publishing a retraction partially eases the sting of libel is an old notion. For many years, a number of states have attached significant legal consequences to the publication of a retraction. Wisconsin, for example, requires that a demand for retraction precede a libel action and provides that publication of the retraction bars any claim for punitive damages.[17] A number of other states also have statutes which bar punitive damages if a retraction is published. These and similar statutes do not require publication of a retraction. However, they do substantially reduce the risk involved for a publication sued for libel.

Before the 1960s, when the controversy over broad rights of access surfaced, proposals had been advanced for compulsory publication of retractions as either a substitute for a judicial determination of libel, or a remedy subsequent to such a determination. The narrowest proposal of this kind would have allowed a person defamed in the traditional sense—that is, whose reputation was damaged by a false statement of fact—to bring an action for a vindication of reputation.[18] If defamation were established in a judicial proceeding, the court would enter a judgment to that effect, and the defendant publication would be required to publish the judgment. Proof of malice toward public officials under *Sullivan* or negligence toward private persons under *Gertz* would not be required to gain judgment and compulsory publication.

Broader statutes granting a right of reply to persons mentioned in any fashion are common in Europe. However, the only comparable law in the United States was a Nevada statute repealed in 1969.[19] Countries having some variant of such a broad reply law include France, Germany, Norway, Hungary, Austria, Japan, and several South American and African countries.[20] Although these broad laws survived a lengthy analysis by the esteemed First Amendment scholar Zachariah Chafee without being considered unconstitutional,[21] the Court's decision in *Miami Herald* indicates that such statutes would not be sustained here in the United States.

Sullivan and its successors generated concern that the constitutional equilibrium between freedom of the press and the rights of individuals had been tilted unfairly in favor of the press. Some have urged implementation of a right to vindication through mandatory publication of a retraction as a means of counteracting this effect. This narrow form of access, triggered by a judicial finding of a false and damaging statement of act, does not appear to be a significant intrusion on editorial autonomy. The burden of proving defamation should be on the person seeking vindication. The court's determination would eliminate any question of vagueness, and limiting the access obligation to defamation would reduce the occasions for mandatory publication to a minimum. If protecting the reputations of individuals is a substantial enough social interest to justify recovery of damages for negligent or reckless defamations, it should also be sufficient to uphold the minimal intrusion into editorial autonomy of a judicially enforced right of vindication. *Miami Herald* should not be regarded as a bar to mandatory publication of retractions in cases where defamation has been established.

Antitrust is the other area of law which suggests that narrow access guarantees might possibly be sustained. Legislation designed to remedy refusals to deal could require a publication which accepts ads from certain enterprises to accept ads from others in the same business. It is doubtful that *Miami Herald* would bar such legislation.

An opinion that relies on the leading precedent holding the press subject to the antitrust laws, *Associated Press,* should not be thought to reverse by implication other leading antitrust decisions, such as *Lorain Journal*, which support access as a remedy for anticompetitive behavior. Any such statute should provide that publishers may refuse commercial ads that they disapprove of for other than noncompetitive or capricious reasons. No statute should be sustained that flatly requires a publisher to accept all ads for any general activity. For example, a publisher who accepts an ad for a Walt Disney movie should not be required to run an ad for an X-rated film. When one conceives of all the legimate reasons publishers might object to particular films—violence, crime, fascism, socialism, atheism, and religion, the list is almost endless—one can see the narrow focus that would be required for an acceptable access statute dealing with commercial advertising. Any publisher disapproval conceivably relating to the substance of an ad or the activity of the advertiser should be protected.

The Supreme Judicial Court of Massachusetts recently upheld the right of the *Boston Globe* to refuse an ad for an escort service.[22] The court held that it could not judge a trade practice to be unfair, nor could it decide that a refusal to deal violated antitrust laws, unless there was evidence "of a purpose or motive either to exclude a person or group from the market or to accomplish some other anticompetitive objective."[23] To similar effect, the Federal Trade Commission has held that a newspaper may properly refuse an ad when "acting in accord with the exercise of its own independent judgment and not in concert with others."[24] Any broader obligation to accept commercial ads would entail serious constitutional questions. Nevertheless, there is room for a narrow access statute aimed at anticompetitive refusals to deal that would not impinge upon legitimate publisher autonomy.

Although a narrow, contingent access statute of this type dealing with commercial advertising might be sustained, there is much reason to doubt the constitutionality of a similar access obligation aimed at political ads. A contingent access requirement applicable to political advertising is dubious on policy and constitutional grounds. Contingent access proposals requiring newspapers and magazines to sell advertising space to all candidates for an office, if they sell to any candidate, have been advanced recently on both federal and state levels. During debates on the Federal Election Campaign Act of 1971,[25] the House Judiciary Committee recommended a provision of this kind that would apply to candidates for federal office.[26] The bill also would have required newspapers and magazines to charge the lowest unit rate for political advertising.[27] The House passed this provision,[28] and a Senate version, applicable only to the broadcast media, became law.[29]

Two similar proposals in the Massachusetts Legislature were considered by the Supreme Judicial Court of Massachusetts under that state's unusual procedure which allows the highest court to issue an advisory opinion on legislative proposals. The Massachusetts Court ruled that such a contingent access requirement for political advertising was a violation of the First Amendment.[30]

It seems likely that the Supreme Court would follow the Massachusetts ruling and strike down a measure of the kind passed by the House. Admittedly, there is substantial public interest in having a candidate's ad disseminated. This interest is demonstrated by the existence of a contingent access requirement for candidates' ads and other information, applicable to the electronic media. However, we have seen that radio and television do not enjoy the constitutional autonomy that has traditionally been recognized for print media. Few rights could be more central to the autonomy of the press under the First Amendment than the right to prefer one political candidate to another. Moreover, the Supreme Court has given political ads the full degree of First Amendment protection accorded to political expression.

In summary, reasoning by reference to antitrust law supports a contingent access obligation applicable to commercial advertising where a medium has accepted other ads dealing with the same activity, and cannot claim that its refusal to take an ad reflects disapproval of the ad or the underlying activity. Antitrust has little relevance to access obligations applicable to political advertising.

Antitrust law also offers little support for broader rights of access, which deal with editorial content instead of advertising. Any effort to guarantee access to the print media for views not sufficiently expressed along the lines of the Fairness Doctrine would require a degree of official editorial supervision which is inconsistent with the maintenance of an autonomous press. Such a radical perspective cannot find support in antitrust principles. The serious problem of media concentration calls for policies designed to increase the number of autonomous publishers, not attempts to impose "balance" or "fairness" on existing outlets of expression.[31] This is the teaching of *Associated Press:*

> [T]he widest possible dissemination of information from diverse and antagonistic sources is essential to the welfare of the public. . . a free press is a condition of a free society.[32]

Professor Emerson's rejection of broad access requirements as a remedy for concentration is persuasive:

> But any effort to solve the broader problems of a monopoly press by forcing newspapers to cover all "newsworthy" events and print all viewpoints, under the watchful eyes of petty public officials, is likely to undermine such independence as the press now shows without achieving any real diversity. Government measures to encourage a multiplicity of outlets, rather than compelling a few outlets to represent everybody, seems a far preferable course of action. Such a goal cannot be reached by mere enforcement of the antitrust laws. It will undoubtedly be necessary to go to the economic roots of the problem and either by government subsidies or other devices create an open market with a new form of economic base.[33]

With respect to the sort of narrow access rights for commercial advertising to protect competition that antitrust principles would support,[34] the countervailing First Amendment interests of publishers are weakest. As previously discussed in Chapter 3, a long line of decisions has held that advertising, or commercial speech, is generally beyond the reach of First Amendment protection.[35] The distinction between commercial advertising and other forms of expression may have significance in terms of a publisher's constitutional freedom from statutory access obligations. No case has been decided on this point, but the 1973 *Pittsburgh Press* decision suggests the possibility that legislation granting access rights for commercial advertising might be sustained.

Pittsburgh Press, it will be recalled, upheld the power of a municipal human relations commission to prohibit a newspaper from segregating help-wanted ads for jobs into male and female columns, since sex discrimination in hiring was unlawful.[36] The Supreme Court, in a close five-four decision, rejected the newspaper's claim of freedom to arrange help-wanted ads as it wished: "Under some circumstances, at least, a newspaper's editorial judgments in connection with an advertisement take on the character of the advertisement."[37]

Does this statement, and the *Pittsburgh Press* holding generally, mean that a newspaper's decision not to publish a commercial ad is subject to reduced First Amendment protection, as is the right of commercial expression? The *Miami Herald* opinion avoids this question, although some statements in the opinion suggest contradictory answers. In citing *Pittsburgh Press* as one precedent in support of its holding, the Court quoted the language set out in the previous chapter, which drew a sharp distinction between the protected editorial judgment for ads and "stories or commentary originated by Pittsburgh Press, its columnists, or its contributors."[38] On the other hand, in the concluding paragraph of the *Miami Herald* opinion, the Court stated: "A newspaper is more than a passive receptacle or conduit for news, comment, *and advertising.*"[39] Thus, *Miami Herald* contains conflicting suggestions as to whether a statutory right of access for commercial advertising, or at least a right of nondiscrimination with respect to such advertising, would be consistent with the First Amendment. In any event, it is clear that *Miami Herald*'s holding that access for political replies may not be imposed on newspapers does not dispose of the constitutionality of access obligations for commercial advertising.[40]

Access and Journalistic Responsibility

Newspapers and, in a qualified sense, the electronic media, should celebrate their newly won guarantee of autonomy with a commitment to journalistic responsibility. The demise of access obligations on a constitutional level is a good reason to practice access on an operational level. To open the press to outside points of view, to institutionalize methods of correction and self-criticism, and to support responsible, external, nonofficial bodies for review of the press' performance are not simply the best way to protect the constitutional freedoms of the press. These measures are also good business and make for more interesting publications. Responsibility and self-interest can combine to produce diversity and fairness on a voluntary basis.

There is heartening evidence of a trend among leading newspapers to adopt mechanisms for access to the press. The *New York Times'* "Op-Ed" page is open to writers who are not on the *Times'* staff. The *Salt Lake City Tribune* has a "Common Carrier" column for outsiders and pays a community panel to screen copy.[41] A number of papers, following the excellent example of the *Louisville Courier Journal* and *The Washington Post,* have appointed reporters as "house critics" to review the performance of the paper and serve as a sounding board for complaints. Other papers, also following *the Louisville Courier Journal*'s and the *Louisville Times'* example, have appointed "reader advocates" to receive, investigate, and do something about readers' complaints.[42] *The Chicago Sun-Times* and *The Chicago Daily News* have established a "Bureau of Fairness and Accuracy." In 1972, *the New York Times* began publishing corrections on page 1 of the second section, rather than on page 37.[43] *The Kansas City Star* in a recent city election offered equal space on its editorial page to opponents of candidates it had endorsed in editorials.[44] Moreover, one survey suggests that most newspapers are willing to print replies to personal criticisms. In 1973, William F. Buckley, Jr. attacked a priest for supporting a union boycott, and some 195 newspapers ran his syndicated column. When the priest submitted a reply to the syndicate, that syndicate distributed it to the same papers. Seventy-two percent of them ran the reply.[45]

This trend toward access and self-correction is a hopeful sign that journalism is mitigating what many critics have called the press' leading defect: the absence of a tradition of self-criticism. However, as of 1975, only about a dozen of the 1750 newspapers in this country are known to have appointed reader advocates.[46]

Besides establishing mechanisms for criticism and correction, newspapers should encourage a robust and substantial "letters to the editor" section. Reader surveys have shown these letters to be a favorite item. In small-town papers, letters to the editor are extremely popular, often the best-read item in the paper.[47] In large metropolitan papers, letters to the editor are less well-read than front-page items, but still tend to draw large audiences.[48] For example, recent surveys have indicated that as many people read the letters published by *The Washington Post* as read Jack Anderson's column. In fact, in most papers, letters are better read than any columnist.[49]

Interestingly, *The Miami Herald* had published numerous statements and letters from Mr. Tornillo before its refusal to run his reply that produced the landmark case.[50]

Radio and television can also open avenues for access that will serve the public interest and make for interesting and diverse programming. Although time constraints for broadcasters are more severe than are space restraints for newspapers, representative approaches to public access are possible. In the San Francisco area, a number of broadcasters support "access centers" which produce "free speech messages" by representatives of local organizations and community groups. The stations undertake voluntarily to present five or six one-minute "free speech messages" each day. The Citizens Communications Center, a public interest law firm devoted to citizen participation in radio and television, has proposed that broadcasters who voluntarily devote a total of one hour per week to "free speech messages" and other types of access programming should be relieved of Fairness Doctrine obligations. Whatever the outcome of this proposal, broadcasters should try to emulate the trend to ombudsmen, self-correction, and voluntary public access that appears to be building among leading newspapers.

Another hopeful sign is the growth of institutions outside the press that have provided both a source of external criticism of the press' performance and a stimulus to greater responsibility within the media. In the long run, the most significant trend in this area may be the emergence of journalism as an important academic discipline. With some 55,000 students currently enrolled, some observers believe journalism is the fastest growing discipline in American universities.[51] Academic study breeds self-examination and the serious pursuit of ethical concerns.

A more concrete example of an outside monitoring agency is the formation, in 1973, of the National News Council. The Council is a nonofficial body that reviews complaints of unfairness, inaccuracy, or bias by the national suppliers of news, including the wire services. the weekly news magazines, national newspaper syndicates, and the broadcasting networks. In its first two years, the Council completed action on 59 complaints, upholding the complaint in five cases. Most observers have given the Council high marks for its handling of complaints.[52]

It is still too early to tell whether the council will receive the cooperation from the national news media that it must have in order to perform its function. However, its creation and subsequent survival for three years signal the possibility of corrective mechanisms that do not involve the heavy hand of government. It is worth noting that the Supreme Court made repeated reference to the National News Council in the *Miami Herald* decision. Other local press councils exist in Minnesota and in several cities.[53]

A third encouraging sign of a constructively critical spirit about the press is the establishment of journalism reviews, such as the excellent *Columbia Journalism Review*. In 1973, there were twelve such journalism reviews,[54] although their financial stability tends to be precarious.

These efforts at openness and self-criticism on the part of the news media should be given new force by the *Miami Herald* decision and the trend away from access and program-by-program oversight in the regulation of broadcasting. The press would be wise to support responsible outside entities which, without governmental sanction, review and evaluate press performance. A line from a Bob Dylan song nicely fits the controversy about access to the press: "To live outside the law you must be honest." And you must be accessible. The press should take that thought to heart.

Notes

PART I
ACCESS TO THE MEDIA:
GENERAL PERSPECTIVES

1 *Palko* v. *Connecticut*, 302 U.S. 319 326-27 (1937)
2 Barron, *Access To The Press—A New First Amendment Right*, 80 HARV. L. REV. 1641 (1967).
3 KALVEN, THE NEGRO AND THE FIRST AMENDMENT 4 (1965).

Chapter 1   Access and the Supreme Court: A Brief Overview

1 395 U.S. 367, 390 (1969).
2 418 U.S. 241, 258 (1974).
3 395 U.S. at 390.
4 *Columbia Broadcasting System Inc.* v. *Democratic National Committee; Business Executives' Move for Vietnam Peace* v. *FCC*, 450 F. 2d 642 (D.C. Cir. 1971).
5 *Tornillo* v. *Miami Herald Publishing Co.*, 287 So. 2d 78 (Fig. 1973).
6 *Id.* at 83 (emphasis deleted).
7 376 U.S. 254 (1964).
8 BARRON, FREEDOM OF THE PRESS FOR WHOM? (1973); Barron, *Access to the Press—A New First Amendment Right*, 80 HARV. L. REV. 1641 (1967); Barron, *An Emerging First Amendment Right of Access to the Media?*, 37 GEO. WASH. L. REV. 487 (1969).
9 Canby, *The First Amendment Right to Persuade: Access to Radio and Television*, 19 U.C.L.A. REV. 723 (1972); Johnson and Weston, *A Twentieth Century Soap-box: The Right to Purchase Radio and Television Time*, 57 VA. L. REV. 574 (1971). A full review of access commentary in legal literature can be found in Lange, *supra*, footnotes 5 and 21.
10 See, *e.g.*, *Office of Communication of the United Church of Christ* v. *FCC*, 425 F. 2d 543 (D.C. Cir. 1969). The Court of Appeals for the District of Columbia has forced the Federal Communications Commission to grant standing to citizen-audience groups to challenge a wide range of administrative action in the broadcasting field. That Court has also forced the Commission to allow licensee reimbursement of citizen group expenses. See Chapter 14, *infra*. One of the most effective of these public interest law firms is named in the above case. Others that have vigorously pursued legal rights of access, especially to the electronic media, include the Citizens Communications Center, the Public Media Center, and the Media Access Project.
11 See, *e.g.* Obledo and Joselow, *Broadcasting: Mexican-Americans and the Media*, 1 CHICANO LAW REVIEW 85 (1972). This area is discussed in Chapter 14, *infra*.
12 *Columbia Broadcasting System, Inc.* v. *Democratic National Committee; FCC* v. *Business Executives' Move for Vietnam Peace*, 412 U.S. 94 (1973).

13 *Lehman* v. *City of Shaker Heights*, 418 U.S. 241 (1974).
14 418 U.S. 298 (1974).
15 *Id.* at 254.
16 *Id.* at 258.
17 *Id.* at 256.

Chapter 2   Sorting Out the Concept of Access

1 HOLMES, COLLECTED LEGAL PAPERS 293 (1921).
2 *See,* Donnelly, *The Right of Reply: An Alternative to an Action for Libel,* 34 U. VA. L. REV. 867 (1948); Note, *Vindication of the Reputation of a Public Official,* 80 HARV. L. REV. 1730 (1967).
3 *See* 47 U.S.C. 315 (a) (1970) for a statute imposing such an obligation on radio and television when the initial appearance is not a *bona fide* news event, interview, or documentary.
4 *Cf. Tornillo* v. *Miami Herald Publishing Co.* 287 So. 2d 78 (Fla. 1973); *rev'd* 418 U.S. 241 (1974).
5 *Cf. Columbia Broadcasting System, Inc.* v. *Democratic National Committee; Business Executives' Move for Vietnam Peace* v. *FCC,* 450 F. 2d 642 (D.C. Cir. 1971); *rev'd* 412 U.S. 94 (1973).
6 EMERSON, THE SYSTEM OF FREEDOM OF EXPRESSION 9 (1970).
7 1 HOLMES-LASKI LETTERS 653 (M. Howe ed. 1953). I owe the quote to Kurland, *Foreward: "Equal in Origin and Equal in Title to the Legislative and Executive Branches of the Government,"* 78 HARV. L. REV. 143, 162 (1964).
8 Again, I owe the phrase to Professor Kurland, *supra.*
9 FREUND, THE SUPREME COURT OF THE UNITED STATES 44 (1961).

Chapter 3   Access in First Amendment History and Theory

1 TOQUEVILLE, 1 DEMOCRACY IN AMERICA 337 (Langley ed. 1841).
2 For example, *New York Times Co.* v. *Sullivan*, which will be discussed in Chapter 6, justified a major advance in First Amendment doctrine by drawing fresh significance from the Sedition Act controversy at the turn of the eighteenth century.
3 The best discussion of the English system of licensing is SIEBERT, FREEDOM OF THE PRESS IN ENGLAND, 1476-1776 (1952).
4 The leading, but controversial, assessment of freedom of the press in early American history is LEVY, FREEDOM OF SPEECH AND PRESS IN EARLY AMERICAN HISTORY: LEGACY OF SUPPRESSION (1963).
5 BLACKSTONE, 2 COMMENTARIES ON THE LAWS OF ENGLAND 112-113 (18th ed. 1836). The continuing force of the Blackstonian heritage can be seen most recently in the *Pentagon Papers* decision: several of the Justices who refused to enjoin the *Times* reached beyond the parameters of the case to suggest the appropriateness of post-publication criminal sanctions. *New York Times Co.* v. *United States,* 403 U.S. 713 (1971). See generally Edgar and Schmidt, *The Espionage Statutes and Publication of*

Defense Information, 73 COL. L. REV. 929, 935 *et seq.* (1973).

6 Jerome Barron has suggested newspapers might be required to publish letters to the editor, but it seems doubtful that he means the *New York Times* must publish the more than 40,000 letters to the editor which it receives yearly. *See,* BARRON, FREEDOM OF THE PRESS FOR WHOM ch. 5 (1973).

7 Siebert, *supra* at 38.

8 *Id.* at 71.

9 The famous statement of the House of Commons attributed to John Locke, which justified the expiration of the Printing Act in 1694, was an attack on the inexpediency of printing monopolies rather than an appeal to the principles of free expression. Indeed, Locke supported elimination of licensing because of the greater efficiency of seditious libel prosecutions in preventing dangerous expression. In fact, a flood of successful seditious libel prosecutions followed the repeal of the Printing Act. *Id.* at 260 *et seq.*

10 HANSON, GOVERNMENT AND THE PRESS, 1695-1763 119 (1936).

11 283 U.S. 697, 718 (1931).

12 TOCQUEVILLE, 1 DEMOCRACY IN AMERICA *lix* (Reeve ed. 1862). Compare, BURKE, REFLECTIONS ON THE REVOLUTION IN FRANCE, in 3 WORKS OF EDMUND BURKE 358 (Beaconsfield ed. 1901): To avoid, therefore, the evils of inconstancy and versatility, ten thousand times worse than those of obstinacy and the blindest prejudice, we have consecreated the state, that no man should approach to look into its defects or corruptions but with due caution; that he should never dream of beginning its reformation by its subversion; that he should approach to the faults of the state as to the wounds of a father, with pious awe and trembling solicitude.

13 COHEN, LAW AND THE SOCIAL ORDER 191 (1933).

14 *Cf. Brown* v. *Board of Education,* 347 U.S. 483 (1954), where the Supreme Court freed itself from the burden of Fourteenth Amendment history.

15 *Branzburg* v. *Hayes,* 408 U.S. 665 (1972).

16 *Red Lion Broadcasting Co.* v. *FCC,* 395 U.S. 367 (1969). The chilling effect problem dealt with in *Red Lion* is discussed in Chapters 13 and 14.

17 *E.g., Valentine* v. *Chrestensen,* 316 U.S. 52 (1942).

18 *SEC* v. *Texas Gulf Sulpher Co.,* 446 F. 2d 1301 (1971), *cert. denied* 404 U.S. 1005 (1971).

19 Whenever the Federal Trade Commission has "reason to believe" an unfair or deceptive practice (including deceptive advertising) is being used it may issue, after a hearing a cease and desist order. 15 U.S.C. §456 (1970. Note, *Corrective Advertising—The New Response to Consumer Deception,* 72 COL. L. REV. 415 (1972).

20 Note, *Advertising, Solicitation, and Legal Ethics,* 7 VAND. L. REV. 677 (1954); *Kelley v. Texas State Board of Medical Examiners,* 467 S.W. 2d 539 (Tex. Ct. of Civil Appeals 1971).

21 United States v. Hunter, 459 F. 2d 205 (4th Cir. 1972), *cert. denied* 409 U.S. 934 (1972).

22 *See generally,* Note, *Developments in the Law—Deceptive Advertising,* 80 HARV. L. REV. 1005 (1967); Note, *Freedom of Expression in a Commercial Context,* 78 HARV. L. REV. 1191 (1965).

23 *Pittsburgh Press Co.* v. *Pittsburgh Commission on Human Relations*, 413 U.S. 376 (1973).

24 See discussion at Chapter 6, *infra*.

25 *See, e.g.*, Barron, *Access to the Press—A New First Amendment Right*, 80 HARV. L. REV. 1641 (1967); Johnson and Weston, *A Twentieth Century Soapbox: The Right to Purchase Radio and Television Time*, 57 VA. L. REV. 574 (1971).

26 *See, e.g.*, Lange, *The Role of the Access Doctrine in the Regulation of the Mass Media*, 52 N. CAR. L. REV. 1 (1973).

27 COMMAGER, ed., DOCUMENTS OF AMERICAN HISTORY 125 (4th ed. 1948).

28 BURY, A HISTORY OF FREEDOM OF THOUGHT 188 (1913).

29 Reprinted in POLLAK, 2 THE CONSTITUTION AND THE SUPREME COURT: A DOCUMENTARY HISTORY 58 (1966).

30 Quoted in LEVY, FREEDOM OF SPEECH AND PRESS IN EARLY AMERICAN HISTORY: LEGACY OF SUPPRESSION 188-89 (1960).

31 *Id.* at 167. However, Levy asserts in another book that Jefferson did not apply the overt-acts test to political, as opposed to religious opinions. LEVY, JEFFERSON AND CIVIL LIBERTIES: THE DARKER SIDE 44 (1963).

32 MALONE, JEFFERSON AND THE ORDEAL OF LIBERTY 483 (1962).

33 Letter to Mrs. Adams, July 22, 1804, 4 JEFFERSON'S WORKS 555-56 (Washington ed.)

34 Article VI of the Constitution provides: "no religious Test shall ever be required as a Qualification to any Office or public Trust under the United States."

35 319 U.S. 624 (1943).

36 *Id.* at 642.

37 *Id.* at 634.

38 *Minersville School Dist.* v. *Gobitis* 310 U.S. 586, 594 (1940).

39 367 U.S. 740 (1961).

40 *Id.* at 749.

41 *Id.* at 788.

42 KALVEN, THE NEGRO AND THE FIRST AMENDMENT 61 (1965).

Chapter 4   Access as a Remedy for Concentration of the Media

1 *United States* v. *Associated Press*, 52 F. Supp. 362, 372 (S.D.N.Y. 1943), *aff'd*, 326 U.S. 1 (1945).

2 NEW YORK TIMES, Nov. 21, 1969, at 22.

3 ROSSITER, SEEDTIME OF THE REPUBLIC 29 (1953); TEBBEL, THE MEDIA IN AMERICA 36 (1974).

4 Tebbel, *supra* at 49.

5 BAKER & BALL, VIOLENCE AND THE MEDIA (Staff Report to the National Commission on the Causes and Prevention of Violence) 68 (1969).

6 1974 EDITOR AND PUBLISHER YEARBOOK.

7   1974 STATISTICAL ABSTRACT OF THE UNITED STATES 507.

8   *Id.* at 503.

9   Bogart, *How the Mass Media Work in America,* in Baker & Ball, *supra* at 165.

10 Baker & Ball, *supra* at 68, 3.

11 Barron, *Access to the Press—A New First Amendment Right,* 80 HARV. L. REV. 1641 (1967).

12 Bishop, *The Rush to Chain Ownership,* 11(4) COLUMBIA JOURNALISM REVIEW 10 (Nov.-Dec. 1972).

13 Statement of Donald F. Turner to Subcommittee on Antitrust & Monopoly of the Senate Commission on the Judiciary, Hearings on S. 1312, 90th Cong. 1st Sess., pt. 7, at 3105-3112 (1967).

14 Newspaper Preservation Act, Report of the Committee on the Judiciary, H. Rept. No. 91-1193 91st Cong. 2d Sess.

15 *Id.*

16 Turner, *supra* at 3107-08.

17 Johnson & Hoak, *Media Concentration,* 56 IOWA L. REV. 267, 269-70 (1970).

18 Barnett, *Cable TV and Media Concentration,* 22 STAN. L. REV. 221, 278 (1970).

19 Barnett, *supra* at 278.

20 Goodman, Katz, & Moncharsh, *Concentration of Ownership in the Media,* paper on file in the Columbia Law Library, at p. 4.

21 Barnett, *Programs for the Many, Airwaves for the few,* NEW YORK TIMES, Oct. 23, 1974.

22 In 1970, the *First Report and Order, Multiple Ownership of Standard, FM & TV Broadcast Stations,* 22 FCC 2d 306 (1970), prohibited common ownership of more than one unlimited-time broadcast station in the same area. The rule was amended in 1971 to apply only to combinations including VHF television stations. *In the Matter of Amendment of Sections 73.35, 73.240, and 73.636 of the Commission's Rules Relating to Multiple Ownership of Standard, FM and Television Broadcast Stations,* 28 FCC 2d 662 (1971).

23 *Second Report and Order, Docket No. 18110,* 32 RR 2d 954 (1975).

24 *See,* dissent of Commissioner Robinson, *id.* at 1024.

25 Informative discussions of the 1975 cross-ownership rules can be found in Note, *Diversity Ownership in Broadcasting,* 27 U. FLA. L. REV. 502 (1975); Mills, Moynahan, Perlini, McClure, *The Constitutional Considerations of Multiple Media Ownership Regulation by the Federal Communications Commission,* 24 AM. U. L. REV. 1217 (1975).

26 *WHDH, Inc.,* 16 FCC 2d 1 (1969).

27 *Greater Boston Television Corp.* v. *FCC,* 444 F. 2d 841 (D.C. Cir. 1970).

28 *Chronicle Broadcasting Co.,* 27 RR 2d 743 (1973); *Columbus Broadcasting Coalition* v. *FCC,* 505 F. 2d 320 (D.C. Cir. 1974). *See also, Second Report and Order, Docket No. 18110,* 32 RR 2d at 998.

29 In 1969 the Hearst chain owned major newspapers in New York, Los Angeles, San Francisco, Baltimore, Boston, Albany, Seattle, and San Antonio and TV and radio interests in Milwaukee, San Juan, and Pittsburgh.

Goodman *et al.*, *supra* at 8. Cowles Communications controls an AM-FM-TV group and the only two general circulation dailies in Minneapolis-St. Paul—the three largest and most influential media outlets in the state—as well as a monopoly newspaper with AM-FM-TV combination in Des Moines and several other midwestern newspapers. *Id.* at 39.

30 Bishop, *supra* at 10. As Bishop concludes, "it is easy to see that a fairly small community controls a tremendous share of America's communications network." *Id.* at 14.

31 Statement of William J. Farson in Hearings on S.1312 before the Subcommittee on Antitrust and Monopoly of the Senate Committee on the Judiciary, pt. 1, p. 202 90th Cong., 1st Sess., (1967).

32 Johnson & Hoak, *supra* at 272.

33 TELEVISION FACTBOOK NO. 42 (1972-73 edition).

34 Barnett, *supra* at 277.

35 Levin, *Competition, Diversity, and the Television Group Ownership Rules,* 70 COLUM. L. REV. 791 (1970).

36 Bagdikian, THE EFFETE CONSPIRACY AND OTHER CRIMES BY THE PRESS 64 (1972).

37 *Id.*

38 Goodman *et al.*, *supra* at 8-9.

39 Bagdikian, *supra* at 66.

40 Bishop, *supra* at 10.

41 Bagdikian, THE INFORMATION MACHINES 90 (1971).

42 *Id.* at 103.

43 *Id.* at 97.

44 *Id.* at 128.

45 Epstein, NEWS FROM NOWHERE 142 (1973).

46 Bagdikian, *supra* at 143.

47 *Associated Press* v. *United States,* 326 U.S. 1, 20 (1945).

48 Turner, *The Definition of Agreement under the Sherman Act: Conscious Parallelism and Refusals to Deal,* 75 HARV. L. REV. 655, 686 (1962).

49 Levi, *The Parke, Davis-Colgate Doctrine,* 1960 SUP. CT. REV. 258, 326.

50 *United States* v. *Lorain Journal Co.,* 92 F. Supp. 794 (N.D. Ohio 1950); *aff'd.* 342 U.S. 143 (1951).

51 342 U.S. at 155-156.

52 See *Klor's Inc.* v. *Broadway-Hale Stores, Inc.,* 359 U.S. 207 (1959), where a group boycott of a local retailer by national manufacturers and distributors of appliances (at the urging of a department store chain) was held to be forbidden by the Sherman Act.

53 *United States* v. *Colgate Co.,* 250 U.S. 300 (1919). For an excellent discussion of the antitrust implications of refusals to deal and of the evidentiary difficulties of proving these cases, see Turner, *supra.*

54 Turner, *supra* at 689.

55 *Valentine* v. *Chrestensen,* 316 U.S. 52 (1942).

56 *Pittsburgh Press Co.* v. *Human Relations Comm'n.,* 413 U.S. 376 (1973).

57 *Pittsburgh Press Co.* v. *Human Relations Commission,* 413 U.S. 376 (1973), distinguishes commercial advertisements, as in *Chrestensen, supra,* from ads

carrying a political message, as in *Sullivan, supra.*

58 The right of political candidates to airtime equal to the opportunities given their rivals is discussed in Chapter 10.

59 *See* Posner, ECONOMIC ANALYSIS OF LAW 140 (1972).

60 284 F. 2d 582 (1st Cir. 1960).

61 284 F. 2d at 584.

62 Codified at 15 U.S.C. §§ 1801 *et seq.* (supp. 1971).

63 15 U.S.C. § 1803 (supp. 1971).

64 *Citizen Publishing Company* v. *United States,* 394 U.S. 131 (1969).

65 Ben Bagdikian has pointed out that not only is the typical American newspaper a local monopoly, but that saturation in local communities and tax incentives for investing profits elsewhere have fueled the development of newspaper chains.

Chapter 5   Access and Current Perceptions of the Press

1 The president of the Washington Post Company made these comments in a speech to the Southern California Distinguished Achievement Awards Dinner in 1969. Quoted in BALK, A FREE AND RESPONSIVE PRESS 15 (1973).

2 SAFIRE, BEFORE THE FALL: AN INSIDE VIEW OF THE PRE-WATERGATE WHITE HOUSE 342 (1975).

3 *Id.* at 352.

4 *Id.* at 360.

5 *Id.* at 356-57.

6 Graham & Landau, *The Federal Shield Law We Need,* COLUMBIA JOURNALISM REV. 26 (March-April 1973).

7 Schor, *The FBI and Me,* COLUMBIA JOURNALISM REV. 8 (Nov.-Dec. 1974).

8 Fulbright, *Fulbright on the Press,* COLUMBIA JOURNALISM REV. 41 (Nov.-Dec. 1975).

9 Reeves, *Journal Square,* NEW YORK MAGAZINE 45 (July 20, 1975).

10 Weaver, *The New Journalism and the Old-Thoughts after Watergate,* 35 PUBLIC INTEREST 67 (1974).

11 *Id.* at 69.

12 Cater, *Toward a Public Philosophy of Government-Media Relations,* ASPEN NOTEBOOK ON GOVERNMENT AND THE MEDIA 6 (1973).

13 See Weaver, *supra* at 72 *et seq.*

14 *Id.* at 75.

15 *Id.*

16 *The New York Times* discovered the plans for an invasion of Cuba, but President Kennedy persuaded the paper not to print the story on grounds of national security. After the invasion fiasco, the President stated that the nation would have been better off if *The Times* had printed the story, thus killing the invasion. In 1966 the managing editor of *The Times,* Clifton Daniel, stated that *The Times* had been wrong not to print the story and would not repeat the error. *Id.* at 76. There has been speculation that

second thoughts about the Bay of Pigs story was partly behind the decision of *The Times* to run the *Pentagon Papers*. Ungar, THE PAPERS & THE PAPERS 102 (1972).

17   See, generally Edgar & Schmidt, *The Espionage Statutes and Publication of Defense Information*, 73 COL. L. REV. 929 (1973).

18   The classic exception to this general rule was the publication by the *Chicago Tribune* of an account of the Battle of Midway during World War II that indicated that the United States had broken the Japanese Naval code. Roosevelt was infuriated, and reportedly wished to prosecute the paper under the espionage statutes, but Attorney General Biddle convinced the President that prosecution would be impolitic. The Japanese apparently never noticed the story. See, BIDDLE, IN BRIEF AUTHORITY (1962). *See also*, Ungar, *supra* 115.

19   Quoted in KNIGHTLEY, THE FIRST CASUALTY 373 (1975).

20   *See generally*, Schmidt, *Journalists' Privilege: One Year after Branzburg*, in THE FIRST AMENDMENT AND THE NEWS MEDIA (Roscoe Pound-American Trial Lawyers Foundation 1973).

21   Weaver, *supra* at 84.

22   BLASI, PRESS SUBPOENAS: AN EMPIRICAL AND LEGAL ANALYSIS 33 *et seq.* (1972).

23   *Id.*

24   Moynihan, *The Presidency & The Press*, 51 COMMENTARY NO. 3 at 41 (March 1971).

25   Quoted in De Sola Pool, *Newsmen and Statesmen: Adversaries or Cronies?* in ASPEN NOTEBOOK ON GOVERNMENT AND THE MEDIA 21 (1973). [Emphasis in original]

26   *Id.* [Emphasis in original]

27   *Id.* at 23.

28   PHILLIPS, MEDIACRACY 28 (1975).

29   BAGDIKIAN, THE EFFETE CONSPIRACY AND OTHER CRIMES BY THE PRESS 80 (1972).

30   *Id.* at Chapters 7 and 8.

31   *Id.* at 47 *et seq.*

32   Littlejohn, *Communicating Ideas by Television*, TELEVISION AS A SOCIAL FORCE 65 (1975).

33   BOWER, TELEVISION AND THE PUBLIC 99 *et seq.* (1973).

34   BAGDIKIAN, THE INFORMATION MACHINES 274 (1971).

35   Weaver, *Newspaper News and Television News*, TELEVISION AS A SOCIAL FORCE 87 (1975).

36   *Id.* at 87-88.

37   *Id.* at 89.

38   EPSTEIN, NEWS FROM NOWHERE 148 (1973).

39   *Id.* at 16.

40   Weaver, *supra* at 93-94.

41   Robinson, *American Political Legitimacy in an Era of Electronic Journalism*, TELEVISION AS A SOCIAL FORCE 97, 117 (1975).

42   The legal and policy questions raised by presidential television addresses are discussed in Chapter 10.

43   See De Sola Pool, *supra* at 24.

44   See Chapter 10.

45   Right of reply 'access rights' are discussed in Chapters 6 and 15.

46   The equal opportunities rights of political candidates to radio and television coverage are discussed in Chapter 10.

47   BELL, THE COMING OF POST-INDUSTRIAL SOCIETY (1973).

48   Phillips, *supra* at 227.

49   *Id.* at 31.

PART II
ACCESS AND FIRST AMENDMENT DEVELOPMENTS IN LIBEL AND THE "PUBLIC FORUM"

Chapter 6   Defamation and Access: The Claims of Equilibrium

1   Nationwide radio broadcast, March 8, 1974. The President's address was excerpted in the NEW YORK TIMES, March 9, 1974, at 11. I have corrected the spelling and altered the paragraphing.

2   Quoted in Kalven, *The New York Times Case: A Note On "The Central Meaning of the First Amendment,"* 1964 SUP. CT. REV. 191, 221.

3   *Id.* at 194.

4   *See generally*, WECHSLER, THE NATIONALIZATION OF CIVIL LIBER-TIES AND CIVIL RIGHTS (1968).

5   Green, *The Right to Communicate*, 35 N.Y.U. L. REV. 903. 907 (1960). Professor Donnelly estimated that less than one-half of one percent of the libel cases started were actually tried. Donnelly, *The Right of Reply: An Alternative to an Action for Libel*, 34 U. VA. L. REV. 866, 869 n. 5 (1948).

6   *E.g., Coleman* v. *MacLennan* 78 Kan. 711, 98 P. 281 (1908).

7   An excellent discussion of pre-*Sullivan* defamation law can be found in HARPER AND JAMES, 1 THE LAW OF TORTS, § 5.1, at 354 *et seq.* (1956).

8   CHAFFEE, 1 GOVERNMENT AND MASS COMMUNICATIONS 97 (1947).

9   *Id.* at 101.

10   Donnelly, *supra* at 870.

11   EMERSON, THE SYSTEM OF FREEDOM OF EXPRESSION 519 (1970).

12   376 U.S. at 269.

13   *Id.* at 279.

14   *Id.* at 279-80.

15   *Coleman* v. *MacLennan, supra.*

16   HARPER AND JAMES, I THE LAW OF TORTS § 5.26 (1956).

17   *Rosenblatt* v. *Baer*, 383 U.S. 75 (1966) (county recreation area supervisor).

18   *Associated Press* v. *Walker*, 388 U.S. 130, 134 (1967) (prominent person leading protest demonstration); *Curtis Publishing Co.* v. *Butts, id.* (university athletic director).

19   *Rosenbloom* v. *Metromedia*, 403 U.S. 29 (1971) (magazine distributor arrested on obscenity charge).

20   376 U.S. at 304-05.

21   *Id.* at 300.

22   *Associated Press* v. *Walker, Curtis Publishing Co.* v. *Butts*, 388 U.S. 130 (1967).

23   *Id.* at 155.

24   *Id.* at 164.

25   Kalven, *The Reasonable Man and The First Amendment: Hill, Butts, and Walker*, 1967 SUP. CT. REV. 267, 299-300.

26   403 U.S. 29 (1971).

27   *Id.* at 45-46.

28   *Id.* at 46-47.

29   *Id.* at 47.

30   *Id.* no. 15.

31   Justices Marshall and Stewart argued that the values of the First Amendment should be served in cases of defamation of private persons by allowing recovery only of damages based on actual injury, with punitive damages disallowed.

32   403 U.S. at 70.

33   *Gertz* v. *Robert Welch, Inc.*, 418 U.S. 323, 344 (1974).

34   *Id.* n. 9.

35   418 U.S. at 345.

36   *Id.*

37   *Curtis Publishing Co.* v. *Butts*, 388 U.S. 130, 155 (1967).

38   418 U.S. at 352.

39   Indexing services disclosed no empirical studies on the impact of *Sullivan* on the number and outcome of libel actions. Nor are the Association of Newspaper Publishers and the libraries of the University of Missouri and Columbia Journalism Schools aware of any such studies.

40   Generally, settlement has been the rule in libel suits. Even in the days when the First Amendment had no impact on the law of defamation, it was estimated that less than 0.5 percent of the libel cases initiated were actually tried. *See* Donnelly, *The Right of Reply: An Alternative to an Action for Libel*, 34 U. VA. L. REV. 867, 869 n. 5 (1948).

41   *Curtis Publishing Co.* v. *Butts*, 388 U.S. 130 (1967).

42   *Id.* at 155.

43   *Goldwater* v. *Ginzburg*, 414 F. 2d 324 (2d Cir. 1969), *cert. denied* 396 U.S. 1049 (1970).

44   *See, e.g., Snowden* v. *Pearl River Broadcasting Corp.*, 251 So. 2d 405 (Ct. App. La. 1971); *Firestone* v. *Time, Inc.*, 271 So. 2d 745 (Fla. 1972). Other cases are collected in GILLMOR AND BARRON, MASS COMMUNICATION LAW 277 *et seq* (1969).

45   *See* Donnelly, *The Right of Reply: An Alternative to an Action for Libel*,

34 U. VA. L. REV. 867 (1948); Note, *Vindication of the Reputation of a Public Official*, 80 HARV. L. REV. 1730 (1967).

Chapter 7   Access and "Public Forum" Cases: The Power of Analogy

1 LEVI, AN INTRODUCTION TO LEGAL REASONING 2 (1949).

2 *See*, BARRON, FREEDOM OF THE PRESS FOR WHOM Ch. 9 (1973).

3 *See generally*, Barron, *supra* at Ch. 5. A leading judicial statement of this view is the opinion of Judge J. Skelly Wright in *Business Executives' Move for Vietnam Peace* v. *FCC*, 450 F. 2d 642 (D.C. Cir. 1971), which was reversed by the Supreme Court, 412 U.S. 94 (1973). *See* discussion in Chapter 12, *infra*.

4 BICKEL, THE MORALITY OF CONSENT 78 (1975).

5 *See*, GUNTHER, CASES AND MATERIALS ON CONSTITUTIONAL LAW 1145 (1975).

6 Kalven, *The Concept of the Public Forum: Cox* v. *Louisiana*, 1965 SUP. CT. REV. 1, 4.

7 Levi, *supra* at 3 *et seq.*

8 *See*, Kalven, *supra* at 1.

9 *Id.* at 2.

10 WECHSLER, PRINCIPLES, POLITICS AND FUNDAMENTAL LAW 3 *et seq.* (1961).

11 CHAFEE, FREE SPEECH IN THE UNITED STATES 399 (1969).

12 Kalven, *supra* at 2.

13 303 U.S. 444, 451 (1938).

14 *Id.* at 452. Although Paine was and is commonly thought to have been an atheist, (Theodore Roosevelt once referred to him as "that filthy little atheist"), he was in fact a sort of unitarian deist who believed in a concept of God, although he vigorously attacked every vestige of organized religion—including the Bible. 14 DICT. AM. BIOG. 159 *et seq.* (1943).

15 *Cantwell* v. *Connecticut*, 310 U.S. 296, 310 (1940).

16 326 U.S. 501 (1946).

17 *Id.* at 503.

18 *Id.* at 505-06.

19 *Id.* at 508.

20 *Id.* at 509.

21 *Id.*

22 *Nixon* v. *Herndon*, 273 U.S. 536 (1927).

23 *Nixon* v. *Condon*, 286 U.S. 73 (1932).

24 *Grovey* v. *Townsend*, 295 U.S. 45 (1935).

25 *Smith* v. *Allwright*, 321 U.S. 649, 660 (1944).

26 345 U.S. 461 (1953).

27 345 U.S. at 484.

28 *See*, Wechsler, *supra* at 40.

29 Chafee, *supra* at 405.

30 My analysis here and at other points owes much to Kalven, *supra*.

31 *Davis* v. *Massachusetts*, 162 Mass.   ℐ (1885).

32 167 U.S. 43 (1897).

33 The Supreme Court first assumed the applicability of the First Amendment to the states in 1925 in *Gitlow* v. *New York*, 268 U.S. 652 (1925).

34 *Hague* v. *C.I.O.*, 307 U.S. 496, 515 (1937).

35 *See, Schneider* v. *State*, 308 U.S. 147 (1939); *Cox* v. *New Hampshire* (1941); *Jamison* v. *Texas*, 318 U.S. 413 (1943). An excellent discussion of these holdings and the public forum decision generally is Stone, *Fora Americana: Speech in Public Places*, 1974 SUPREME COURT REV. 233.

36 379 U.S. 536 (1965).

37 379 U.S. at 555.

38 *See, e.g.*, *Bachellar* v. *Maryland*, 397 U.S. 564 (1970); *Coates* v. *Cincinnati*, 402 U.S. 611 (1971); *Colten* v. *Kentucky*, 407 U.S. 104 (1972).

39 *Brown* v. *Louisiana*, 383 U.S. 131 (1966).

40 *Adderley* v. *Florida*, 385 U.S. 39 (1966).

41 *Tinker* v. *Des Moines School District*, 393 U.S. 503 (1969).

42 *Grayned* v. *City of Rockford*, 408 U.S. 104 (1972).

43 *Chicago Police Dept.* v. *Mosley*, 408 U.S. 92 (1972).

44 *See, e.g.*, the reversal of the convictions for obstructing public passages in *Cox* v. *Louisiana*, 379 U.S. 536 (1965).

45 *See, e.g.*, Barron, *An Emerging First Amendment Right of Access to the Media*, 37 G.W.L. REV. 487 (1969).

46 Cox, *Foreword: Constitutional Adjudication and the Promotion of Human Rights*, 80 HARV. L. REV. 91 (1966).

47 *See, e.g.*, *Burton* v. *Wilmington Parking Authority*, 365 U.S. 715 (1961).

48 WECHSLER, THE NATIONALIZATION OF CIVIL LIBERTIES AND CIVIL RIGHTS 27(1970).

49 *See, e.g.*, the discussion of legislative power in the opinions of Justices Brennan and Clark in *United States* v. *Guest*, 383 U.S. 745, 777, 762 (1966).

50 *See,* the Civil Rights Act of 1968, codified at 18 U.S.C § 245 (1970). *Compare* Cox, *supra* at 91, 120, *with* Wechsler, *supra* at 30.

51 *Jackson* v. *Metropolitan Edison Company*, 95 S. Ct. 419 U.S. 345 (1974).

52 *Amalgamated Food Employees* v. *Logan Valley Plaza*, 391 U.S. 308 (1968).

53 *Lloyd Corporation* v. *Tanner*, 407 U.S. 551 (1972).

54 KALVEN, THE NEGRO AND THE FIRST AMENDMENT 146 (1965).

Chapter 8   Nonstatutory Access to the Print Media

1 Black, *Foreword: "State Action," Equal Protection, and California's Proposition 14*, 81 HARV. L. REV. 69 (1967).

2 418 U.S. 241 (1974).

3 418 U.S. 298 (1974).

4 299 F. Supp. 102 (S.D.N.Y. 1969).

5 *Id.* at 105.

6 306 F. Supp. 1097 (W.D. Wis. 1969), *affirmed,* 441 F. 2d 1257 (7th Cir. 1971).

7 "Thus," the Court of Appeals noted, "the appeal does not present the question of whether there is a constitutional right of access to press under private ownership." 441 F. 2d at 1258.

8 385 F. 2d 151 (3rd Cir. 1967); *cert. denied,* 390 U.S. 920 (1968).

9 Avins has written a long string of "original understanding" articles, many published in leading law reviews.

10 483 U.S. 438 (1954).

11 385 F. 2d at 153-54.

12 324 F. Supp. 268 (W.D. Tex. 1970).

13 324 F. Supp. at 270. Apparently, no appeal was taken by the *Journal.*

14 *Cf., Munn* v. *Illinois,* 94 U.S. 113 (1877), which elaborates the concept of "private property affected with the public interest."

15 *Uhlman* v. *Sherman,* 31 Ohio Dec. 54, 62, (Defiance C.P. 1919).

16 This occurred, rather in passing, in 1925 with *Gitlow* v. *New York,* 268 U.S. 652 (1925).

17 *E.g., Bloss* v. *Federated Publications, Inc.,* 380 Mich. 485 (1968). The head of the Motion Picture Association stated in 1970 that 32 daily newspapers refused to publish ads for either "X" or "R" rated movies. BARRON, FREEDOM OF THE PRESS FOR WHOM 60 (1973).

18 440 F. 2d 133 (1971).

19 435 F. 2d 470 (7th Cir. 1970); *cert. denied,* 402 U.S. 973 (1971).

20 435 F. 2d at 474.

21 322 F. Supp. 1100 (D. Colo. 1971).

22 322 F. Supp. at 1105.

23 *Id.*

24 Now codified as 42 U.S.C. §§ 1981, 1983 (1970).

25 323 F. Supp. 1212 (M.D. Ala. 1971), *affirmed,* 458 F. 2d 1119 (5th Cir. 1972). The initial round of this litigation went forward on the assumption by the district court that the statutes under which the plaintiffs sued could not be violated unless the newspapers were acting "under color of law." The plaintiffs made the ingenious argument that in claiming the protections of the First Amendment as a shield against plaintiffs' access to the white society page, the papers were acting "under color of law." The district court rejected the argument, holding that "under color of law" should encompass only "state action." Private newspapers were not state action.

26 Quoted at 458 F. 2d at 1121.

27 *Id.* at 1124.

28 The title of this Act is the Labor-Management Reporting and Disclosure Act of 1959. The provisions that Yablonski claimed had been violated are codified at 29 U.S.C. §§ 481(c), 501 (1970).

29 305 F. Supp. 868 (D.C. D.C. 1969).

30 305 F. Supp. at 872.

31 307 F. Supp. 1226, 1227.

32 *Kissinger* v. *Transit Authority,* 274 F. Supp. 438 (S.D.N.Y. 1967).

33 *Wirta* v. *Transit District,* 64 Cal. 2d 430, 434 P. 2d 982 (Sup. Ct. Calif. 1967).

34 *Hillside Community Church, Inc.* v. *City of Tacoma,* 76 Wash. 2d 63, 455 P. 2d. 350 (Sup. Ct. Wash. 1969).
35 94 S. Ct. 2714 (1974).
36 *Id.* at 2717.
37 *Id.*
38 *Id.* at 2717-18.
39 *Id.* at 2718.
40 *Id.* at 2719.

PART III
ACCESS TO TELEVISION AND RADIO

1 *Kovacs* v. *Cooper,* 336 U.S. 77, 97 (1949) (concurring opinion).
2 DAVIS, ADMINISTRATIVE LAW TEXT 5 (1972) (emphasis added).
3 BOORSTIN, THE AMERICANS: THE DEMOCRATIC EXPERIENCE 393 (1974).
4 Adler, *Understanding Television,* in TELEVISION AS A SOCIAL FORCE 25 (1975).
5 Robinson, *American Political Legitimacy in an Era of Electronic Journalism, id.* at 105.
6 EPSTEIN, NEWS FROM NOWHERE 9 (1973); Robinson, *supra* at 105.
7 Robinson, *supra* at 107.
8 *Id.* at 109.

Chapter 9   An Overview of Broadcast Regulation

1 65 CONG. REC. 5735 (1924).
2 Coase, *The Federal Communications Commission,* 2 J. LAW & ECON. 1, 7 (1959).
3 48 Stat. 1064 (1934), as amended 47 U.S.C. § 151 *et seq.* (1970).
4 An excellent and concise description of the physical characteristics of the radio spectrum and the statutory basis for its allocation can be found in JONES, REGULATED INDUSTRIES, 1019-76 (1967).
5 S. Rep. No. 659, 61st Cong., 2d Sess. 4 (1910). An excellent short description of the development of law governing radio and television is Coase, *The Federal Communications Commission,* 2 J. LAW & ECON. 1 (1959).
6 37 Stat. 302 (1912).
7 BARNOUW, A TOWER IN BABEL 32 (1966). This work is an exciting history of the development of broadcasting.
8 *Id.* at 79.
9 Coase, *supra* at 4.
10 Barnouw, *supra* at 95. One of the few details on which the Conference seemed to agree was that advertising over the air should not be

countenanced. Hoover wrote of his feeling that "[i] t is inconceivable that we should allow so great a possibility for service to be drowned in advertising chatter." *Id.*

11 *Id.* at 96.

12 *Id.* at 121.

13 *Hoover* v. *Intercity Radio Co.,* 286 Fed. 1003 (D.C. Cir. 1923).

14 *United States* v. *Zenith Radio Corp.,* 12 F.2d 614 (7th Cir. 1926).

15 Barnouw, *supra* at 190.

16 44 Stat. 917 (1926).

17 44 Stat. 1162 (1927).

18 Dr. Brinkley's rise to prominence apparently stemmed from his recommendation that goat glands be transplanted into men complaining of failing potency. Barnouw, *supra* at 168 *et seq.*

19 *KFKB Broadcasting Association* v. *Federal Radio Commission,* 47 F.2d 670, 672 (D.C. Cir. 1931).

20 *E.g., Trinity Methodist Church, South* v. *Federal Radio Commission,* 62 F.2d 850 (D.C. Cir. 1932). where renewal was refused because the licensee, a minister, denounced Jews and Catholics, committed contempt of court under California law, attacked judges and the local bar association, blackmailed unnamed persons for contributions to his church, and spoke freely of pimps and prostitutes—all in broadcasts.

21 Quoted in DILL, RADIO LAW x (1938). A slightly different version of Chief Justice Taft's remark to Senator Dill appears in Barnouw, *supra* at 258.

22 78 CONG. REC. 8828-29 (1934).

23 The current regulations of affiliation agreements and other network program practices can be found in 47 C.F.R. 73.658 (1973).

24 319 U.S. 190 (1943).

25 319 U.S. at 213, 215-17.

26 *Id.* at 226-27.

27 The phrase is Harry Kalven's, *Broadcasting, Public Policy and The First Amendment,* 10 J. LAW & ECON. 15, 30 (1967).

28 Coase, *The Federal Communications Commission,* 2 J LAW & ECON. 1, 7 (1959).

29 In rare cases, the height of permissible structures is another limitation of land ownership.

30 A helpful comparison of land and the spectrum in terms of these issues can be found in Malone, *Broadcasting, the Reluctant Dragon: Will the First Amendment Right of Access End the Suppressing of Controversial Ideas?* 5 U. MICH. J. L. REF. 193, 241 *et seq.* (1972). *See also* Jones, *supra* at 1020 *et seq.* and Coase, *supra.*

31 However, our capacity to "find" and effectively use more spectrum space has grown in a fashion similar to our capacity to find and effectively use iron ore. *See,* Jones, *supra* at 1021.

32 Jones, *Use and Regulation of the Radio Spectrum: Report on a Conference,* 1968 WASH. U. L. Q. 71, 87 (1968).

33 Kalven, *Broadcasting, Public Policy and the First Amendment,* 10 J. LAW & ECON. 15, 30 (1967). Although my conclusions about broadcasting and the

First Amendment are substantially different from those of Professor Kalven, my analysis owes a great deal to his excellent treatment.

34 See Malone *supra* at 245.

35 47 U.S.C. § 301 (1970). *See also*, 47 U.S.C. § 309(h) 1970).

36 47 U.S.C. §§ 302(a), 303(f), 307(a), 316.

37 MINOW, EQUAL TIME 9 (1964).

38 47 U.S.C. § 307(b).

39 This language was added by a 1959 amendment, which was intended to codify the FCC's administrative practice. 73 Stat. 557 (1959), *amending* 47 U.S.C. § 315(a) (1970).

40 LE DUC, CABLE TELEVISION AND THE FCC 44 (1973).

41 47 U.S.C. § 315(a).

42 47 U.S.C. § 153(h) (1970).

43 47 U.S.C. § 326 (1970).

44 A trust is a legal conception whereby the incidents of ownership and control over property can be given to a person subject to duties to administer the property for the benefit of others. *See*, SCOTT, ABRIDGMENT OF THE LAW OF TRUSTS, sec. 2.1 *et seq.* (1960).

Chapter 10   Politics and Access: The "Equal Opportunities" Provision of Section 315

1   Quoted in H. Rep. No. 464, 69th Cong., 1st. Sess. 16 (Minority Views) (1926).

2   *Id.* at 17.

3   *Id.*

4   The proposal is set out at 67 Cong. Rec. 12503 (1926), and described in S. Rep. No. 772, 69th Cong., 1st Sess. 4 (1926) (emphasis added).

5   67 CONG. REC. 12503 (1926).

6   *Id.* at 12504.

7   *Id.* at 12505.

8   68 CONG. REC. 2589 (1927).

9   *See, e.g.* S. 2910, 73d Cong., 2d Sess. § 315(a)(1934); H.R. 7716, 72d Cong., 1st Sess. § 315 (1932).

10 H.R. 7716, 72d Cong., 1st Sess. (1932), passed 76 Cong. Rec. 3768 (1933).

11 S. 3285, 73d Cong., 2d Sess. (1934).

12 The proposed provision is set out in S. Rep. No. 781, 73d Cong., 2d Sess. 8 (1934). This legislative history is admirably discussed in *Felix v. Westinghouse Radio Stations, Inc.*, 186 F. 2d 1 (3rd Cir. 1950).

13 H. Rep. No. 1918, 73d Cong., 2d Sess. 49 (1934).

14 66 Stat. 717 (1952).

15 The words "under this subsection" were added by Public Law 92-225, 86. Stat. 3 (1972). Earlier the Statutes at Large showed the word "hereby" before "imposed" but the United States Code did not. *Compare*, 66 Stat. 717 (1953) *with*, 47 U.S.C. § 315(b) (1970). See Friedenthal and Medalie, *The Impact of Federal Regulation on Political Broadcasting: Section 315 of*

the Communications Act, 72 HARV. L. REV. 445, 446 n. 6 (1959).

16   *Id.* at 447. In 1952, Congress added a provision to section 315 to the effect that broadcasters could not charge higher rates for political advertising by candidates than for commercial advertisements. 66 Stat. 717 (1952), codified as 47 U.S.C. § 315(b) (1970).

17   *See, Felix* v. *Westinghouse Radio Stations, Inc., supra;* this hard-and-fast rule is criticized in Singer, *The FCC and Equal Time: Never-Neverland Revisited,* 27 MD. L. REV. 221, 225 (1967).

18   For example, problems can arise if a candidate for the first time demands equal opportunities late in a campaign, when the result of granting equal opportunity would be to give that candidate predominant air-time just prior to the election. Unfairness may also result because each primary and central election is treated separately under the statute. One candidate in a primary election can therefore get much more exposure than his or her ultimate opponent in the general election, without the ultimate opponent having a right to equal opportunities. These and other problems of administration are thoughtfully discussed in Friedenthal and Medalie, *supra.*

The Commission rules provide that the broadcaster need not notify other candidates but most make facilities available on request. *See* 47 C.F.R. §§ 73.120, 73.290, and 73.657 (1973).

19   These and other FCC rulings are discussed in Singer, *supra* at 228.

20   *Columbia Broadcasting System,* 18 RR 238, *reconsideration denied,* 18 RR 701 (1959).

21   S. Rep. No. 562, 86th Cong., 1st Sess. 10 (1959).

22   The 1959 amendment provided:
"Appearance by a legally qualified candidate on any—
   "(1) bona fide newscast,
   "(2) bona fide news interview,
   "(3) bona fide news documentary (if the appearance of the candidate is incidental to the presentation of the subject or subjects covered by the news documentary), or
   "(4) on-the-spot coverage of bona fide news events (including but not limited to political conventions and activities incidental thereto),
shall not be deemed to be use of a broadcasting station within the meaning of this subsection. Nothing in the foregong sentence shall be construed as relieving broadcasters, in connection with the presentation of newscasts, news interviews, news documentaries, and on-the-spot coverage of news events, from the obligation imposed upon them under this Act to operate in the public interest and to afford reasonable opportunity for the discussion of conflicting views on issues of public importance."
73 Stat. 557 (1959), 47 U.S.C. § 315 (1970).

23   *The Goodwill Station, Inc.,* 40 FCC 362 (1962); *see also, National Broadcasting Co.,* 40 FCC 370 (1962).

24   *Columbia Broadcasting System, Inc.,* 40 FCC 395 (1964).

25   74 Stat. 554 (1960).

26   For an entertaining and thoughtful account of fringe parties in our history, see Hesseltine, THIRD PARTY MOVEMENTS IN THE UNITED STATES (1962).

27   Other proposals to deal with this problem are described in Friedenthal and Medalie, *supra,* at 460 *et seq.*

28 MINOW, MARTIN & MITCHELL, PRESIDENTIAL TELEVISION 54 (1973). (Hereinafter cited as Minow).

29 *See, Hearings on Section 315,* Senate Subcommittee on Communications, 88th Cong., 1st. Sess. (1963).

30 *Petition of the Aspen Institute and CBS, Inc., for Revision or Clarification of Commission Rulings under Section 315(a)(2) and 315(a)(4),* FCC 75-1090 (released September 30, 1975).

31 *See,* 15 *Television Digest* No. 39 (1975).

32 *See* Friedenthal and Medalie, *supra* at 476 *et seq.*

33 For example, the FCC has held that the licensee may not censor a political advertisement preaching racial hatred or other inflammatory material unless the ad would be likely to produce violence or imminent lawless action. *Letter to Lonnie King,* FCC 72-711, August 3, 1972.

34 *Farmers Educ. and Cooperative Union* v. *WDAU, Inc.,* 360 U.S. 525 (1959).

35 86 Stat. 4 (1972).

36 This Act's effort to regulate the charges by newspapers and broadcasters for political ads, as well as broader access proposals discussed during debate on the Act, will be discussed in chapter 15, *infra.*

37 Unless the President is an announced candidate for re-election at the time of his appearance, the "equal opportunities" rights of section 315(a) are not triggered. *McCarthy* v. *FCC,* 390 F. 2d 471 (D.C. Cir. (1968).

38 The statistics are provided in Minow, 171 *et seq.*

39 Minow, Foreword ix.

40 *Id.*

41 Fred Friendly has written:
    The drafters of the American Constitution strove diligently to prevent the power of the president from becoming a monopoly, but our inability to manage television has allowed the medium to be converted into an electronic throne. *Id.* at vii.

42 Quoted in Note, *Televised Presidential Addresses and the FCC's Fairness Doctrine,* 7 COLUM. J. LAW & SOC. PROBL. 75, 103 (1971).

43 Mr. Albert drew 17 million on one broadcast and 15 million on another; Senator Humphrey drew 15 million. NEW YORK TIMES, January 25, 1975, at 55, col. 5.

44 *Id.*

45 Under the Commission's separate election theory an address by a President who is an announced candidate for renomination would trigger only equal opportunities rights for other candidates for his party's nomination, not for candidates of the opposition party. See Friedenthal and Medalie, *supra* at 455.

46 *Columbia Broadcasting System,* 14 RR 720 (1956).

47 *Republican National Committee,* 3 RR 2d 647 (1964).

48 *Committee for the Fair Broadcasting of Controversial Issues,* 19 RR 2d 1103 (1970).

49 *See, Televised Presidential Addresses and the FCC's Fairness Doctrine, supra* at 93.

50 Quoted *id.* at 80.

51 25 FCC 2d 739 (1970).

52 *Columbia Broadcasting System, Inc.* v. *FCC* 454 F. 2d 1018 (1971).

53 *Id.* at 1027.

54 24 RR 2d 1917, 1926 (1972).

55 *Minow*, supra at 107.

56 For an excellent discussion of the pros and cons of televising congressional proceedings, *see generally,* OPENLY ARRIVED AT (Twentieth Century Fund 1974).

57 Minow, *supra* at 151.

58 *Id.* at 147.

59 Quoted *id.* at 103.

60 A critique of opposition party access proposals and the analysis underlying them can be found in Whitehead, *Media Chic*, 83 YALE L.J. 1751 (1974).

61 *Minow et al, supra* at 148.

Chapter 11   The Fairness Doctrine and Access to the Electronic Media

1 *Columbia Broadcasting System, Inc.* v. *Democratic Nat'l Comm.*, 412 U.S. 94, 117 (1973).

2 *Red Lion Broadcasting Co.* v. *FCC*, 395 U.S. 367 (1969).

3 *Great Lakes Broadcasting Company*, 3 F.R.C. Ann. Rep. 32 (1929).

4 13 FCC 1246 (1949).

5 73 Stat. 557 (1959).

6 105 CONG. REC. 14457 (1959).

7 *Id.*

8 *Id.* at 14458.

9 Conf. Rep. No. 1069, 86th Cong., 1st Sess. (1959).

10 *See, Letter to the Honorable Oren Harris*, 40 FCC 583 (1963).

11 *Cullman Broadcasting Co.*, 40 FCC 576 (1963).

12 *Clayton W. Mapoles*, 23 RR 586, 591 (1962):

Our singling out this area of the problem of fairness for specific treatment reflected not only our concern but our decision that a licensee must act with an especially high degree of responsibility where his broadcast facilities are used to attack a person or group. In appropriate recognition of the serious nature of such attacks, we pointed out that fairness may dictate that "time be allocated" to the person or group attacked. Where, as here, the attacks are of a highly personal nature which impugn the character and honesty of named individuals, the licensee has affirmative duty to take all appropriate steps to see to it that the persons attacked are afforded the fullest opportunity to respond.

13 *Billings Broadcasting Co.*, 23 RR 951 (1962).

14 *Times-Mirror Broadcasting Co.*, 24 RR 404 (1962).

15 47 CFR § 73.123 (1973).

16 *National Broadcasting Co.* v. *United States*, 319 U.S. 190 (1943), discussed in Chapter 9, *supra*.

17 *Red Lion Broadcasting Co.* v. *FCC*, 381 F. 2d 908 (1967).

18 381 F.2d at 924.

19 See, Friendly, *What's Fair on the Air?*, NEW YORK TIMES MAGAZINE 12 (March 30, 1975).

20 *Radio & Television News Directors Ass'n v. United States,* 400 F.2d 1002 (1968).

21 395 U.S. 367 (1969). Justice Douglas did not participate in the decision.

22 *Id.* at 378-79.

23 *Id.* at 388, 389-90.

24 *Id.* at 393.

25 *Id.*

26 *Id.* at 393-94.

27 *Associated Press v. United States,* 326 U.S. 1 (1945). *See,* discussion at Chapter 5, *supra.*

28 395 U.S. at 387.

29 *Id.* at 390.

30 *Id.*

31 *Id.* at 386-87 n. 15.

32 *Id.* at 401 n. 28.

33 Barron, *Access—The Only Choice for the Media?* 48 TEXAS L. REV. 766, 769-71 (1970):
    Red Lion launches the Supreme Court on the path of an affirmative approach to freedom of expression that emphasizes the positive dimension of the first amendment. In fact, the access-for-ideas rationale practically replaces the original legal justification for broadcast regulation—that broadcasting is a limited-access medium.
    ... (T)he opinion is studded with observations that give it a radical undertone throughout and that display the constant tension in the opinion, and perhaps in the Court, between a rationale for broadcast regulation based on limitation of the spectrum and one based on maximizing opportunities for expression.
    .... The *Red Lion* case therefore finds the law of freedom of expression in mid-passage. Old and new theories of broadcast regulation walk into each other in the case.

34 *Red Lion* leaves room for First Amendment claims where outright suppression of expression is the issue. By positing First Amendment interests as belonging to listeners rather than broadcasters, *Red Lion* invites active judicial scrutiny of suppression problems. But even in this area, the courts are much more relaxed about FCC intervention than would be expected in the case of print media. *See, Yale Broadcasting Co. v. FCC,* 478 F.2d 594 (D.C. Cir. 1973) *cert. denied,* 414 U.S. 914 (1973), where the FCC, noting potential adverse effect of songs glorifying drug use, stated that "the broadcaster could jeopardize his license by failing to exercise licensee responsibility in this area." 31 FCC 2d 377 (1971). The Commission's action was upheld in the courts.

35 Barron, *supra* at 771.

36 *Committee for the Fair Broadcasting of Controversial Issues,* 25 FCC 2d 283 (1970).

37 *First Report,* Docket No. 19260, 36 FCC 2d 40 (1972). The failure of the Fairness Doctrine to provide a right of reply to presidential broadcasts has led to the statutory proposals by Minow *et al.* discussed in the preceding chapter.

38 Matter of *WCBS-TV*, 8 FCC 2d 381 (1967), *aff'd on rehearing, Application of the Fairness Doctrine to Cigarette Advertising*, 9 FCC 2d 921 (1967); *aff'd. sub. nom. Banzhaf* v. *FCC*, 405 F.2d 1082 (D.C. Cir. 1968); *cert. denied, sub. nom. Tobacco Institute* v. *FCC*, 396 U.S. 842 (1969).

39 *See, e.g., Sam Morris*, 11 FCC 197 (1946); *Broadcast of Programs Advertising Alcoholic Beverages*, 5 RR Radio Reg. 593 (1949): *Letter to Senator Edwin C. Johnson*, 5 RR Radio Reg. 597 (1949).

40 *Matter of WSBA*, 20 FCC 2d 557 (1969).

41 *Complaint Against NBC*, 16 FCC 2d 956 (1969).

42 *Report on Cigarette Advertising*, 16 FCC 2d 284 (1969).

43 The provision is codified at 15 U.S.C. 1335 (1970); the constitutionality of this ban was upheld in *Capital Broadcasting Co.* v. *Mitchell*, 333 F. Supp. 582 (D.C. D.C. 1971), *aff'd. mem.* 405 U.S. 1000 (1972). In 1973 Congress amended section 1335 to include little cigars in the statutory ban on electronic media advertising. 87 Stat. 352 (1973).

44 The Commission refused to order pollution counter-commercials in response to car and gasoline ads in *Friends of the Earth*, 24 FCC 2d 743 (1970). The Court of Appeals for the District of Columbia reversed in *Friends of the Earth* v. *FCC*, 449 F.2d 1164 (1971). But the FCC still balked, in *Friends of the Earth* 33 FCC 2d 648 (1972), and the parties finally settled the dispute.
     The Commission also refused to order counter-commercials in rulings on phosphate-based detergent ads: 30 FCC 2d 640 (1971); on deceptive gasoline ads: 29 FCC 2d 807 (1971); on Alaska pipeline ads: 30 FCC 2d 643 (1971); on the military draft: 24 FCC 2d 171 (1971).

45 *The Handling of Public Issues under the Fairness Doctrine and the Public Interest Standards of the Communications Act*, Docket No. 19260, FCC 74-702 (July 12, 1974). 30 RR 2d 1261, 1265.

46 *Id.* at 1264-65.

47 *Report on Personal Attacks and Political Candidates*, 8 FCC 2d 721, 725 (1967).

48 47 CFR § 73.123 (1973).

49 *Rome Hospital and Murphy Memorial Hospital*, 40 FCC 2d 452 (1972).

50 *In re Complaint of Philadelphia Federation of Teachers*, FCC 74-1272, released Nov. 27, 1974.

51 *Compare In re Complaint of John J. Salchert*, released Aug. 12, 1974, *with In re Complaint of Leonard W. Moss*, FCC 74-859, released July 31, 1974.

52 *Compare University of Houston*, 11 FCC 2d 790 (1968), *with J. Allen Carr*, 30 FCC 2d 894 (1971).

53 *Compare WMCE, Inc.*, 26 FCC 2d 354 (1970), *with WCMP Broadcasting Co.*, 41 FCC 2d 201 (1973).

54 *Compare Storer Broadcasting Co.*, 11 FCC 2d 678 (1968), *and WIYN Radio, Inc.*, 24 RR 2d 505 (1972), *with CBS, Inc.*, 21 RR 2d 497 (1971).

55 *Compare In re Complaint of Philadelphia Federation of Teachers*, 31 RR 2d 36 (1974), *with In re Complaint of Benjamin S. Rosenthal*, FCC 75-22, released January 8, 1975. The author is of counsel to the broadcaster in the above case. The FCC decision in *Rosenthal* was reversed by the Court of Appeals. *See,* Chapter 12, *infra.*

56 *Compare Storer Broadcasting Co., supra, and WIYN Radio, supra, with Dorothy Healy*, 24 FCC 2d 487 (1970) *aff'd., Healy* v. *FCC*, 460 F.2d 917 (D.C. Cir. 1972).

57 *Compare National Association of Government Employees and Mr. Kenneth T. Lyons,* 41 FCC 2d 965 (1973), *with Dr. John Gabler,* 27 RR 2d 1249 (1973).

58 *In re Complaint of Morris Gardner,* FCC 74-1163, released Oct. 29, 1974. Cf. the statement of Professor Barrow:

> (T)he attack must not be private, but public in the sense that it is a factor in the listener's decision on the controversial issue; and in no event do the rules apply to a personal attack made during a bona fide newscast, on-the-spot coverage of a bona fide news event, bona fide news interview, and news commentary or analysis in a bona fide newscast.

Barrow, *The Equal Opportunities and Fairness Doctrines in Broadcasting: Pillars in the Forum of Democracy,* 37 U. CINN. L. REV. 447, 498 (1968).

59 *In re Complaint of Benjamin S. Rosenthal, supra,* dissenting opinion by Commissioner Robinson.

60 GELLER, THE FAIRNESS DOCTRINE IN BROADCASTING 71 (1973).

61 32 FED. REG. 11531 (1967).

62 *See,* the discussion of the Seventh Circuit Court of Appeals on these exemptions. 400 F.2d at 1007 *et seq.*

63 Geller, *supra* at 72.

64 See Geller, *supra* at 73 *et seq.*

65 47 U.S.C. § 399 (1970).

66 Geller, *supra* at 74 n. 3.

67 *Columbia Broadcasting System, Inc.* v. *Democratic Nat'l Comm., 412 U.S. 94, 117 (1973).*

68 *Democratic National Committee* 25 FCC 2d 21 (1970). The FCC did grant limited approval to the right of political parties to have ads accepted for the purpose of soliciting funds. This ruling was not appealed. *See also Business Executives' Move for Vietnam Peace,* 25 FCC 2d 242 (1970).

69 *Business Executives' Move for Vietnam Peace* v. *FCC; Democratic Nat'l. Comm.* v. *FCC,* 450 F.2d 642 (D.C. Cir. 1971).

70 Judge Wright's conclusion that broadcasters should be treated as state action rested on two theories: (a) that the process of licensing established a relation of "interdependence" with government, and (b) that the electronic media have become "our foremost forum for public speech." *Id.* at 651.

71 Judge McGowan dissented for the reason, among others, that the majority was imposing on the FCC a task that could not be discharged. *Id.* at 666.

72 *Id.* at 654. An excellent discussion of the possible ways of implementing a right of access to broadcast advertising may be found in Malone, *Broadcasting, The Reluctant Dragon: Will the First Amendment Right of Access End the Suppressing of Controversial Ideas?* 5 MICH. J.L. REF. 194, 252 *et seq.* (1972).

73 450 F. 2d at 650.

74 *The Supreme Court, 1972 Term,* 87 HARV. L. REV. 1, 178 (1973).

75 412 U.S. at 120-21.

76 412 U.S. at 126-27.

77 *Id.* at 131.

78 *Id.* at 117-18. The broadcasters in *B.E.M.-DNC* did not argue that such access obligations as the plaintiffs sought would violate the broadcasters' First Amendment rights; rather they contended that such obligations were

neither required nor supported by the Communications Act, nor mandated by the First Amendment.

79   *Id.* at 138.

80   *Id.* at 146.

81   *Id.* at 145 (emphasis in original).

82   *Id.* at 148, 154, 160.

83   *Id.* at 177 (emphasis in original).

84   *Id.* at 193.

85   *Id.* at 199.

Chapter 12   Access, Autonomy, and the Public Interest in Broadcasting

1   *Citizens Committee to Save WEFM v. FCC,* 506 F.2d 246, 281 (1974).

2   *In the Matter of the Handling of Public Issues,* 30 RR 2d at 1292 (1974).

3   *First Report-Handling of Political Broadcasts,* 24 RR 2d 1917, 1926 (1972).

4   *Id.* at 1929.

5   *In the Matter of the Handling of Public Issues, supra,* at 1297-98.

6   Friendly, *What's Fair on the Air?,* NEW YORK TIMES MAGAZINE 12 (March 30, 1975).

7   *Id.* at 37.

8   *Letters,* NEW YORK TIMES MAGAZINE 70 (April 27, 1975).

9   *Office of Communication of United Church of Christ v. FCC,* (I) 359 F.2d 994 (D.C. Cir. 1966); (II) 425 F.2d 543 (D.C. Cir. 1969). The station was not actually judged to be unqualified to hold the license, but renewal was denied and WLBT was reduced to the status of one of several applicants for the license it had previously held.

10   473 F.2d 16 (D.C. Cir. 1972). In response to Judge Bazelon's dissent, Judge Wright filed an opinion, with which Judge Tamm concurred, that the refusal to renew rested adequately and independently on the licensee's filing of deceptive papers with the Commission. *Id.* at 81.

11   *In re Applications of Alabama Educational Television Commission,* 32 RR 2d 539 (1975).

12   *Id.* at 546. The Commission examined the amount of "integrated programming," defined as programs on which at least one black person appeared. It also found a pattern of precluding black-oriented programs made available by NET. *Id.* at 550.

13   Because of the improvements, the Commission allowed AETC to file as an applicant for the stations again, though without any preferred position, of course. *Id.* at 561.

14   *Id.* at 562. The dissenters were Commissioners Lee and Reid.

15   *In re Applications of Star Stations, Inc.,* 32 RR 2d 1151 (1975).

16   *In the Matter of the Handling of Public Issues, supra* at 1276.

17   *Stone v. FCC,* 466 F.2d 316 (C.A. D.C. 1972); *Bilingual Bicultural Coalition of Mass Media, Inc. v. FCC,* 492 F.2d 656 (1974). The Commission has promulgated section 73.680 of its rules, requiring all licensees to afford equal opportunity in employment.

18 *See generally,* Obledo & Joselow, *Broadcasting: Mexican-Americans and the Media,* 1 CHICANO L. REV. 85 (1972). A typical agreement of this kind might commit the station to employ roughly the proportion of the minority group equal to that of the population served by the station, to meet regularly with community representatives to discuss programming, to require key personnel to participate in sensitivity training to better understand minority groups, to broadcast a minimum number of specials aimed at the needs of the minority group, etc. One agreement commits the station to hiring members of a minority for specific personnel slots, such as the anchorman on a designated news program.

19 *Office of Communication of United Church of Christ v. FCC,* 465 F.2d 519, 527 (D.C. Cir. 1972).

20 GELLER, THE FAIRNESS DOCTRINE IN BROADCASTING 51 (1973).

21 Geller reasons that the campaign context is one area where Congress intended fairness violations to be corrected promptly, before the election, as indicated by the equal opportunities requirement of section 315(a).

22 Geller's position on personal attacks is spelled out in an amicus brief in *Straus Communications, Inc. v. FCC,* No. 75-1084-(D.C. Cir. decided January 16, 1975).

23 Geller, *Supra* at 69.

24 *Brandywine-Main Line Radio, Inc. v. FCC,* 473 F.2d 16, 64 (1972).

25 *Id.*

26 *Id.* at 68.

27 *Id.* at 70.

28 *Id.*

29 *Citizens Committee to Preserve the Voice of the Arts in Atlanta v.FCC,* 436 F.2d 263 (1970).

30 506 F.2d 246 (1974).

31 *Id.* at 273.

32 *Id.* at 275.

33 Bazelon has amplified his views on reform of broadcast regulation in *FCC Regulation of the Telecommunications Press,* 1975 DUKE L.J. 213.

34 *National Broadcasting Company, Inc. v. FCC,* 516 F.2d 1101 (1974). The Commission decision is reported at 44 FCC 2d 1027 (1973).

35 395 U.S. at 393.

36 412 U.S. at 117.

37 516 F.2d at 1118.

38 *Id.* at 1120.

39 516 F.2d at 1122.

40 *Id.* at 1153.

41 Employee Retirement Income Security Act of 1974, Public Law 93-406.

42 516 F.2d 1182.

Chapter 13   Access to Cable Television

1 THOREAU, WALDEN 67 (1950).

2 *The Wired Island: The First Two Years of Public Access to Cable Television*

in Manhattan 4 (The Fund for the City of New York 1973).

3 In practice, the standard cable in use today carries 20 to 25 channels, but two cables are frequently installed in larger metropolitan areas to double this total.

4 "Grandfathering" refers to the common arrangement in which new administrative rules are made applicable only to newly created entities, with existing entities exempted either indefinitely or for a specified time.

5 CABLE: CABINET COMMITTEE REPORT ON CABLE COMMUNICATIONS Ch. 1, p. 4 (1974).

6 *Id.* at 5.

7 ON THE CABLE 38-39 (Sloan Commission on Cable Communication 1971).

8 *Broadcasting*, April 14, 1975. Cable penetration is not generalized throughout the nation, but rather massive saturation of the homes in certain areas where cable has been successful.

9 LE DUC, CABLE TELEVISION AND THE FCC 6 (1973). I am greatly indebted to Professor Le Duc for giving an early version of this chapter the benefit of his expert review. He saved me from many errors and contributed greatly to the ideas presented in the chapter. He is, of course, not accountable for the ideas presented here, nor for errors that remain.

10 *Id.*

11 A useful survey of opinion on the immense social implications of cable television can be found in GILLESPIE, PUBLIC ACCESS CABLE TELEVISION IN THE UNITED STATES AND CANADA (1975).

12 Le Duc, *supra* at 9. A microwave link involves the transmission of a narrow beam signal aimed at the receiver. A microwave relay system involves a series of such point-to-point transmissions.

13 Le Duc, *supra* at 121. An excellent account of the FCC's regulation of cable is La Pierre, *Cable Television and the Promise of Programming Diversity*, 42 FORD. L. REV. 25 (1973). This article was initially submitted as part of the requirements for the Columbia Law School Seminar in Electronic Media and the First Amendment.

14 The Commission's power to regulate microwave relays under its authority to regulate communications common carriers was sustained in *Carter Mountain Transmission Corp. v. FCC*, 321 F.2d 359 (D.C. Cir. 1963); *cert. den.*, 375 U.S. 951 (1963).

15 *See*, Le Duc, *supra* at 132.

16 *First Report and Order*, 38 FCC 683 (1965). This Report is discussed in detail in Le Duc, *supra* at 141 *et seq.*

17 *Second Report and Order*, 2 FCC 2d 725 (1966). The carriage and nonduplication rules adopted in 1966 were sustained by the Supreme Court in *United States v. Southwestern Cable Co.*, 392 U.S. 157 (1968).

18 ON THE CABLE, *supra* at 29.

19 La Pierre has pointed out that the distant signal rule was waived in 105 cases, but that waivers were concentrated in the lower part of the top 100 markets. La Pierre, *supra* at 52 n. 165.

20 Le Duc, *supra* at 154.

21 La Pierre, *supra* at 54.

22 *Fortnightly Corp. v. United Artists Television*, 392 U.S. 390 (1968). This ruling was reaffirmed in 1974. *Teleprompter Corp. v. Columbia Broadcast-*

ing System, 94 S. Ct. 1129 (1974).

23 392 U.S. 157 (1968).

24 Le Duc, *supra* at 182.

25 *Notice of Proposed Rulemaking and Notice of Inquiry into Rules and Regulations Relative to CATV Systems,* 15 FCC 2d 417 (1968).

26 La Pierre, *supra* at 58.

27 Price, *Requiem for the Wired Nation: Cable Rulemaking at the FCC,* 61 U. VA. L. REV. 541 (1975).

28 The sort of revolutionary social potential some saw in the emergence of cable television is suggested by the names of such cable-oriented publications as GUERRILLA TELEVISION and RADICAL SOFTWARE. *See,* Gillespie, *supra* at 38.

29 *See,* Le Duc, *supra* at 195 *et seq.*; Price, *supra* at 560.

30 *Cable Television Report and Order on Rules and Regulations Relating to CATV Systems,* 36 FCC 2d 143 (1972).

31 These are described in La Pierre, *supra* at 63.

32 *See,* Price *supra* 553 *et seq.*

33 *First Report and Order on Rules and Regulations Relative to CATV Systems,* 20 FCC 2d 201 (1969).

34 *Midwest Video Corp.* v. *United States,* 441 F. 2d 1322 (8th Cir. 1971). The Supreme Court reversed the Eighth Circuit decision, primarily on the ground that the Commission could legitimately regulate cable systems to "assure that in the retransmission of broadcast signals viewers are provided suitably diversified programming." *United States* v. *Midwest Video Corp.,* 406 U.S. 649, 669 (1972).

35 39 FED. REG. 43302 (1974).

36 47 CFR § 76.251 *et seq. (1972). See,* La Pierre, *supra* at 92. The 20 channel minimum applies throughout the top 100 markets.

37 La Pierre, *supra* at 93.

38 *Docket No. 20363,* 34 RR 2d 723, 736 (1975).

39 *FCC Report on Cable Television Service,* 37 FED. REG. 3252 (1972).

40 47 CFR § 76.251 (a)(4)(1972).

41 *Columbus Communications Corp.,* 26 RR 2d 368 (1973). However, the Commission approved the use of the public access channel for technical testing or leasing so long as public access use is given priority. *Metro Cable Co.,* 26 RR 2d 734 (1973).

42 *Stark County Communications, Inc.,* 26 RR 2d 371 (1972), 26 RR 2d 722 (1973).

43 Le Duc, *supra* at 204.

44 Price & Morris, *Public Access Channels: The New York City Experience,* Appendix C, ON THE CABLE 230.

45 *Id.* at 237.

46 *Id.*

47 *Id.*

48 *The Wired Island: The First Two Years of Public Access to Cable Television in Manhattan* 1973.

49 *Id.* at 5-6.

50 *Id.* at 19. A useful comparison is that the budget for Channel 13, New York's public VHF television station is $15-20 million. *Id.*

51 *See* Gillespie, *supra* at 70.

52 Dystel, *Public Access Cabletalk Becomes Doubletalk*, ARGUS, (Pacific Northwest Weekly) 5 (April 18, 1975).

53 MAYER, ABOUT TELEVISION 372 (1972).

54 *Amendment and Clarification of Television Service Rules*, 29 RR 2d 1621, 1631 (1974).

55 Mayer, *supra* at 359.

56 *The Wired Island* at 37.

57 Several commentators have proposed that the Fairness Doctrine and equal opportunities rules be eliminated from cablecasts generally since, in contrast to broadcasting, there is no scarcity of outlets to create barriers to access. *e.g.,* Simmons, *The Fairness Doctrine and Cable TV*, 11 HARV. J. LEGIS. 629 (1974). For a contrary view, *see,* Barrow, *supra* at 702.

58 *Report on Cable Television Service*, 37 FED. REG. 3252 § 145 (1972). A person attacked on an open access channel need only apply to have access in any case, and thus open access makes rules that require access in certain circumstances meaningless.

59 *Id.* § 135.

60 *Id.* § 141.

61 *See,* La Pierre, *supra* at 104 n. 442.

62 *The Wired Island* at 19.

63 Gillespie, *supra* at 84.

64 Mayer, *supra* at 388.

65 These ideas are based on a letter of May 2, 1975, from Professor Le Duc to the author.

66 47 C.F.R. §§ 76.205, 76.209 (1972). Rules respecting obscenity, sponsorship identification, and lotteries are likewise parallel. 47 C.F.R. §§ 76.215, 76.221, 76.213 (1972).

67 *Memorandum Order and Opinion (Cablecasting)*, 23 FCC 2d 825 (1970).

68 *See,* discussion in Chapter 9, *supra.*

69 *See,* Bazelon, *FCC Regulation of the Telecommunications Press,* 1975 DUKE L.J. 213, 223 (1975).

70 ON THE CABLE, *supra at 92.*

71 CABLE: CABINET COMMITTEE REPORT ON CABLE COMMUNICATIONS Ch. I, p. 14, Ch. II, p. 13 (1974). The Cabinet Committee's excellent 1974 report recommends that cable operators should control the distribution of channels, but should have no control over the programming that goes out over the channels. Channels would be leased by anyone having a program or other communications service to provide. This separations policy would eliminate the need for government oversight of programming, would offer unrestricted access to those who wished to use cable channels, and would provide cable customers with a rich diversity of choice. Unfortunately, the Cabinet Committee Report was released in January 1974, during the Watergate time when the Nixon administration was not looked to for serious policy initiatives; nor was Clay Whitehead, the committee chairman, identified at the time with progressive communications policy. Hopefully, the report will receive serious consideration.

PART IV
THE *MIAMI HERALD* DECISION
AND THE FUTURE OF ACCESS

1   418 U.S. 241 (1974).

Chapter 14   Miami Herald Publishing Co. v. *Tornillo*

1   Bickel, The "Uninhibited, Robust and Wide-Open" First Amendment, 54 COMMENTARY 60, 61 (1972).

2   F.S.A. § 104.38 (Supp. 1972). The statute was enacted as part of a general effort to prevent electoral abuses. *See generally,* Keen, *Brief History of Corrupt Practice Acts of Florida,* 9 FLA. L. J. 297 (1935).

3   *State* v. *News-Journal Corp.,* 36 Fla. Supp. 164 (Volusia County Judges Ct. 1972).

4   38 Fla. Supp. 80 (1972).

5   287 So. 2d 78 (1973).

6   *Id.* at 81 (emphasis deleted).

7   *Id.* at 80.

8   *Id.* at 82 (emphasis deleted).

9   *Id.* 83 (emphasis deleted).

10   *Id.* at 86. This construction drew a dissent from one justice. *Id.* at 89.

11   416 U.S. 312 (19740.

12   418 U.S. at 250-51.

13   418 U.S. at 254, 56.

14   418 U.S. at 256-57.

15   418 U.S. at 258.

16   *Associated Press* v. *United States,* 326 U.S. 1, 20 n. 18 (1945).

17   418 U.S. at 254.

18   408 U.S. 655, 681 (1972), cited at 418 U.S. at 254-55.

19   *Pittsburgh Press Co.* v. *Human Relations Comm'n.,* 413 U.S. 376, 391 (1973), cited at 418 U.S. at 255.

20   *Columbia Broadcasting Sys., Inc.* v. *Democratic Nat'l. Comm.,* 412 U.S. 94, 117 (1973), cited at 418 U.S. at 255.

21   418 U.S. at 258.

22   *Id.*

23   418 U.S. at 261.

24   *See, e.g., New York Times Co.* v. *Sullivan,* 376 U.S. 254 (1964) (Black, J., concurring); *New York Times Co.* v. *United States,* 403 U.S. 713, 714 (1971). (Black, J., concurring).

25   *See, e.g., New York Times Co.* v. *United States,* 403 U.S. at 714.

26   315 U.S. 568, 571-72 (1942).

27   *Beauharnais* v. *Illinois,* 343 U.S. 250 (1952).

28   *Roth* v. *United States,* 354 U.S. 476 (1957).

29   *Chaplinsky* v. *New Hampshire, supra.*

30 The definitional approach continues to mark constitutional adjudication about obscenity; *see, e.g., Miller v. California*, 413 U.S. 15 (1973).

31 Barron, *An Emerging First Amendment Right of Access to the Media?*, 37 GEO. WASH. L. REV. 487 (1969); *Access to the Press—A New First Amendment Right*, 80 HARV. L. REV. 1641 (1967).

32 *Cf., Report of the Study Group on the Caseload of the Supreme Court* (the *"Freund Commission Report"*) (Federal Judicial Center 1972).

33 418 U.S. 683 (1974).

34 *See generally*, Professor Kurland's discussion of "decision by deadline" in POLITICS, THE CONSTITUTION, AND THE WARREN COURT 194 *et seq.* (1970).

Chapter 15   Conclusion: Access, Autonomy, and the First Amendment

1 Gilmore, *The Truth about Harvard and Yale*, YALE L. REP. (1964).

2 The central portion of Justice Stewart's Yale speech is published in Stewart, *Or of the Press*, 26 HASTINGS L. REV. 631 (1975).

3 *See generally*, Nimmer, *Introduction—Is Freedom of the Press Redundancy: What Does It Add to Freedom of Speech?*, 26 HASTINGS L. REV. 639 (1975).

4 *See*, Chapter 11, *supra.*

5 *See*, Chapter 9, *supra.*

6 *Id.*

7 *Id.*

8 *See generally*, Winter, *The Equal Protection Clause*, 1972 SUP. CT. REV. 41, 44 *et seq.*

9 *National Broadcasting Company, Inc. v. FCC*, 516 F.2d 1101, 1193 (1974). The case is discussed in Chapter 12, *supra.*

10 The case is *Straus Communications, Inc. v. FCC*, No. 75-1083, in which a Congressman was called a coward and the FCC found a violation of the personal attack rules by a radio station. The author was counsel to the broadcaster in this case. *See*, Chapter 11, *supra.*

11 *In the Matter of the Handling of Public Issues*, 30 RR 2d 1261 (1974).

12 *Columbia Broadcasting System, Inc. v. Democratic National Committee*, 412 U.S. 94, 148 (1973).

13 Bazelon, *FCC Regulation of the Tele-Communications Press*, 1975 DUKE L. J. 213. *See generally*, Chapter 12, *supra.*

14 *See*, Chapter 12, *supra.*

15 Geller, *Does* Red Lion *Square with* Tornillo?, 29 U. MIAMI L. REV. 477, 479 (1975).

16 *See*, the discussion in Chapter 9.

17 W.S.A. 895.05(2) (1966).

18 *See*, Note, *Vindication of the Reputation of a Public Official*, 80 HARV. L. REV. 1730 (1967).

19 N.R.S. 200.570 (1965), *repealed.*

20 Donnelly, *The Right of Reply: An Alternative To An Action For Libel*, 34 U. VA. L. REV. 867, 884 (1948).

21   CHAFEE, I GOVERNMENT AND MASS COMMUNICATIONS 145 *et seq.* (1947).

22   *PMP Associates, Inc.* v. *Globe Newspaper Co.,* 321 N.E.2d 915 (Sup. Jud. Ct. Mass. 1975).

23   *Id.* at 918, citing *America's Best Cinema Corp.* v. *Fort Wayne Newspapers, Inc.,* 347 F.Supp. 328 (N.D. Ind. 1972).

24   F.T.C. Advisory Opinion No. 93, 70 F.T.C. 1877 (1966); *see generally,* 16 CFR 15 (1974).

25   H.Rep.No. 92-565, pp. 11-12.

26   *Id.* at 2.

27   117 CONG. REC. 43164 (1971).

28   S. Conf. Rep. 92-580.

29   This provision is now codified in 47 U.S.C. 312(a)(7) (Supp. 1974).

30   The first ruling struck down the proposal on vagueness grounds, *Opinion of the Justices,* 284 N.E.2d 919 (1972). The second proposal was judged to violate the First Amendment and a comparable state provision because of possible chilling effects. *Opinion of the Justices,* 298 N.E.2d 829 (1973).

31   *See,* EMERSON, THE SYSTEM OF FREEDOM OF EXPRESSION, 667 *et seq.* (1970).

32   326 U.S. at 20.

33   Emerson at 671.

34   For a useful discussion of the advertising access and antitrust laws, *see, Note, Commercial Access to the Newspapers* 35 MD. L. REV. 115 (1975).

35   *See,* Chapter 3, *supra.*

36   *Pittsburgh Press Co.* v. *Human Relations Comm'n.,* 413 U.S. 376 (1973).

37   *Id.* at 386.

38   *Id.* at 391.

39   418 U.S. 241, 258 (1974).

40   For a general discussion of the commercial access question, *see* DeVore & Nelson, *Commercial Speech and Paid Access to the Press,* 26 HAST. L. J. 745 (1975).

41   *See* BALK, BACKGROUND PAPER, A FREE AND RESPONSIVE PRESS 20 (1973).

42   *See generally,* DILLIARD, READER ADVOCATES, IN THE PUBLIC INTEREST: A REPORT BY THE NATIONAL NEWS COUNCIL (1975).

43   Holmes, *Ethics in Journalism: A Growing Awareness* 31 (Report for the Senior Seminar in Foreign Policy 1974-75).

44   *Id.* at 24.

45   Cranberg, *Testing Fairness,* COLUMBIA JOURNALISM REV. 56 (Nov.-Dec.

46   *Id.* at 31.

47   Surveys by two small Massachusetts papers, *The Southbridge Evening News* (a daily) and *The Webster Times* (a weekly) showed 80-90 percent readership, higher than for any other items.

48   *See,* BRUCKER, COMMUNICATION IN POWER: UNCHANGING VALUES IN A CHANGING JOURNALISM 292 *et. seq.* (1973).

49   Conclusions based on Carl J. Nelson National Readership Surveys for 1973.

50   Fisher, *And Who Will Take Care of the Damrons of the World,* THE TRIAL

OF THE FIRST AMENDMENT (Missouri Freedom of Information Center, 1975).

51 Holmes, *supra* at 42.

52 *See,* Ritter & Leibowitz, *Press Councils: The Answer to Our First Amendment Dilemma,* 1974 DUKE L.J. 845; Kriss, *The National News Council at Age One,* COL. J. REV. 31 (Nov.-Dec. 1974).

53 On the Minnesota press council, *see* Petersen, *Press Councils—A Look Towards the Future,* 29 U. MIAMI L. REV. 487 (1975).

54 Balk, *supra* at 19.

Index

A